M

ANN ARBOR DISTRICT LIBRARY

31621011450240

WITHDRAWN

D1544209

Loss within Loss

The Estate Project would like to thank the Hale Matthews Foundation
as well as Ted and Betty Rogers for their generous support.

Loss within Loss

Artists in the Age of AIDS

Edited by
Edmund White

in cooperation with
*The Estate Project
for Artists with AIDS*

A project of the Alliance for the Arts

THE UNIVERSITY OF WISCONSIN PRESS

The University of Wisconsin Press
2537 Daniels Street
Madison, Wisconsin 53718

3 Henrietta Street
London WC2E 8LU, England

Copyright © 2001
The Board of Regents of the University of Wisconsin System
All rights reserved

1   3   5   4   2

Printed in the United States of America

Quotations from Joe Brainard's letters are used by permission of
John Brainard, Executor of the Estate of Joe Brainard.

Previously unpublished work by James Merrill
is copyright of the Literary Estate of James Merrill
at Washington University and is used by permission.

Library of Congress Cataloging-in-Publication Data

Loss within loss : artists in the age of AIDS / edited by Edmund White ;
in cooperation with the Estate Project for Artists with AIDS.
pp. cm. — (Living out)
ISBN 0-299-17070-5 (cloth : alk. paper)
1. AIDS (Disease) and the arts.   2. AIDS
(Disease)—Patients—Biography.   3. Arts, Modern—20th century—United
States.   I. White, Edmund, 1940–   II. Estate Project for Artists with
AIDS.   III. Series.
NX180.A36 L67   2001
700'.87—dc21   00-011012

Contents

Loss within Loss

The American Sublime
Living and Dying as an Artist
Edmund White

When I hold these essays in my hand I can feel the heat rising off them—the intense, baked terra-cotta heat of longing and desire, or the headachy, sobbing heat of grief writhing on the mattress, pounding it like a defeated wrestler. And I can feel the simple, blunt fact of the heat of human presence—of eyelashes brushing the pillowcase, of breath held, heart bursting, of another head on the pillow, drinking it all in, a bit stunned by such voluminous and cruel information but observant nonetheless, memorizing the moment.

Longing, grieving, observing—these are three gerunds that imply an object. *Whom* are you longing or grieving for? *Whom* are you observing? For these are essays devoted to another person now dead, once loved and admired and necessary and now painfully missed but partially forgotten.

In some cases the writer nearly effaces himself or herself and turns a bright, objective light on the dead subject (John Berendt on the landscape architect Bruce Kelly, for instance); the tribute here is research and reportage, lucidity itself, held up like a clear pane through which the accomplishments of the young artist can be seen—without distortion or occlusion, virtually unmediated by another temperament. The very *professionalism* of such an essay is an offering to a life cut short.

In other cases (Alexander Chee on the painter Peter Kelloran, say, or Ramsey McPhillips on photographer Mark Morrisroe), the relationship was intensely personal and cannot be deferred or distanced. In both instances the writer of the essay was young, susceptible, and in love with the subject as soon as they met; and, as we can see, a love affair that is still alive, ongoing, and *tender* (as an injury is said to be tender) contains conflicts as well as resolutions, hidden wounds as well as open celebrations. The story has not come to a peaceful end. It's apparent that Alex Chee is still in love with

Kelloran's blue hair and weathered leather jacket, just as McPhillips's memories of Mark Morrisroe's bum leg and strident claims to be the son of the Boston Strangler go on existing in a medium undefined by time.

Most of these memoirs, however, are about a specific time, one that Benjamin Taylor calls "the sunlit late seventies." Many of the subjects in this volume were different from the people one meets now. They were eccentrics, sometimes geniuses, who believed in immortality more than public relations, in quality hard won more than a lucky hit, in originality rather than re-runs, re-treads, sampling, and "appropriations." They were young men who were intensely serious about their art, whether it was poetry, film, painting, puppetry, or dance. They'd come of age, for the most part, after Stonewall and took their homosexuality in stride if not for granted. Sometimes it was the central theme of their work, although sometimes it was peripheral. But what they did not deny was desire itself—incorrect, irrepressible, anarchic: artesian.

I suppose we should never forget that the one social milieu that was open to the homosexual in the period before Stonewall was the bohemian—and this acceptance defined much of subsequent gay artistic history. The whole idea of making art—of setting up shop in workaday America and declaring oneself an artist—was as unthinkable to most Americans of that epoch as was sexual dissidence. In the 1950s (I'm speaking of the generation that preceded the subjects of these essays), American poets and painters had to break with society before they could begin to do their work. This radical break with convention, this deliberate choice of the status of outsider, was also a break with America's two most venerable activities—getting and spending. Most artists were poor, but at least there was a tradition then of honorable poverty amongst artists and intellectuals.

Not for a moment do I want to play down the homophobia of the New York Action Painters, who were mostly male and hoped to prove they could be as macho as the most red-blooded American man—at a time when practicing an art was still considered effeminate in the States. But that homophobia was specific to New York (two of the leading Bay Area figurative painters, Paul Wonner and Theophilus Brown, had become lovers and open about it by 1960). And in any case the *next* generation, the one that included Warhol, Jasper Johns, and Rauschenberg, was primarily gay, though none of them advertised it and some went to considerable lengths to conceal it.

Moreover, the Beats were extraordinarily gay-friendly. Allen Ginsberg and William Burroughs were fearless about their homosexuality, and Jack Kerouac could be had. Ginsberg harked back to the manly, democratic queerness propounded by Whitman. The Beats consoled themselves for their years of poverty, obscurity, and freakishness by comparing themselves constantly to Blake and the romantics (just as Blake had compared his contemporary Henry Fuseli to Michelangelo). The Beats also aligned themselves with Buddhism, which seemed to confuse all distinctions in an exotic nihilism.

In the 1950s I attended a strict, English-style boarding school that, luckily for me, was just across the street from an art academy for college-age and post-graduate students. Although it was against my school's rules, I constantly slipped across the street in the late afternoon and visited the studios and even dorm rooms of the painters, weavers, sculptors, and stained-glass makers. They liked me because I was arty and a bit desperate for their approval. I quickly learned not to chatter while looking at their canvases but to stare and grunt knowingly—or to say nothing. With them I'd listen to Indian ragas, American folk music, Bach, and Scarlatti. We'd drink espresso and even rotgut wine, they'd show me reproductions of the latest de Koonings or Klines, and they'd even lend me English translations of Jung or *The Songs of Maldoror.*

I never got laid at the academy, but I felt that out of all these men wearing their hair long, their trousers paint-stained, arrayed with bits of Indian finery and round, black glasses such as those Le Corbusier wore, *one* of them might just put out one day. No one had a viable defense of homosexuality back then, and all those artists respected Freud and Jung, but if psychiatry wasn't invoked they would take a neutral, let's-not-be-uncool stance toward homosexuality. They never talked about women as objects, domestic or sexual, and seemed alive to the individuality of their friends—everyone, that is, who wasn't a square or a member of the detested bourgeoisie.

In the 1970s a new *gay* bohemianism appeared, though it wasn't called by that label; it is *this* bohemianism that is half-glimpsed in several essays in this collection. This movement sprang up in New York and San Francisco, the two cities where most of our subjects lived or ended up. This milieu was compounded out of the Beat and hippie movements, out of cool, jazz-loving, heroin-shooting New Yorkishness, out of the new gay liberation movement and the New Left in general. Like their predecessors, these gay artists thought that living differently was a condition for making art—living wildly, wickedly, using drugs, dressing bizarrely, embracing poverty, substituting day for night. And many of them considered promiscuity a given, one of the continuing adventures necessary for stimulating, even lacerating, the imagination. "We have become the people our parents warned us about," was a popular slogan of the day. Of course my highly colored description would have struck the participants as ludicrous, since their verbal style was cool, ironic, jokey.

Perhaps in Europe, at least Catholic Europe, few artists would have felt they had to reject conventionality in order to make art. For them, high culture was—and is—all too annoyingly an ornament of the *grande bourgeoisie*, the smug expression of what Thomas Bernhard, the Austrian novelist, contemptuously called the Old Masters and located in hateful Salzburg. Art was a national industry in most European countries, not a weird act of rebellion as in America. Artists were acceptable figures in the European city, whereas in the States an acceptable artist was only a best-seller or a box office hit. In America only money, in other words, could redeem such a bizarre personage. Although American bohemians might look for heroes toward a largely imaginary Europe (the nineteenth-century Europe that had created bohemianism), they would have been surprised to see, for instance, a certain group portrait of the French surrealists—clean-shaven and wearing coats and ties, resembling brokers more than explorers of the unconscious.

I just want to underline what so many of these essays allude to—Brad Gooch on Howard Brookner, Philip Yenawine on David Wojnarowicz, Sarah Schulman on David Feinberg and Stan Leventhal, Randall Kenan on John C. Russell, Ramsey McPhillips on Mark Morrisroe, Felice Picano on Robert Ferro and Michael Grumley—that for the generation of gay artists of the seventies and early eighties, the old bohemian ideal was still going strong, a spirit that seems to have vanished from the world for good now. As Gooch points out, someone of his generation would have felt bad if he hadn't recognized the music of Busoni; today a sophisticate rejects a boyfriend for not having seen all of the episodes of *Rhoda*.

The subjects of many of these essays united in their work and lives high and low culture (John C. Russell's plays blurred "the boundaries between Roland

Barthes and *Tiger Beat* magazine, between Peter Brook and *Entertainment Tonight*") and fused mainstream ambitions with subculture strangeness (Scott Burton's chairs were shown in major museums all over the world, but he and his lover John were covered with tattoos and piercings, and Scott could be spotted wearing either Savile Row suits or S/M grunge). Joe Brainard, as Keith McDermott explains, was generous to the point of saintliness—a *serious* eccentricity in a society that worships greed and encourages selfishness. David Feinberg, Sarah Schulman writes, wrote carefully structured novels such as *Eighty-Sixed*, but he thought nothing of giving a "dying party" during which he had the bad taste nearly to die in front of casually socializing friends.

Of the people mentioned in this book, I knew Bruce Kelly, Joe Brainard, Howard Brookner, James Merrill, Henry Post, Maurice Grosser, Harry Kondoleon, John C. Russell (a student of mine), Paul Monette, Robert Ferro, Michael Grumley, Scott Burton, Warren Sonbert, and Stan Leventhal. I suppose it's a sign of how small the gay arts scene was that I met so many of these men. Also, it may reflect on how many years I lived in New York (from 1962 to 1983). All of these men (except Merrill) went to the bars and could be cruised or chatted up. I had a brief affair with Joe Brainard before Keith did (and Keith and I lived together for several years). Robert Ferro and Michael Grumley were members of a writers' club I belonged to. One of my ex's, Chris Cox, hung out with Brad Gooch and Howard Brookner after I moved to Paris in 1983. Howard filmed me in New York for his last movie, in which I read a chapter from Brad's novel *Scary Kisses*.

The history of the gay arts scene in New York and San Francisco during the seventies and eighties has yet to be written, though any history must now take into account the following essays. It was a period and a movement as vital and influential as any other artistic moment in postwar America—and one of the few that was both a social and artistic phenomenon. It was a time of interlocking love affairs and friendships, of a slowly emerging sexual identity, a time when gay bookshops were thriving community centers (instead of declining and disappearing porn dispensers as they are at the dawn of the twenty-first century). It was a time when intellect and accomplishment were *almost* as prized as physical beauty, when certain hot writers, painters, and filmmakers would cause a stir when they entered a bar or gay restaurant, when gay writers didn't yet teach on remote campuses (no university wanted them), when they lived in Manhattan where they supported themselves as advertising copywriters, as gallery employees, as magazine and book editors (even editors of porn magazines), as fashion models or actors—or with welfare and unemployment benefits they'd somehow scammed. Warren Sonbert lived off grants as an avant-garde film director. They seldom came from artistic or intellectual backgrounds (dancer and choreographer Joah Lowe was the son of watermelon farmers from Henderson, Texas, and his case was in no way atypical). These gay artists were sophisticated men with their ears to the ground, alert to signal events in all the arts—the emergence of Robert Wilson's visually sumptuous "operas" or of Charles Ludlum's campy updates of classic plays (his *Camille* was a crucial event in New York theater history, as were Ethel Eichenberger's drag performances). Of course the gay aesthetic was not shaped just by gay art; everyone in the arts, straight or gay, was influenced by the continuing evolution of George Balanchine at the New York City Ballet (Balanchine was arguably the only undisputed genius working in New York in the second half of the twentieth century). Balanchine may have been notoriously heterosexual, but his greatest apologist, Edwin Denby, incidentally, happened to be gay.

Interior decoration, theatrical lighting, fashion, graphics—all the facets of contemporary design impinged on the gay consciousness and emanated from it. The breakdown of distinctions between the pure arts and the applied, between the seriousness of high art and the sensory blandishments (or assault) of rock music, discos, or the baths—this breakdown had already been foreshadowed by camp in the fifties and sixties, with its confusion of genres, its enshrinement of old movies, bad actresses, and failed glamour.

The younger gay artists of the seventies and eighties had their elder statesmen. James Merrill set an unreachably high standard of excellence by integrating his own gay experience (loves and friendships) into his superbly eloquent and all-embracing poems and finally into his book-length epic, *The Changing Light at Sandover*. As one of the heirs to a brokerage firm he was also able to fund a foundation that made many small grants to poets and novelists, many of them gay. Richard Howard—a powerhouse who'd translated dozens of books from the French, who'd written a massive critical study of forty-one contemporary poets, *Alone with America*, and who'd won the Pulitzer Prize for his own verse—was tireless in promoting the talents of his friends, straight or gay (he arranged for my first novel to be published, for instance, and I am only one person among many he helped). Virgil Thomson, who'd lived in Paris for fifty years and written two operas with Gertrude Stein, had an apartment in the Chelsea Hotel where he entertained musicians, poets, and painters. Chris Cox worked for Virgil, arranging his archives for Yale, and through Virgil, he and I met Christopher Isherwood and Don Bachardy, the ultimate gay artistic couple. (Virgil himself went to great lengths in public to deny his own homosexuality, which was ludicrous, since everyone was hip to him.) John Ashbery—who'd won all the prizes for his enigmatic poetry—was the link between younger gay poets of the ever-growing New York School (Brad Gooch, Tim Dlugos, John Ash) and the older founding generation of such gay poets as Frank O'Hara and James Schuyler. No matter that Ashbery himself rejected the label "gay poet" as too limiting (just as Elizabeth Bishop had refused to be defined by her sexuality or even her gender).

All of these people could be met in the meltdown of gay bars or prowling the lobby of the New York State Theater or at readings at Three Lives Book Shop. Many of them formed couples, short-lived or enduring, but there was an unspoken prejudice against fidelity and domesticity, which was too close to Mama-Papa coziness to seem bohemian. And just as promiscuity is nature's way of spreading advantageous genetic mutations, by the same token the sexual and social confusion of gay artistic Manhattan or San Francisco was the quickest, surest way of maximizing contact and consolidating alliances.

This world died out with AIDS. In the late eighties magazines liked to publish full spreads of photos picturing all the talent wiped out by the disease, but what these photos didn't suggest was that a way of life had been destroyed. The experimentalism, the erotic sophistication, the prejudice against materialism, the elusive humor, the ambition to measure up to international and timeless standards, above all, the belief that art should be serious and difficult—all this rich, ambiguous mixture of values and ideas evaporated. It's a world that a few novelists have tried to preserve (Felice Picano in *Like People in History*, Brad Gooch in *The Golden Age of Promiscuity*, I myself in *The Farewell Symphony*), but the whole period is crying out for a lively, detailed, multifaceted social history.

What has prevailed after the demise of this splendid period is a new queer Puritanism—the appearance of many gays who want to marry, to adopt, to blend in, and to become virtually suburban. In the arts an edginess, a quirkiness, even a violence has given way to stylistic blandness. Gay fiction has now become a wading pond for minor talents to dabble in; the novels often sound transcribed from the film scripts they long to become: novel as novelization. Publishers, who recognize that few gay novels can be expected to sell more than twenty thousand (or even ten thousand) copies, are now content to throw dull genre fiction out into the world and let it sink—or paddle—unaided. Gay bookshops are closing down (from seventy-five two years ago to fifty now), and most of the serious gay literary publications (with the exception of the *James White Review* and the *Gay and Lesbian Review*) have stopped publishing. A tackiness, a sort of steroid-injected sex-shop conform-ism, has replaced the old transgressiveness of gay art.

At the movies more and more gay characters are appearing, but they are either adolescents struggling to come out or side-splitting drags—or beautiful men dying horrible AIDS deaths. In other words, in Hollywood ac-ceptable gay characters either aren't yet gay or are holy-fool cross-dressers or are soon to be dead: pre-gay, not really gay, or soon to be no longer gay.

What isn't being shown are gay men in a gay world, people as fully ex-pressed socially as sexually. We never see two gay friends, two gay buddies; at the cinema the gay's only function is to come out, camp it up, and die (or murder, in the case of *The Talented Mr. Ripley*).

The essays in this book mark a void—the collapse of a creative world that flourished in the recent past and the end of the promise these gay artists were never able to fulfill. What if Warren Sonbert or Howard Brookner were still making movies? What if Robert Ferro (or Allen Barnett or Tim Dlugos) were still writing?

Into one essay after another in this anthology the word *immortality* creeps in uneasily; the idea is that all this suffering—the poverty and public fear and contempt and the long agonies of a brief life cut short by AIDS—would be redeemed if only the artist's work would turn out to be immortal, or at least widely known right now. Four different essays mention the obitu-ary pages of the *New York Times*, as though that paper were the absolute mea-sure of fame. But was Rimbaud's name mentioned in the papers at the time of his death? Was Van Gogh's? Conversely, no one could have been more fa-mous at the end of his life than James Gould Cozzens, but no one reads him

now. Nor Giambattista Marino, the most celebrated poet of the Italian Renaissance. Nor Ivan Bunin, the Russian short story writer, who won a Nobel
Prize in the 1930s but is completely, and unjustly, forgotten now.

I suppose we could ask if anyone's reputation is secure today. Was
Andy Warhol the last painter whose name became a household word? (And
is it any accident that he was a master of self-promotion?) Maybe more titles
are published now than ever before, but this very proliferation means only
that fewer and fewer copies of each title are read by everyone literate. In
France and England the literary prizes are such media events that a handful
of books are discussed and read by "everyone" every year, yet in America
there is no comparable prestige or concentration or attention. In America
we have many great writers but few great readers (France has the opposite
problem).

No, America (despite its cult of celebrity) has become a country not
of lasting celebrity but of ephemeral cults, enclaves, fanzines, and Web sites.
We're always shocked when we discover (usually too late) neo-Aryans in our
midst, the child prostitution rings, ashrams full of urine drinkers, body modification clubs, and fisting seminars, the Halley-Bopp suicide sects and S/M
boot camps. The arts in America are just as fragmented—by region, even language, as well as by the fault lines of identity politics. The quintessential
American moment occurs when the poet laureate of New Hampshire is introduced to the leading literary guru of Silicon Valley—and they've never
heard of each other! The entire literary scene has lost its coherence. No wonder the public is confused. Immortality?

Any project that attempts to come to terms with artistic expression
arising from AIDS must confront a host of questions. Is a collection of essays
such as this one only serving to marginalize still further what is already a
minority subject (and enterprise)? What about quality? Surely an essay by
someone with AIDS or about someone who died of AIDS isn't necessarily
good; as a recent discussion on this subject in France put it, "One cannot confuse the question of homosexual visibility with the question of literature."
And then what about an essay that presents a point of view that strikes one
as weird, or even possibly offensive?

I haven't even begun to answer these questions to my own satisfaction. I do know that I was never concerned to censor the essays as they came
in. As the editor of this anthology I commissioned most of the authors,

although many of them were suggested by the Estate Project for Artists with AIDS, which sponsored the entire project. I am especially grateful to Patrick Moore, the director, and Randall Bourscheidt, the president. They helped me on a nearly day-to-day basis.

As I read straight through the essays in this book as a totality and not in a piecemeal fashion, I am moved by the feeling and intelligence and the seriousness about bearing witness to those who have died. To my mind, at least, this is a tribute both to a vanished sense of artistic vocation and to the enduring and transforming beauty of friendship.

Through the
Looking Glass
Sarah Schulman

The present does not resemble the past. We went through a mass death experience and then we took a break. Instead of constant morbidity there was puking, diarrhea, never-ending adjustments to toxic drug combinations, a lot of swallowing and a certain facsimile of robustness, everyone feeling "great." Back to the gym. The funerals slowed or stopped and the neighborhoods changed, a new kind of AIDS body modification came into being. No more KS and wasting syndrome on the street, now we have the Crixovan Look: sunken eyes and a pot belly. Guys who are HIV can bulk up the way the steroid-pure cannot. Now they're larger than ever. Some men got their power back. We could not, did not face what we had really endured.

Looking clearly at the gay dead, locked in their youth, their youth is now locked in the past. Eighties haircuts, ACT UP demonstrations, tentative first novels from defunct presses. I find that my memories fade. Men are increasingly reduced to specific moments played over again and many are moments of dissipation.

John Bernd, the dancer, the performance artist. Something was wrong with his blood, but he didn't know what it was. GRID. His skin fell apart. He got sick so early in the scheme of things and seemed to live on will alone. But was it truly will that made some people live longer than others, or was that a placebo. Did they just have a weaker strain of virus? ARC. One day on the subway I offered him a sip of my orange juice. He thought twice and then refused. Whom was he protecting? AIDS. He came into the coffee shop where I was working. "How can I get better if you say I have AIDS?" I didn't know the answer. I know there is more there. We were in two shows together, all that backstage banter. I saw his collaboration with Anne Bogart on a version of *Picnic* and we had a long, long talk about it. I saw him perform many times including his last piece with Jennifer Monson—he was so disoriented he could barely follow her. He waved at me crossing the street. I went to his funeral.

The world before protease inhibitors is clearly The Past, emotionally for me now. That was the world of the helpless well watching the ill fade, suffer, and disappear. I think of my artist friends who are healthy today: Jack Waters, Peter Cramer, Mark Ameen, Dudley Saunders, Scott Tucker, Harvey Redding—I am so grateful for their presence on this earth as equals. And my dearest, the writer Joe Westmoreland, struggling with endless medical poisonings, swollen tongue, frozen retinas, IVs, toxifying, detoxifying. They live in another time from the dead. It has ceased to be a continuum.

Of course memory is a reflection of the self. I recall the moments that meant the most to me; they are unrepresentative and historically subjective. Massaging Phil Zwickler's feet in the hospital while he explained to his mother that "that's what we do for the dying." Traveling with Michael Callen in Germany, watching Customs trying to cope with his gym bag filled with pills. Despite his claim of having had three thousand penises up his rectum, Michael was sure that he knew who infected him, and he was mad about it. Assotto Saint's family at his funeral. His mother knew all his friends' names. "When he received an award from the Black Lesbian and Gay Leadership Forum," said a young conservatively dressed Haitian woman at the church podium, "I was so proud of my cousin." Bo Houston, the writer. He died while we were angry at each other. Vito Russo in the hospital with an ACT UP button on his striped pajamas. He wanted to know everything that was happening out there in his beloved world. Others couldn't bear to hear about what they were missing.

There are two guys in particular whom I think about a lot. The one who was my real friend was a writer named Stan Leventhal. All of his books are out of print now. And the harsh truth is that Stan never really became a great writer. But he wanted to be. My favorite story of his was in the final book published in his lifetime, *Candy Holidays and Other Short Fictions*, where Stan remembers the last man he unknowingly infected. However, Stan was a great friend. He liked to have a Jack Daniels and a cigarette; he took AZT with bourbon sometimes. A tall skinny guy, clean shaven with short brown hair, he was kind of a hippie, wore a jean jacket, T-shirt and had a backpack. Stan read everything and was one of the first men I'd met who actually read lesbian fiction and loved it.

Stan Leventhal. Courtesy of the estate of Stan Leventhal.

He lived in a filthy apartment on Christopher Street overlooking the park. It was packed with books and CDs, his guitar and TV. He'd come to the city from Long Island to be a singer and started out on the folk circuit. He'd broken up with the love of his life right before we made friends and plunged himself into the creation of Amethyst Press, which probably published the most interesting collection of gay male writing in the history of our literature. He published books by Dennis Cooper, the late Bo Houston, the late Steve Abbott, Kevin Killian, Patrick Moore, Mark Ameen—all important, underappreciated artists. After working at porn magazines like *Torso* for years, Stan had a formula. He'd publish a highly intellectual, formally innovative novel by a gifted writer and then slap a piece of beefcake on the cover so it would sell. His favorite writer was Guy Davenport, to whom he'd written a comprehensive and adoring monograph.

Near the end of Stan's life, Amethyst got wrested away from him in a power play, and then the new bosses destroyed and folded it. This depressed him deeply; he was filled with anger. I remember one lunch at a Chinese restaurant when I saw tears splash into his food, only to look up and discover it was sweat; he had such a high fever but was still running around. His true love died. My final visit to his apartment, the place stank. The toilet bowl was black and there were no sheets on the bed. Stan gave me one of his books, *Resurrection of a Hanged Man* by Denis Johnson, which unfortunately I didn't care for. I was surprised, actually—usually we agreed on books.

I saw him in Beekman Hospital the week that he died. He was bald and shaking, could barely sit up, but did. That was the first time I met his mother, Pearl, an old uncomprehending woman. "There's so much to say," Stan told me. Then he told me something I won't repeat here. I stepped out into the hallway as the doctor fiddled with his body and Pearl followed. "Stanley always wanted a hard cover," Pearl said. Then he was dead. Stan's best friends were Chris Bram and Michelle Karlsberg. Later Michelle told me about her final conversation with Pearl.

"Should I ask Stanley if he wants to be buried in Florida?" Pearl asked.

"Stan doesn't give a shit where he's buried," Michelle told her.

Like all the dead and the living, I think I see him everywhere. But it is just new versions, young versions of guys like Stan. Most of us seem to be re-created every fifteen years. I see a twenty-year-old me almost once a month, and a twenty-year-old, forty-year-old, sixty-year-old Stan passes by on the street often enough.

The other guy I think about a lot is David Feinberg. He's famous for being the guy who was so creepy to his friends that when he died they were all mad at him and never got over it. He forgot that people have responsibilities to others until they are dead. He thought he was absolved. The great thing about David is that his work gets better as the years pass. He wasn't sentimental and now, neither are we. We've caught up with the sarcasm, hatred, and resentment of the dying for the living. We're not ashamed of it anymore. In fact, it's funny. That's the thing about gay people—we're not really especially caustic or campy, we just get bored very easily and move on to whatever sensibility is waiting around the corner. So David's books, *Queer and Loathing, Eighty-Sixed,* and *Spontaneous Combustion,* have become documents of justifiable anger and the guts it takes to have it.

There are famous stories about David, famous lines. "You can't wear a red ribbon if you're dead." Or the time he hauled himself out of Saint Vincent's Hospital and across the street to the ACT UP meeting to tell everyone there that we had failed because he was dying. The way he'd stop people on the elevator and tell them that he had AIDS. How he went to a department store covered in KS and asked for a free makeover. How he went to see *Love! Valor! Compassion!* with his portable IV and slept through the show. There was a lot of pain there and a lot of expression of it—two things that are not supposed to go together. He was a real Jew in that way.

I remember when David threw a dying party. He invited his closest friends and had us stand around eating and drinking while we watched him, emaciated, lying in the living room dying in front of us. Then, he had diarrhea accidentally on the couch and ran screaming to the bathroom. Stan Leventhal was there, and after David shit his pants, Stan left. That's when I realized the cruelty of David's act. He wanted to make everyone else who had this in his future stare it down now. No mercy.

I visited him in the hospital once when he called his mother and asked her to send him some cookies. She sent them parcel post because it was cheaper. Another time I was there, American Express called up to ask if he was the one buying plane tickets and charging hotel rooms on his card. No, David was busy dying. It was an ex-boyfriend who was ripping him off.

This is a story I heard, so I'm no witness, but after he died his parents decided that they wanted him to have a Jewish funeral. The friends were so shell shocked by his abusive behavior, they had lost all judgment and went along with it, getting a lesbian rabbi. The whole works. But the parents got caught in traffic coming from upstate and were hours late, so the lesbian rabbi had to leave and the house rabbi was called in to take her place. When the family finally arrived he started the service.

"David was a great . . . athlete."

Oh my God, his friends thought.

"He loved to go to the gym."

These are stories but the pain they contain is immeasurable. The impact of these losses requires a consciousness beyond most human ability. We grow weary, numb, alienated, and then begin to forget, to put it all away just to be able to move on. But even the putting away is an abusive act. The experiencing, the remembering, the hiding, the overcoming—all leave their scars.

Early this year I was in the political funeral for Matthew Shepard. Of the five thousand gay men and lesbians who showed up there were a lot of guys in suits, a lot of younger people who'd never been in a real demonstration before, and a lot of friends from the old ACT UP. The feeling in the crowd was so unusual. It was something I've never experienced in a demonstration before. A certain calm. There was an absorbed alienation, a lack of concern, really. We'd seen it all. It was an action of the emotionally experienced. No matter how stupidly the police behaved we all knew just what to do. There was a beautiful nonverbal communication. We just stepped around them, kept going forward, ignored them, their horses, their stupid threats. And I realized that this was the result of compartmentalized grief. This alienation, this total disregard, this lack of fear, this common understanding, this quiet perseverance, the impossibility of either being stopped or getting upset about anyone trying. Our disappeared friends have taken our fear with them. After all, they knew what we did, who we were. Without them, so much of what we, the living, have done, also goes unremembered. Increasingly I vaguely recall my dead friends and in those ways I vaguely recall myself.

Rereading Stan's books for this essay was a strange experience. This good man who was a loyal friend, who had impeccable taste in literature, who started a literacy program at the Lesbian and Gay Community Center to teach gay people how to read, who has a library named after him, who published some of the most important gay male writers of our day—this guy could not really write. I feel guilty saying that because I know how much Stan wanted to be a great writer. But on the other hand, one of the paradigms we've created about AIDS is that of the dead genius. And of course, most of the people who died were not great artists. They were just people who did their best or didn't try at all. Some of them were nasty and lousy, others mediocre. Some knew how to face and deal with problems, others ran away and blamed the people closest to them. Stan was unusual because he gave so much to other people, both personally and in his never-ending contributions to the community. These actions alone make him exceptional. But as an artist, he had, as one colleague put it "an ear of lead." That's partially why

I decided to focus this essay on him, because his death is just as horrible even though he never wrote a great book and possibly never would have.

I'm older now than I was when we were friends and when Stan died. I've suffered more and learned more about people. This makes me appreciate him so much more. Looking over the Davenport monograph, I'm impressed all over again. How many writers take the time to praise another living writer? Most people can't; they're too small. They resent everyone else's achievement. I honestly believe that most people have not realized their dreams, cannot face and deal with the problems that obstruct them, and consequently feel inadequate. For these reasons most people resent other people's strengths, unless they've fully realized their own. Because Stan did not become the kind of writer he wanted to be and yet was able to see and praise beauty in someone else's work, he was an exception. That's what made him such a great reader and publisher. He had that rare maturity to not project.

I think I can see that maturity, retrospectively, in the way he died. For those of us who are experienced death watchers, we know that many people die resenting the living. But up until the last moment I saw him, Stan appreciated other people, he did not begrudge them. When they were evil, like the guys who destroyed Amethyst Press, he knew it and had appropriate anger. But when people had integrity and depth, he loved his friends. How many others can have that said about them?

After Peter

Alexander Chee

In memoriam, Peter David Kelloran
17 December 1961–10 May 1994

I slept but my heart was awake.
Song of Songs 5:2

1.

His name was Peter David Kelloran, Peter D. Kelloran, as he liked to appear in print, and he was a painter. He died in his bed at the Maitri Hospice in San Francisco at the age of thirty-three on the afternoon of May 10, after he decided he could no longer care for himself in his apartment at the edge of town, where he had lived until then. There was a solar eclipse that day, and his passing occurred during it. He had spoken with his mother that morning on the phone. His dementia had parted enough for him to tell her he loved her. "And then he started to go," his friend Laura Lister says. The room was full of women friends of Peter's and they laid hands on him in a circle. Laura recalls the phone ringing, and she took her hands off him to answer it. "He lunged up off the bed." He went slowly. "I begged him to go, begged him to let go at that point. He needed to go. He wouldn't go, though," Laura says. "And then one of the male volunteers came in and he took Peter's hand in his. You could see the change. Like a light came over him. And he was gone."

"All the people there with him at the end, I can never thank them enough. They were all so beautiful, so strong," his mother, Jill Kelloran, says from her home in Chicago. "They did what I physically could not do. Peter's death was tearing me apart and I literally could not be there. They cared for him to the end. And I will always be grateful to them, for that."

Peter D. Kelloran. Courtesy of Patrik Rytikangas.

"We were there until he grew cold," Peggy Sue, a friend who was present, says. "Maitri being a Buddhist place, you lie in state. So we sat with him."

I am a minor character in Peter's story. I first saw Peter when I worked in the Castro at a bookstore, A Different Light, a gay and lesbian bookstore that in those days doubled as a reference library and community center. The store was the first to have a section devoted entirely to AIDS/HIV issues; it was located at the front of the store, beside the register. I supposed, the first day I saw him, he'd either seroconverted recently, or had recently decided to do something about it. I saw many people in this way, on their first few days, and I was forever inventing some story about them, never mentioned to anyone, simply to fill the hours. I was often the first person they had to deal with, a bookstore clerk who would show them the short shelf of books, expanding weekly, but, still short.

I was twenty-two years old then. Peter was twenty-eight, tall and broad shouldered and thin; he had a wide, Irish frame and usually wore leather: a motorcycle jacket, leather boots. A dyed-blue tuft of hair glowed across his forehead. I'd seen him walking through the Castro, and I'd see him at demonstrations. A year would pass before I'd hear his voice, speaking to me. Today he simply ran through the books and selected a few on strengthening the immune system, and he paid when someone else was at the register. I saw him leave. His blue eyes had a searchlight intensity, and it seemed clear what he saw and what he didn't. He didn't see me. I saw that my mission would be to be seen by him. I felt called and commanded by him immediately and to this day I cannot say why it was, only that it was immediate, and thorough.

That day in the store he didn't look at me, moving quickly instead back out into the hurrying sidewalk, the afternoon sunlight making long crowded shadows. I didn't know his name then, or anything about him, except that he was beautiful, and he was hurrying and possibly, probably, positive.

Peter, in fact, at the time that I first saw him, had been positive for three years. "He wrote to me from Morocco," Laura says, of a trip he'd taken in 1986. "And he could only write about how sick he had been. And after he got back and he tested positive, that was when we figured out, that was his onset."

He would keep it a secret for years, not telling anyone besides Laura, who kept his secret as well. "A lot of people were angry at me for that," she says, about her keeping his secret. "But people thinking about your death, that'll put you in the grave. And besides," she adds, "if you didn't get your business dealt with when someone dies, that's your own fault. You had every day before then to deal."

When I arrived in San Francisco, there was no way to find the Castro on any maps. People were forever calling the bookstore for directions to the neighborhood. I remember that in my group of friends there was the sense that we were a wave arriving on this coastal city from farther inland: postcollegiate young men and women arriving to find cheap apartments, thrift stores bursting with the old athletic T-shirts and jeans and flannel we all prized. I remember when I put the empty clothes together with the empty apartments, on an ordinary sunny afternoon walking down a sidewalk to work: there on a blanket stood a pair of black leather steel-toed boots, twelve-hole lace-ups.

They gleamed, freshly polished, in the light of the morning. As I approached them, feeling the pull of the hill, I drew up short to examine the rest of the sidewalk sale. Some old albums, Queen and Sylvester; three pairs of jeans; two leather wristbands; a box of old T-shirts; a worn watch, the hands still moving; a pressed-leather belt, Western style; and cowboy boots, the same size as the steel-toes. I tried the steel-toes on and took a long look at the salesman as I stood up, to feel at that moment that they were exactly my size.

This man was thin. He was thin in a way that was immediately familiar. Hollowing from the inside out. His skin reddened, and his brown eyes looked over me as if lightning might fall on me out of that clear afternoon sky. And I knew then, as I paid twenty dollars for the boots, that they'd been recently emptied. That he was watching me walk off in the shoes of the new dead. And that all of this had been happening for some time now.

I lived in San Francisco for two years right after leaving college in 1989. When I say I was part of a group, I mean I was part of a group of activists who divided our time and energies between a number of organizations and affinity groups. ACT UP and Queer Nation were the seeds for a great deal of what happened there and what happens there to this day. We engaged in direct-action protests, spent free time discussing new protests and the way in which past protests had been perceived, and thought about politics and its relationship to our personal lives to the point that our lives inverted entirely into this realm: the personal as political because that was all there was. We had bitter feuds and disputes, we had angry meetings. We had raucous celebrations. We had vigils and parties, we made mistakes and made amends. The average member was twenty-three, HIV-negative, white and college educated, usually gay or lesbian and from another part of the country.

At the time, I was twenty-two, HIV-negative, Amerasian, college educated, and from another part of the country. Pictures of me at the time show a thin dark-haired young man who seems inordinately happy for someone who spent a good deal of his time wanting to be dead. Every picture of me from this time shows me smiling. This young man I was drove a motorcycle, worked at a bookstore, hung out with drag queens who didn't attend meetings of any kind, and was known to dance on a bar or two. He was a member of ACT UP/SF before the bitter split of the group, a member of Queer Nation, and a somewhat pesky intern at *Out/Look*, a queer academic journal of the time. He was on the media committee of ACT UP and had a reputation at first for dating no one, and then, for having dated everyone. He hollowed his desire to die with the knowledge that other people were dying who wanted to live, and this was the single strongest motive for his participation in direct-action AIDS activism. Being an activist meant, among other things, never being alone, and being alone was where he got into trouble. And so he made sure he was never alone.

At this time in San Francisco, the world seemed like it might either go up in fire or be restored in a healing past imagining. The world seemed ripe for fixing and rescue. Those of us in ACT UP and Queer Nation were accused at one point of a gay Zionism, and it was true only in that, in a way similar to Jewish thought, we believed we could fix the world and do it by staying together, working together. Why am I telling this story? As a minor character, out of place here in this narration, this is what has happened, since AIDS, for me at least: the major characters have left, in these stories from the first ten years of the epidemic. The men I wanted to follow are dead: David Wojnarowicz, Derek Jarman, Peter. Finding them had made me want to live, and I did, do. The world is not fixed and the healing is still just past my imagining, though, perhaps, closer. The minor characters are now left, to introduce themselves and take the story forward.

2.

Electric blue Mohawk. Blue eyes carrying the light like a filament. Something energy would force its way through. Blue. Peter.

I saw him next on Market Street at five in the morning under the giant Safeway sign there in the middle of the city, where our ACT UP activist affinity group had gathered in the parking lot for a "non-ACT-UP-related action," which was to say, all the same members, different team for the occasion. I was a participant in a handful of these sorts of actions. This morning, we were going to wrap false newspaper fronts over a thousand copies of the *San Francisco Chronicle.* 9000 DEAD IN THE CITY, read the headline on the false newspaper front we'd created for the occasion. Clever group members had imitated the font and layout, and the false front wore the name *San Francisco Chronic Liar.* Readers reading closely would read that this was the number of people who had died thus far in the AIDS epidemic, but the cover photograph, a shot of the city from the sky, was meant to evoke a natural disaster or terrorist news story, which, to us, the AIDS death story was. The action's purpose was to increase the accurate coverage of AIDS in the media.

About thirty or forty of us were gathered there, and we split the bales of false fronts up into groups. Each team had a neighborhood. The plan was to wrap the false fronts over the papers after sneaking them into the car. Each car had a squad of three. One of us had coins, to get the paper box open, one of us drove, one of us was on lookout. As we split the bales of papers from the box, what we were doing felt dangerous. But when we wrapped the fronts it was only tedious, or silly, or funny, and my team, after we wrapped the last one up, sat and waited for twenty minutes for a pedestrian to come up to the paper box, open it, and read the headline. This person puzzled over the paper and walked off, to catch the train.

I did not meet Peter that morning. Instead, I ached as he walked the parking lot, oblivious to me, his leathers shiny in the dark, his hair flashing occasionally above the perfect white of his scalp. I asked my friend Choire about him. Peter Kelloran, he said. Dreamboat. Jason's boyfriend. I didn't mention my memory of him, from the store, afraid of violating his privacy.

As I wrapped the papers in the dark, as we went from box to box, I tried to tell myself, There's nothing you can do, other than what you are doing. I felt then a very personal responsibility to end the AIDS crisis. I was a literalist and remain a literalist. When someone had said to me, shortly after I arrived, you need to help end the AIDS crisis, I thought, okay, and this is what happened: I became an AIDS activist, a fairly direct outgrowth of my college activism for gay and lesbian causes. My Korean forebears, in previous times, when asked directions, would take their questioners all the way to their destinations, sometimes traveling miles out of their way. I took this new destination, the end of the AIDS crisis, as my own; this seemed ordinary. That someone wouldn't do this seemed extraordinary to me. But there in the dark morning Peter's face, so like the future, merged with this mythic end to become a private horizon line, hidden inside every view I had of my days afterward in San Francisco. The immanent hidden inside everything. There was nowhere, it seemed, where I might not see him, and I tried to stay vigilant, for awhile. Peter seemed beyond me: too handsome, too adult, too cool to want me, and, certainly, unapproachable. There would be other men for me while I was there, but the sight of him on the back of a friend's motorcycle, or

3 1621 00930 4839

at the wheel of his VW Thing, his head settled low as he drove by, caught me every time, and this was, for a few more months, how I always saw him.

I knew the Jason mentioned to me by my friend Choire that day, as he was also an activist and we were friendly. He had a long narrow face, attractive in the way of a soldier from World War I, but done up in punk drag: Dr. Martens, leather jacket, torn jeans. He had what seemed to me to be an enviable sexual success, and I do recall on occasion feeling the contrast when we sat next to each other, his dyed blond hair making my dark hair seem darker, his lighter. In other words, we were not similar, we were opposites of a kind, and that we would end up having not one but two men in common was a sort of bizarre square dance, but in those times, ordinary.

Peter first asked me out at brunch at the Baghdad Café, on a morning after we had all eluded capture by the police downtown for a Gulf War street action. He walked up to my table and asked for my phone number. I tried to write my number, took his, and he waited as I wrote, grinning a little. He walked off with a look over his shoulder and a wave, to me, more or less ignoring my tablemates. He never asks for anyone's number, my friend Miguel said. He's still hung up on Jason.

People change, I said.

He had asked in a manner so calm, so at odds with my reaction, that I wondered at the time what on earth could have been the reason. For it didn't seem like desire. He had seemed like he was asking if I wanted to go shopping or something.

My days and nights in San Francisco tend to run one into the other: separating them takes an act of will. For years afterward, I recalled my time there as one long day and night, the night full of dancing on bars and long motorcycle rides, the day full of the eerie sunlight, coffee in enormous amounts, dusty used bookstores and, of course, earthquakes and police riots. It was half dream, half nightmare, and in this odd construction, for all the men I had there, Peter's face would remain, clear, at the center of it: Imagine a valentine made from earthquake rubble, spray-painted boots, dollar books, and gasoline, Peter's smile the center of it. Peter at Café Flore, sitting in a sunlit window, surrounded by friends; Peter walking a dark sidewalk, wheat paste in a bucket in his hand, for flyers; Peter at meetings, standing in the back of the room, scowling slightly; Peter's clean body, no marks or tattoos, shining in the reflection of the mirror in his apartment as he approached his bed.

A memory I have of Peter is of protesting the filming of Sharon Stone's vehicle to fame, *Basic Instinct.* Peter and I and Fernando, an ex-boyfriend of mine, stood under the overpass where they were filming and created a discordant trio howl. Peter and I were both formerly in boys' choirs, and Fernando couldn't carry a tune but was quite loud. The sound was haunting, a tone that climbed the bridge's belly and flew everywhere around us. I remember Peter's smile in the San Francisco night, his handsome face slightly contorted by a swollen gland.

Our shriek apparently caused so much distress on the set that Michael Douglas drove his car into a bank of lights. He was not harmed. Later, some of us had fake set passes and got onto the set during the filming. Riot police hidden inside emerged and handcuffed us and brought us all down to the precinct house, where we were held. Peter and Fernando both avoided arrest, I recall. They were technically legal observers and waited for us as we left the police garage. I remember sashaying out of the garage to the howls and whistles of my waiting friends, and that may have been the first time that Peter saw me. He was standing at street level, talking to Jason. But I saw his eyes find me, smile, and go back. A few weeks later, he would ask me out.

I don't know how Peter saw me. I'll never know.

When I finally met and dated Peter I was breaking up with someone dear to me: a Mexican American metalsmith and activist, who took up with Jason, Peter's ex-boyfriend: two of us dark, two of us light. Some odd trade occurred. Some could call it karma, but in those days, I called it pain, and I left it. This ex had been the only man to make me a ring and put it on my finger (no one else has yet done this). Jason and he would have a commitment ceremony. Peter would up until his passing think sometimes, in his dementia, that Jason, who visited him regularly and well, was still his boyfriend. Peter had not, as I'd said to my friend Miguel, changed: he still loved Jason.

I left this tangle. You are reminded: I am a minor character. You sense the distortion of this story, and you are right to ask, where is the main character? He is gone. I moved to New York, for another man. I could ask myself what might have happened had I stayed, but that's a false question, suitable only for novelists and drunks. I didn't stay. The pain went away and I figured I had left it behind. I was wrong. Peter's story continued without me, to its end.

How do you know someone is dead? One way is when they are referred to in the past tense. Peter lived for a few years after my departure, and his death happened out of my sight, my hearing. I was not part of the group that got called. I was one outside that group, after that departure I'd made. I now understand and accept this as one of the costs of my departure. Years later, in New York, my friend Choire was speaking to me about San Francisco, and he said, "Well, after Peter died. . . ." Peter had been dead three months when he said this.

I felt like he had been cleaning a gun and it had emptied into me. "Sorry," Choire said. "Thought you knew. Hate that, when people don't know."

3.

Peter was born in Albuquerque, New Mexico, and had grown up in Washington, first on Mercer Island and then in Bellevue, where he went to Newport High School. He was a skier and a swimmer in high school, but "not competitive in that way people wanted from athletes," his mother adds. Intelligent, quick-minded, he never had to study hard and school came easily to him. "He used to love to bug me," his sister says of him. She remembers him always taking her back upstairs to re-dress her in the mornings, when she would come down in what he considered inappropriate clothes. He could get away with a great deal of mischief. "He used to leave the house undetected, all the time," his mother recalls. "I didn't know for years that he would get out of the house through his window and go out all night. He started doing it as a child." He graduated from the University of Washington with a degree in graphic design and left for Europe, living for the year in Spain and Portugal. He had been a kind of art prodigy, good at ceramics, drawing, design. He had made, in college, a ceramic relief so large there was no kiln big enough to fire it, and the relief stayed at his home in Washington until his father sold the house. His mother still has a set of plates he made in the shapes of fishes, and one Christmas, she recalls, he sent her copper candlesticks that had once been table legs; each one had been wrapped in brown paper and then the group arranged and tied to make the shape of a star. "I didn't want to open it," she says. "It was like, that was the gift itself, it was so beautiful." He did the artwork for the events posters for the Paradise Lounge, where he worked as a bartender, all done in a psychedelic mode. "So beautiful," Laura says, who bartended there with him. Peter created images for ACT UP's Marlboro boycott. He was personally happy to see earnings reports that showed they had lost money in the quarter the boycott began. He wanted to be a musician, and before he became too ill to do so, he had plans to record. "He had a beautiful voice," Lisa says. "He had a beautiful voice," his mother says.

He is remembered as consistent by anyone who knew him, steady with everyone, and a study in contradictions: he was immensely private, and yet he would say, without provocation, to anyone, "I'm a homo." Serious and grave, he would give in occasionally to a jig, a little hopping dance. Extremely quiet, he could, when he wanted, be the center of attention. "I was called to school by the principal when he was in the fifth grade," his mother recalls, "for a show. A talent show, by the students. And out came this little boy, my boy, so self-possessed. And he emceed the entire show from start to finish, totally confident, a little Johnny Carson." Peter attended his high-school prom in a black tuxedo he splattered with shocking pink paint to match his date's pink dress and the pink shirt he wore with the tux.

In San Francisco, after college, he became part of a punk rock scene that centered on a place called the A-hole, where he befriended the painter Pasquale Semillion, whom he and Laura cared for until his death from AIDS. Peter had turned to photography but still painted abstract canvases. No one is exactly sure who has what pieces of his art now. His sister has three of the Paradise Lounge posters framed in her home, his mother, the plates that he made and paintings and a sketch he had titled "Three Dogs and a Pig" that was actually of four dogs. She likes to remember this as a sample of his humor. Laura has paintings and pictures and tapes. Jason has memories only. "I can't really remember him from before he was sick, don't really remember the art," he says. "Isn't that terrible?"

Jill Kelloran, his mother, has a picture of him, framed, that she looks at regularly, of Peter on the beach in Portugal, waving from the sand in front of a tent he had made from everything he had found on the beach—flags, old jeans, sails—and where he lived for a good part of his time there. His father,

Tom Kelloran, has framed a five-page letter that Peter sent from that Portuguese tent.

His favorite bands: Band Yellow and Adam Ant, Einstürzende Neubauten. His favorite article of clothing: a belt buckle shaped like a bullet. His favorite author: Kurt Vonnegut; in particular, the story "Welcome to the Monkey House," in which Billy the Poet, a lighthearted sexual rhymer, stalks a futuristic America with plans to make Americans enjoy the sex they now all deny themselves. Peter's plan: to become a musician.

When an artist dies young there is always talk of the paintings undone, the books unwritten, but that points to some imaginary storehouse of undone things and not to the imagination itself, the far richer treasure, lost. All of those works are the trail left behind, a path across time left as the sun leaves gold on the sea: you can see it but you can't ever pick it up. What makes us sweat from the sun here on earth is a fraction of the force the sun can bring to bear, and this is what this lost work is to us, these paintings in the apartment with him when died, unfinished: this is faint heat from faraway fire. What we lose with each death is like stars falling out of the sky and into the sea and gone. It is more than nothing that we have left, loss larger than nothingness; the something undone, the something that won't ever be done, remains unendurable to consider. My personal pantheon of heroes from that time are all dead: Peter, Derek Jarman, David Wojnarowicz. I feel more than unequal to any one of them. So instead I stand here and balance them on the tip of a crush a decade old. I feel they would all approve.

More than my other heroes, Peter and I were alike. Both oldest brothers, both with family money, both with a sense of political responsibility. More mundane details: both of us got away with all sorts of misbehavior as children, both of us liked to shock with our way of dressing, both of us liked science fiction. Both of us sang in boys' choirs as children. Both of us worked in ceramics in college. Both of us skied and swam and eschewed team sports, competitive behavior in general. Why should I survive on the earth where he didn't? As I near the age he was when he passed on, I feel a clock count off, though, at this writing, I am still negative. At this writing, no one has yet been cured of AIDS, either.

What can we endure? We cannot help but be reminded of what we do not know from these lost, and what they will never tell us, can never tell us.

And I can't help but long for it still, can't help but long for Peter still, the sight of him, as I once did, love-struck and young, a star in my eye, the top corner of it dyed blue.

What I felt for Peter, I know, may never, if I'd stayed, have added up, but knowing what I know about him makes me believe in love at first sight more rather than less, because I wasn't wrong about him, even though I didn't know him: the truth of him came to me in the sight of him. And so this eye empties out what it saw, and I can't help but want to restore him with memory's pantomime, the imagination's garish theater, the fiction writer's song. And so now he is on this page. He is gone and not gone. Peter D. Kelloran, as he liked to appear in print.

4.

I remember that on our first date Peter took me to see a concert. He picked me up at my apartment on Market Street, we went to the concert downtown, and then we drove back to my apartment, a flat under the Divisadero overpass on Market Street. I don't remember the music. The whole time I was only aware of Peter. I asked him in, and he said sure. In my room he sat down on my bed, a lumber and cement-block affair that I'd made with a friend.

San Francisco nights are always more vivid than the days. The sunlight of San Francisco, for all its color and clarity, has always added to the sense that the city was an illusion. That light shows nothing. The nights in San Francisco are where everything seems its true self and color. Peter seemed much older than me that night. He wore his leather jacket, a coat I loved, and it was one of the few times when I knew him that his hair was blond, his head nearly bare. I remember he kept removing a dropper of astragalus and taking it, which he did just then.

So, he said, as he sat on my bed and tucked the dropper into his jacket. I normally take boys home and tie them up and whip them.

I hadn't turned the light on in my room and we were in the dark there. He smiled as he said this.

Do you want to take me home and tie me up and whip me? I asked.

Do you want to be tied up and whipped? He asked.

No, I said. Not really. Part of me thought he was joking. Part of me knew his reputation.

He lay down next to me on the bed. The two of us lay there, in our coats and boots, and I felt alone with him for the first time. That's fine, he said. We don't have to do that. And he reached his arm around me.

Can you do me a favor? I asked him, after we had lain there awhile, silent and still.

Yes, he said.

Can you lie on top of me? Just, you know, lie there?

He rolled on top of me, in a light embrace, and the weight of him pushed the breath out of me.

Am I crushing you? he asked.

No, I said. This is exactly what I meant. And the weight of him pressed me out. I felt covered, safe; something dark retreated, and, for what felt like the first time in the arms of a man, I felt safe. Which is one of the things that love can feel like. Peter stayed there for some time. He may even have fallen asleep at some point. And so it is that when I hear stories of how thin he became, I can't reconcile them with the weight of the boy who pinned me to myself and made me feel the place in me where I attached to the world.

He got up and went home. We made a plan to see each other again. I was with him in a way that I was with no one else, and from what I understand, this was also true for him. Strange to ourselves and each other, only the feeling of the room, the silence of it, was familiar. All over the city, people were strung into slings, dancing on tables, walking down alleys following strangers, and on my doorstep it felt like we were a young couple out of *Happy Days*, out of the fifties, mild as milk. I watched him go and then turned and went back upstairs to bed.

He had shaved his head, having come back from his sister's wedding, for which he had grown out his hair. I wouldn't know, until years later, that he had just told his mother of his illness. On pictures from that day "he looked gorgeous," his mother says. But his grandmother, Paula Morgan, thought otherwise. "He's sick," she said, after seeing him. She knew before he had told them what was wrong. "He was a very special young man," she says of him now. "It seems to me this happens to special young men."

5.

During his last two years, when he was very sick, he became so thin his pants would fall off him. He went in and out of dementia, regressing. He started smoking again. He would ask Jason, "Does my father know we're boy-friends?" Or he would say, "I met you at high school, right?" He went out from the hospice one day with Janet, his aunt, and went to get cigarettes and burg-ers, and he looked around at the people there and said, "These people, they're all homosexuals! Every one!" He was so thin at that point that even in the Castro, where people were accustomed to the sight of wasting, Peter attracted attention.

"He had wanted," Janet says, "to be at Maitri. And so we went and there was no room and it looked like he was going to have to go somewhere else, and then I called and found him a space there, which was good. It was where he wanted to be." Janet had rented an apartment for Peter to spend Christmas with her down in Carmel, and it was shortly after, upon returning, that Peter called her to say, "It's time. It's my time." He had been living at home until then, getting meals delivered and having home care, and when he called Janet, he gave as his reason, "I can't take care of myself anymore. It's my time."

Imagine all your days running through you, you like a pool of light and sound altering as you encounter them. That all at once you are every age you have ever been. Time is coursing through you, the time you lived, running back and forth through you, a flume of your days. This was Peter's dementia.

"I always knew where he was," Lisa says, of his dementia. "He, God, he would say something and people would say, 'He's crazy,' but he wasn't. No, people thought it was sad, and it was, but it was beautiful, really, because he was back in the days that he loved, just, all at once. I remember he said once, 'I have to give Lisa a baby!' and the people at the hospice really thought he'd lost it, but I knew. We used to talk about having a child, and then, well, he got HIV, and he never talked about it again. And so he mentioned the baby again there and I said, 'No, remember? You got sick. And so we didn't have it.' And he got quiet again."

Jason remembers him saying, "I am supposed to tell you something, Jason. They want me to tell you something." And so Jason waited, and then Peter said, "It's about love. I am supposed to tell you, they want me to tell you, it's about love."

"He was so angry at the end," Laura remembers. "Before Christmas we went out to dinner for his birthday, and he had chocolate. And it made him all warm, as he wasn't eating any sugar and hadn't for a long time. And so we took him home, and I stayed with him and it was then I knew, we'd lost him. That he was going to go. He was very lucid then, very disappointed. He was talking about how he'd never been properly loved by a man and how he wouldn't be, now. He spoke of everything he wouldn't do, the music, everything. And when I heard him talk like that, I knew he wasn't going to make it."

Before this Peter had wanted to live until 1995. Research that Laura and he had done in astrology said that 1995 would be an important year, and it would be. It was the year of the advent of protease inhibitors, the year many people mortgaged their deaths. Laura had done so much research into trying to keep Peter alive that she was awarded a complete scholarship to Mills College to study microbiology, and she received the letter notifying her the Monday after he had died. "It got me out of bed," she says. She had taken to her bed for a week after Peter's passing and would later in the year be hospitalized for two weeks for severe depression. "I've had a number of breakdowns since," she says, over the phone from her new job at a recording studio in San Francisco. "I just felt that I had failed him. That I wasn't able to keep him alive. And it hurt too damn much." Laura divorced her husband later, in part because without Peter she felt her marriage reduced, and she likewise gave up her research. She has lost more friends than Peter to the epidemic, but more than that, she lost the one she loved best. "If I thought for a second," she says, "that I could love like that again. . . ." Her mother and Peter's mother both had not so secretly wished the two of them would marry—Laura was a Lister, as in Listerine, and Peter was a Morgan of the banking family on his mother's side—but eventually both accepted the situation for what it was.

Laura and Peter had divined several significant concordances within their astrological charts, but for Laura the most significant was that he was Aries moon at twenty-seven degrees, she, Aries sun at twenty-seven degrees. "Your moon sign is your relationship to yourself, how you talk to yourself. The way he talked to himself, that was me. And your sun, that is how you greet the world."

Peter was not buried. He was cremated and his ashes spread on a sunny day from a catamaran that sailed out under the Golden Gate Bridge. "There's no marker," Jill Kelloran says. "Just our hearts. We know where he is."

Peter was a member of what was jokingly known at first as the BART 9, a group of nine activists who had handcuffed themselves to the pole at the center of a BART train when the doors were open, stopping the train in the station. This same group had also disrupted the San Francisco Opera opening night and blockaded the Golden Gate Bridge. This same group had done a lot of things over the years, and while many of them were in ACT UP, for most this was simply another in a series of protests designed to draw attention to the AIDS pandemic and the various ways in which companies were looking to exploit the dying. The whole thing had been over very quickly, with the group arrested and taken away. The train was made late but still left the station. Peter missed medication that day as a result of his arrest, Laura recalls. "It was a nightmare." Missing medication was a risk all AIDS activists who had AIDS took constantly. The police denying them their pills, out of whatever rules the jail follows, were murderous.

Peter felt the risk was worthy. At the time, we joked constantly about suicide missions. We have nothing to lose, the HIV-positive contingent of ACT UP would say in those days. We have nothing to lose, having lost everything. Understand that in 1989 there was AZT and that was basically it. Understand that those of us who lived there in San Francisco had the false impression that no one like us had ever existed before, because the ones who might have greeted us when we arrived were already dead. Their lives had been efforts of a transitory nature; they were like those species from the Pleistocene who never waded into the tar pit, who never left behind a fossil record. We lacked models for bravery and were trying to invent them, as we likewise invented models for loving, and for activism. In the writing of an article about love and HIV that I compiled interviews for over this last winter, I interviewed many young gay people who would say, I can't imagine getting older. Most of the people who might have shown them what it would be like to be gay and alive even at forty or forty-five are dead. What happened to me is happening again, ten years later.

When I fell in love with Peter, I fell in love with what I wanted to be next. In the *Odyssey*, Homer describes Poseidon Earthshaker as having blue hair. He is alternately "blue-maned Poseidon" and "Poseidon of the blue brows." Peter returned to the sea makes me think of that, his blue hair like a mark across his brow from an old god. Peter D. Kelloran, resident of San Francisco, a town ruled by earthquakes and inhabited by people who understood some of the value of what the Greeks left for us, Peter the blue-maned, now in the arms of Poseidon Earthshaker—he belongs to a time that already we can't imagine even though we lived through it, when there was one drug and hope was hidden so it wouldn't die. I like to imagine him now like the science fiction characters he favored, in flight through the sky, roaming the night in a nimbus of blue light, a smiling rogue punk rock angel, his wings dyed blue to match, from a Heaven where everyone dresses really well and mercy means love and a man you don't know will hold your hand for you when you die. A Heaven where when there's injustice you chain yourself to a train because you know somewhere, someone feels it. Somewhere along the spirit-chain world-mind over-soul, someone, somewhere, who maybe thought there wasn't a thing called strength, feels how you care enough to stand in front of the passage of a train. As children, we thought Superman was brave to stand in front of a train. That's not brave, though. Superman never stood before anything that could destroy him. Peter did.

Howard, Art, and the Seventies

Brad Gooch

Three nights ago I went with Moses—a twenty-six-year-old Israeli who had just released a dance cut, "Don't Let Me"—to a party at the apartment of friends of his who live above the sex shop the Pleasure Chest, which they own. Their online catalog sales for dildos, candy-flavored panties, and toy handcuffs must be brisk these days because not only did our hosts have hills of shrimp, ham, and turkey, and a bartender pouring stiff drinks, but they'd hired a straight, hairy go-go dancer, moonlighting from his job as a trainer at a gym on the Upper West Side, and another gayer boy dressed only in his Calvin Klein briefs who'd been paid to allow people to touch him wherever they so chose.

I didn't think about Howard or the seventies once that night.

But I did the next day. Background: rain. I thought about how that period, and mood, and its list of names so evocative of love and art, had finally become history. This relegation didn't happen instantly of course. For years I've felt that gay life was defined by the names and places of that era: Robert Mapplethorpe, Rainer Werner Fassbinder, the Mineshaft, the Castro, Christopher Street, David Wojnarowicz, Jack Wrangler. But at the party all these cute kids were talking in a very high-powered-sounding way of writers I sort of knew whose first novels had just come out, and of painters who lived in Williamsburg across the East River rather than in SoHo or the East Village, and of deejays I certainly had never heard of, never having understood the fine distinction between "ambient" and "trip" or "house" and "heavy house." They had their own celebrity system and their own homemade hype. All during seventies' hangover and then seventies' nostalgia I remember thinking and sometimes saying, "When are they going to think of something new?" Wow, I realized that next day, to surprisingly mixed feelings. They *have*. Or at least they've found new names and bodies to fill the old slots.

Thinking about the seventies is like watching a very grainy, handheld black-and-white movie in a world of color. One with lots of exterior downtown shots. And lots of youth. And lots of new people in almost every scene—party scenes, too many party scenes. But to underline the obvious: there are no cell phones in those scenes. No computer chat rooms to enter. To make a phone call you drop a dime in the phone booth at the corner. No CDs are playing. The first time you find out about a new Blondie cut is when you hear it from the radio of a car driving by. Most people don't even have answering machines. There are no phone sex lines. There are just bars. And new clubs opening in big abandoned warehouses, or down steps into a cellar, or up a freight elevator. No one seems to have jobs. And everywhere, everywhere, there is art—but I'll get back to that. It's my theme. That, and Howard. But then Howard, art, and the seventies turn out to be deeply connected, as you'll see. (Especially since for me what I mean when I say "the seventies" doesn't begin until around 1975 and certainly doesn't end on the dot in 1979.)

I first met Howard Brookner at a bar called the Ninth Circle in the West Village in 1977. We were introduced by a mutual friend, Richard Elovich, who was working as an assistant to various poets and artists: Jasper Johns, Allen Ginsberg, John Ashbery. (Name-dropping here is a virtue, a kind of an explanation, not a vice, not mere wallpaper.) Howard was sitting at a table in the back with his film crew. I'd never seen a film crew. But there they were, all NYU Film School students, with their cameras like props laid out on the table and floor, drinking beers and vodkas. I think Howard was shooting the early footage that became his documentary on the writer William Burroughs. "Hellos" were exchanged. He wrote down his number for me on the back of a Taste of Tokyo chopsticks wrapper in squiggly horror movie script. Then he called a few weeks later, when he got back from visiting his parents in Miami.

Actually we'd met a few minutes before we'd been introduced. We just hadn't spoken. He'd somehow squeezed a few minutes away from crew and friends to lean against a low shelf along one wooden wall of the bar. I was standing alone near the ruby jukebox staring at a poster taped on the wall above of Mark Spitz in a swimsuit with Olympic medals hung about his neck. Then suddenly there was Howard: about 5´9˝, curly dark hair, bantamweight toned body, tanned, almost Middle Eastern looking that night. I re-

Howard Brookner. Courtesy of Brad Gooch.

member him in a T-shirt, brown corduroys, and these beat-up blue sneakers with Zs on the sides. I already had a buzz, admittedly. But I felt his brown eyes like lasers staring into me as I was staring into him. I remember seeing a light in my head that almost seemed to be speaking to me in another language. Then the cosmic connection snapped. Romance meets sci-fi. But significantly. I did feel significance here in this young man. (Though I must say I'd felt zapped by quite a few other young men at the time; such zapping seemed a characteristic of either the time or my age, or both.)

As Howard was dying of AIDS in April 1989 I sat by his bed writing out his obituary, which was then retouched by Stephen Holden and printed in the *New York Times*. Only once while I was working away on the yellow tablet did Howard regain consciousness—as John Lennon's "Imagine" began to play on the stereo. He was beyond talking by this point. But he did regain consciousness. I felt his presence as certainly as I had that first night in the bar. And the same zapping from his eyes took place, though this time filled with lots of memories rather than being a pure beam of instant intimacy. He insisted with his eyes that we acknowledge the dark joke of hearing this song right now, and of our sharing it. We cried and hugged until the song was over.

And then I went back to the therapy of figuring out the dates and plot points of his life—

Born 1954. Grew up in Great Neck, Long Island. Went to Phillips Exeter Academy, Columbia, NYU Film School. His *Burroughs* documentary shown at the 1984 New York Film Festival, at festivals in West Berlin, Tokyo, Florence, Rotterdam, and in theatrical release in forty cities around the world. I put in a few lines from Janet Maslin's review in the *Times*, remembering how we'd walked to the corner in the rain to buy the paper at Gem Spa on Second Avenue to find her comments, and adding up very clearly in my mind that he was thirty and that he had somehow made it: "The quality of discovery about 'Burroughs' was very much the director's doing, and Mr. Brookner demonstrates an unusual degree of liveliness and curiosity in exploring his subject." The review was *so* good that I was envious.

There was a PBS documentary in 1986, *Robert Wilson and the Civil Wars*, about Wilson's international avant-garde opera. And there was *Bloodhounds of Broadway*, his first feature film with a cast including Madonna, Matt Dillon, Jennifer Grey, Esai Morales, Rutger Hauer, and Randy Quaid, based on four Damon Runyon stories, that he'd just finished writing, directing, and producing for Columbia Pictures, when he got sick. I knew he wanted to live until his thirty-fifth birthday, the April thirtieth on which he was actually buried.

In the weeks following the *Times* obituary, some feature-style obituaries appeared. *Newsweek* included him in their "AIDS and the Arts: A Lost Generation" issue. But I didn't particularly feel close to Howard as one of a row of death-radiant celebrities. His picture and even name seemed like light from a distant star. I was much more drawn to the earlier period, the "seventies" period, when everyone wanted to be famous, but no one really expected to be. To films that included his friend, Joe, a Hungarian head usher at the Met who played Count Discount in an early effort. Or to footage of Jimmy the Bum, a what-we-now-call "homeless person" whom Howard befriended on the Bowery and used in a long-lost scene. Or to his friend Melinda of the fake English accent, whom he matched up with his favorite prop, a plaster cast rip-off of the Apollo Belvedere—the title of that vehicle designed to show off Melinda's most cinematic qualities now escapes me.

And of course I was, and am, drawn to that period because neither of us yet had date books, so we had lots of spare time just to be together. That's the Howard I want to get close to again here. But to get close to him is to get reacquainted with a time and with lots of people—it's hard to name one person from that time without naming another, because we were so chummy and elitist and given to "We are a family" utopian fantasies. And it's hard for those names not to be the names of poets, painters, and other creative types because art *was* politics in that era before PAC committees and openly gay candidates. A Tom of Finland dirty drawing or an Allen Ginsberg love poem was about the closest we had to a political statement. (I remember the only Gay Pride march I ever participated in being with a bunch of writers whose idea of clout was to run screaming up the steps of the New York Public Library with our posters of Rimbaud, Whitman, and Henry James held high.) The feeling involved in making a world "bigger than the both of us" did keep us pretty alert and sometimes even happy. Whether bona fide artists or not, we lived like artists by making up the rules as we went along.

Certainly the Howard Brookner I met in 1977 was a live wire. Later after he died I found this entry in a diary he'd been keeping after being diagnosed with AIDS: "When I die, my education dies with me. All those years of Latin, French, Italian. We all share the same education, including television, film, music, events. But each person's mix is slightly different. My particular mix will be removed soon from this planet." In those early days, though, Howard's mix was quite evident and could be felt as personally as a signature, or a fingerprint on everything he did and said. Indeed his casual intellect, and eagerness to see every new Godard movie and buy every new Springsteen record, or opera recording for that matter, was what *made* him sexy. I can't imagine any of my friends for whom such a percolating curiosity wasn't a turn-on, if not a requirement. Years later a fellow survivor remarked to me at the gym, "In the seventies, we didn't *have* bodies." Well of course we did. But the emphasis was elsewhere, and Howard's lithe young unworked-out body was fine by me. (I report all this, incidentally, as a true time-traveler who sees his trainer three times weekly and isn't the least bit rattled if someone he's dating hasn't read Proust. That was then; this is now.)

When Howard called a few weeks later after our initial meeting to ask me out on a date I had the nerve (youthful dumbness?) to say no. Why? Not because I hadn't been waiting anxiously for him to return from Miami. But because he asked me to see a Cuban dance troupe—he was working as an usher at the Met that summer, his twenty-fourth, my twenty-sixth, and had scored free tickets. Knowing nothing about it, I'd decided that Cuban dance was lame. He tried again. His friend, Brad, was the lead singer in a punk rock band and they were having a concert in a basement club on Eighth Street. Ping! went my heart, and we were on. He showed up that night at my West Village walk-up all sweaty from having run down by the river. Five minutes later he emerged from the shower with just a towel wrapped around him. I was sitting on oversized floor pillows pretending to read Derrida. I then tried pretentiously to serve him steak tartare (the influence of the Derrida?) and he insisted on cooking it, balking at the notion of uncooked meat. Somehow we were even, and remained even from then on.

The date was fun: a black velvet rope, a guest list, freebie drinks. (We never did become Studio 54 types, sticking more to downtown venues—Paradise Garage, the Mudd Club, the Mineshaft.) But the special segment of the evening occurred afterward when we returned to his vast loft on Prince Street near the Bowery, for which he was paying one hundred dollars a month. One of those kids who'd made a small fortune at his lemonade stand, Howard had brought down his own rent by working out some deal with his Italian landlords, the Bari brothers, to rent out their other undesirable apartments in what was then undesirable SoHo to friends, starting with his best friend at film school, the director Jim Jarmusch. That night Howard sat in a big ugly armchair that had been his grandmother's and I sat on the red vinyl couch and we talked: about nuclear bombs, Kraftwerk, Andy Warhol as a young artist, the films of Nicholas Ray, death, extinction, the use of hypnosis in sex when we were teenage boys, Israel versus the Arabs (Howard was Jewish, I wasn't), Literature versus Film (the sides taken there were obvious).

All this talk was foreplay, of course. The next morning when I woke up two things happened: I noticed the bookshelf that had been looming precariously over us all night as we made love. It was filled with the same books I'd read in freshman humanities class at Columbia University where we'd both been students at the same time, though we hadn't met. I pulled down a copy of *The Collected Poems of D. H. Lawrence* and went into the bathroom to read "The Snake." When I reemerged, Howard's grip from his film crew, this kid named Kevin who was wildly sexual and into dangerous straight boys, had appeared bearing a big Acme bag filled with potato chips and sodas. Howard announced that he was having a barbecue and his friends would be showing up in an hour. (I think it was that day, anyway, or I've telescoped two early dates into one. But then whatever's been left out would only have been a lot of unimportant static that obviously didn't further the plot of my life.)

A lot of Howard's favorite friends-dash-character-actors were there— Joe the usher at the Met, Jimmy the Bum. But there was also Darryl Pinckney, a writer, black, who'd been in college with both of us and became a kind of hinge. Darryl had been more of a protégé of Elizabeth Hardwick, and he was a prose writer. I'd been more of a protégé of Kenneth Koch, and I was a poet. Howard was a wild card, being a filmmaker, which at the time seemed daring, new, thrilling, and a little down-market. Howard and Darryl had been roommates, and had worked together as interns at the *New York Review of Books*. They had lots of funny literary-style anecdotes. Howard Moss, the poetry editor of the *New Yorker*, had apparently made a pass at Howard at one party and Howard (Brookner) had said to Darryl, "A rolling Brookner gathers no Moss." Repeating this jibe would cut them up. Darryl liked to tell the story about his quoting a remark of Hardwick's to someone at a dinner while she was present and her reprimanding him, "Darryl, you are not T. S. Eliot and I am not the Greeks!" I heard both those witticisms for the first time— though certainly not the last—at that barbecue.

Our relation to the preceding generation was interesting. We'd all come to New York to live the bohemian artist life. To take our places in lofts and garrets reading poems, painting, drinking ourselves into the gutter in order to look at the stars, etc. But at the same time we'd already been ventilated in a sense by growing up on TV, by being as much potheads as drinkers, and by being openly gay. Leaving the explanation to sociologists and psychologists, I did notice that our older heroes in poetry and painting were much wittier than we, much sharper, much more diffident, and I felt a bit snobbish about the obvious gaps in our collective cultural files. You had to fake it a bit to sit around the poet John Ashbery's apartment sharing his thrill over his obscure recordings of Busoni or Ravel. (This process has speeded up and intensified to such a degree—and roles have been reversed predictably enough—that I can't say I wasn't shocked in my own way recently when a young friend claimed he'd broken up with a boyfriend because he didn't know what *Rhoda* was—a spin-off of the *Mary Tyler Moore Show*. "How could he be so ignorant of such a big part of American culture?" he'd complained.)

Cultural politics worked itself out in more personal ways as well between me and Howard. By making a film about the Beat author, his bent was more toward a group that included Allen Ginsberg, Gregory Corso, John Giorno. He was always running out to interview Patti Smith, or Terry Southern, even the painter Francis Bacon. Early on I'd visit Howard in the Bunker— Burroughs's basement headquarters on the Bowery—where he'd play scenes on his Steenbeck editing machine for my feedback, or just as an excuse to be on a date and get some work done at the same time. My "set"—at least mindset—was the more urban, or urbane, New York School of Koch, Ashbery, and Frank O'Hara, about whom I later wrote a biography. (These documentaries and biographies were obviously in part a working out of the family dynamics of this high culture we'd adopted and been adopted by.) When we met I lived in the West Village, Howard in the East, and this too was a major divide. The West Village was associated with the "clone" look of flannel shirts and close-cropped beards, and when I'd cross one intersection on my way to Howard's I'd see the message "Clones Go Home" stamped on the street. The East Village was more punk rock than disco, more bohemian than leather-and-Levi's gay. These aesthetic distinctions meant a lot to us then, and led to a certain amount of conflict and stress. Amazingly so, given the virtually undetectable nuances of difference between these relatively similar schools of poetry, and neighborhoods, looked back on from the jumble of today.

We worked matters out though by moving in together after a year and trying to make statements that were "ours." First in a rambling apartment on Bleecker Street near the Bowery—the move forcing me to turn in my West Village passport. Then in an apartment in Paris during a two-year detour I took as a male model, Howard using the occasion to edit his film, the reels of which he brought over in big black steamer trunks we then lugged up the cold spiraling stairs of our beige apartment building near Place Pigalle. Finally, and most perfectly, in the Chelsea Hotel, steeped in bohemian tradition, where with our upstairs neighbor, Chris Cox, a writer and editor, we used to throw "ladies' parties"—getting dressed in drag and drinking oversized martinis. Howard's persona was Lilli Laleen, Italian film directress who dressed in black sunglasses and a thrift-shop Mary McFadden-esque pleated dress. I was June Buntt, the wife of a space-case astronaut, Brad. The writer Dennis Cooper was a black lesbian who cradled his/her baby, Charmin, a roll of toilet tissue wrapped in a blanket. Poet Tim Dlugos, who later studied at an Episcopal seminary before his own death from AIDS in 1990, was

Bernadette of Lourdes. I still have a garish posed snapshot of one of these blotto events taken by Chris, aka Kay Sera-Sera.

When we were apart we kept our what-had-become-love kindled—I had my modeling gigs, and then grad school; Howard was onto his documentary about Robert Wilson that involved filming in Tokyo, Rome, Cologne, Berlin, Paris, New York City, and Los Angeles. He liked calling in that period from the five-franc thirty-second phones on the Champs Élysées. Typical, too, was a call from an airport phone booth that cut off after his opening line, "I'm getting on a plane with Bob and Bianca to go to Tokyo." His life was obviously moving into fast forward. But mostly he kept in touch with letters, poems. He was always a writer, too, of everything from journals, to porn novels for the Mafia briefly to make quick money, to screenplays, including one he was a passionate about based on James Purdy's *Eustace Chisholm and the Works*. The love notes though were always the best, for me at least. I have one here that he wrote early on when he was once again visiting his parents' condo in Miami: "The wind is picking up. The light is rippling on the lake. I hope I can be open enough to be vulnerable to you. I hope I still feel this way when the invisible summer haze is blown away by the reality of an autumn breeze. I hope you like me despite that last horrible line."

After a few years of monogamy, or near monogamy, we became what in retrospect was probably too smart for our own good. We missed the electricity of boy-love and all-nighters and art-inducing self-destructive love affairs. So we decided in 1986 that we were smart enough to be able to live apart, keep a life going with a summer house on the north shore of Long Island, and a planned sunset phase together on some imaginary hill or canyon in Los Angeles. Suddenly we both had boyfriends, several of them. Howard—who had originally been the proponent of fidelity and a marriage modeled on that of his grandparents, whom he often reminded me were never apart one night during their seventy years together—became like a casting director for the very edgy, romantic movie he wanted his life to become. To make things more interesting, he even had a beautiful actress girlfriend in Paris. Curiously though we *were* half-successful at our ambitious project. We never really fought. We remained each other's best friend. And our mutual heart—which was always part art—kept beating with fervor. I detect less of such lifelong expectations in a gay subculture today in which even the hypothetical option of "together forever" seems to have been deleted by the AIDS experience.

The experiment did work in keeping each of us juiced with ambition. As our mutual agent at ICM, Luis Sanjurjo, rightly told someone who was complaining that we'd given up our two-bedroom garret at the Chelsea Hotel, "They both have work to do." By then, however, a disturbing devil's bargain seemed to be setting in. Howard called me one spring evening at dusk to tell me he'd tested positive for HIV, and that his T cells were down. I was in my apartment on West 29th Street, he in a loft he was subletting from Robert Wilson in Tribeca. I cried a bit, but, more important, had a vision while staring into what had become in my eyes the pitiless and unrelenting brown of Eighth Avenue of what was in store. Soon the crock pots appeared filled with special Chinese teas, and the little pills to be taken at irregular hours, and dietary eccentricities that changed by the week.

Simultaneously, however, Howard's brilliance became magically unmuffled. He'd always been exceptional. But suddenly his Mexican jumping bean energy was much more palpable. He was able almost without failure to talk anybody into anything. Soon he wrote a script for *Bloodhounds of Broadway* that became unnaturally hot in Hollywood, and many eager young stars wanted a part—or were charmed into wanting a part. I remember him telling me that when Matt Dillon—a longtime screen crush of Howard's—was wavering about being in the film, Howard invited him to lunch at Umberto's Clam House and at an opportune moment between dessert and coffee had his assistant walk by and drop a manila envelope on the table that he presented to Matt. Inside were vintage photographs of Joey Gallo lying murdered on the floor of the restaurant. Apparently pixilated, the actor signed on. (Later, feeding my own fetishism, Howard slipped me a pair of Dillon's white sox from his dressing room that I still have tucked away in a cedar chest.)

Howard received seed money for the film from the *American Playhouse* series on PBS, but then in one memorable meeting at Columbia Pictures he managed to convince David Puttnam, then chairman of the studio, to back this auteur production of a first-time director with a $4 million budget, and they began filming in December 1987 on the streets of Union City, Newark, and Jersey City. This backing proved to be a mixed blessing, though, when, after the wrap and Howard's quick descent into a wheelchair where he remained, half blind and paralyzed on one side of his body, the studio wrested back control of the editing process. (His symptoms were the result of the virus having crossed the blood-brain barrier.) Interviewed later by the *New York Times* for a story—"A Director's Race with AIDS Ends Before His Movie Opens"—Lindsay Law, the head of *American Playhouse*, recalled that during the early contract negotiations, when his condition was a secret, Howard asked him, "What do we do when Columbia wants final cut? You never allow that do you?" Law answered, "Howard, this is the first feature film of a long career, you can't expect a studio to give you final cut." To which Howard replied, "But what if this is my only film?" "Those words echo now," Law told the reporter.

In near-death as in life, though, Howard remained insistent, and as offbeat as his early films or the daffy characters Hotfoot Harry and Feet Samuels he'd just captured on celluloid. Howard often bragged that he'd been named after his cousin, Moe Howard, one of the Three Stooges. And there was some affinity I guess in Howard's own zany relationship with people and the world "You look like you've seen a ghost," he quipped sardonically to Randy Quaid when he came to visit him near the end. This slightly irrational flair, coupled with practicality, of course, gave him his authority. When he was finally confined to a gray couch in an apartment his parents sublet for him in London Terrace during his last year, he decided that he was going to film a novel I'd just published, *Scary Kisses*, about male modeling. The project was a sort of sweet and final valentine between us. As preparation, everyone who came to visit Howard—Barry Diller, Madonna, Sean Penn—had to endure being videotaped reading a section. Who could refuse? In the face of his own gigantic refusal—the refusal to succumb so easily to the diminishment of death—he pulverized anyone's ability to turn him down on anything. Howard used this dynamic to his advantage, and along the way almost convinced us that he just *might* be up to making another film. As Sarah Driver—Jim Jarmusch's girlfriend—told the *Times* in the article on Howard's race with the clock, "Howard was kind of a weasel in figuring out how to get things done. Jim and I thought he would weasel out of his illness somehow."

Howard was still in and out of the hospital in this final phase, and the movie was still in and out of his hands. Once I walked in on a speaker-phone conference in which he was shouting about his editing rights in words that were by now greatly slurred, while shaking his stiffened arm angrily in the air at no one in particular. He wasn't yelling at Dawn Steel, who'd taken over the studio. He liked her too much. But at someone. The person who seemed to zigzag most fully between these two startlingly disconnected worlds—the hospital room and the movie studio—was Madonna, who was helpful in both capacities, as powerful editing ally and regular visitor. I recently redis-covered a note from her to Howard that brought back this eerie double mo-tif of career and disease as she promised to both watch the new cut of the film and visit the hospital—her visits making Howard as much of a celebrity as she was on the seventh floor of St. Vincent's. "I hope you are not angry w/me for keeping the V.H.S. of Bloodhounds for so long," she'd written in green felt-tip pen. "It was difficult to find time to watch without the peering eyes of my ever curious husband . . . . I'm sure the new editor has made many im-provements and look forward to seeing them. I'm going to try & visit you on Fri and at this time I will be in the possession of a tray of RICE KRISPIE TREATS—sorry for the delay—Hi Sarah—I know you're reading this to Howard. All my love to you & Howard. OXOX. Madonna. OXOX." (Sarah Lin-demann first met Howard when they were both students in a playwriting class at Exeter—where his one-acter with a toilet as its centerpiece won a New England prep school award—and she'd been his most indispensable helper since on several of his projects.)

Funnily enough Madonna became the indirect cause of what I re-member almost fondly as our last fight—not that we were ever big fighters. I was sitting bedside with Howard one night, the only other person in the apartment being his full-time nurse Tony—a queenie black man we'd nick-named Nurse Thing to his exaggerated annoyance. Madonna sent Howard an advance release of her new CD, *Like a Prayer,* and he kept telling Tony to turn up the volume, turn up the volume, until the entire apartment was filled with overwhelming sound. I, though, was teaching freshman comp at Columbia that year and had brought along students' papers to read, my plan having been to keep sick Howard company while prepping for the next day. Prig-gishly, I started complaining about the music. "Turn it off," I insisted. "I loooove her," he insisted loudly. "Then I'll leave," I'll threatened. "Geet ooout," he countered furiously. I did. But by the time I arrived at my own apartment a few blocks away, I realized what had happened and called up immediately. "I'm sorry, I love you," I said. I skipped sharing with him my psychological insights into the linking of rage, sorrow, and frustration. "I'm sooory," he sweetly mimicked me, his syllables much elongated. "I loooove you."

Two weeks later Howard was dead. He was buried near some relatives in a cemetery in New Jersey. I was of course at the funeral. And I went a year later to put a stone on the gravesite with his parents and older brother. But for me he wasn't really there. Anymore than he was there in the *Newsweek* lineup of celebrities brought down in a kind of massacre by AIDS. But I knew what his epitaph really was. Howard was very proud whenever he said anything funny in those last months—and he did make astonishingly funny remarks often. One of these became his favorite, so much so that he asked for it to be written down and taped to the refrigerator by Tony. When I went back to the London Terrace apartment a few days after Howard's death to arrange for his hospital-style bed to be given to another needy AIDS patient, there was Howard's voice taped to the flat white refrigerator door.

"There's so much beauty in the world," he was saying. "That's what got me into trouble in the first place."

Where R U, John Crussell?
Or, Inventing Humanity,
One Play at a Time
Randall Kenan

So here *I* am—where are you? I have a silly job, a funky pad, lots of quasi-great/quasi-marginal theatre going on. NYC is a socio-cultural festival, somewhat overwhelming me. I and love (lack of both) are always the bottom line. But nothing *bad* happening. How's the odyssey going? Please keep me posted.

Peace,
Love,
John

PS. Someday I'll really write you.

This 1991 note came scribbled underneath a photocopied picture of John C. Russell, T-shirt- and jeans-clad, holding his signature glasses, about to get his hair bobbed, or "styled" as the update letter reads:

Starting October 1ˢᵗ Dennis Hanrahan will be styling the hair of JOHN C. RUSSELL at John's new East Village abode which he will share with prominent drag queen/activist . . . Miss Understood. . . .

Hair.
John always did have a strange relationship with his hair.
John C. Russell. John Crussell. John C. Russell.

We met in 1990 in Peterborough, New Hampshire, at the MacDowell Colony, a retreat for composers and painters and writers and artists of all kinds. Located on a farm, its headquarters in a large farmhouse with two smaller buildings alongside, dotted by cabins here and there amid the meadows and fields and forests, it remains a blessed place for makers to escape the demands of the real world, perchance to get work done, perchance to socialize, perchance to goof off if the Muse so dictates, or if the Muse fails to show up at all.

Upon my first sight of John, I suspected he might be some West Coast volleyball player, abandoned in New England by a road-tripping team lost in a haze of weed and Bud Light. He stood over six feet from the ground and possessed inordinately long arms ending in very large hands; his face was large, ovally, and when he smiled he tended to completely close his eyes, uncanny as they were, behind a pair of thick-lensed, black plastic framed glasses, the sort that Aristotle Onassis might have worn.

John had a pixie-like quality and was possessed of a preternatural energy, a maniacal horse's laugh, and the sensitivity of a puppy dog. At first I was wary of him for he was an odd creature, all effusive and chattery and a gamin in his gamboling, the likes of which I had rarely encountered in my travels. From the beginning of my stay at MacDowell, conversations with John, at the family-style dinner tables, seemed to be bathed in celluloid and celebrity gossip—and were always uproariously hilarious. He managed to be the center of chat and to have his share of juicy tidbits. He was forever concocting some fabulous game or ordering some esoteric movie for the colonists to watch, or deciding—higgledy-piggledy—that a fete was in order to raise the group's morale, or just to boogie down till the griffons came flying home. He was a strange man, yet wonderful.

But his hair: that green summer, he later told me, he was attempting to grow it to shoulder's length. This was his goal; this was his mission; this was his obsession. The problem was that John's hair had the wispy fine texture of a baby's new growth, and was not the Tarzanian tangle made to be tossed and tousled and knotted and sun-bleached. He knew this as well as anyone, but the reality didn't matter as much as the illusory might of the beach bum's mane that exercised itself in his imagining. Long tresses he'd have, damnit! so help him Thespis, Patron of Drama! A seemingly superficial fixation—in truth a truly superficial fixation—but that simple fact belied the mind behind the whimsy.

For John C. Russell—and I pioneered calling him John Crussell, which he found initially bemusing and later a badge of friendship—was a playwright of equally illusory might and wild imagining. I would presently discover, that summer of meadow-walking and bug-swatting and late-night conversing, that our John Crussell was much more complex a fellow than his initial superficial veneer suggested. True, he believed and longed for those tresses, but he also longed to write the great American play; he longed for a place in the imaginations of America; he had strong—awfully strong—opinions about the arts of dramaturgy and playwrighting, often at odds not only with the establishment and with the avant garde, but with numbskulls such as myself. I've known many an artist high-strung on the fine wine of "art" in my day, but few seemed so bound up in the everyday quest of marrying their life to their work as did John C. Russell.

I am honored that somehow, somewhy, he took a shine to me; and I to him.

Many an afternoon John would bring his lunch over to my cabin where we would gossip and gather dreams; many a time we would walk down to the town of Peterborough for lunch or dinner there. Our conversations were global in sweep, but would often center around our two mutual obsessions: boys and writing. Though at the time I would have been loathe to admit it, I was only four years out of the small town South, and though I'd done my share of living under big city lights, I had miles and miles to go before I felt anywhere near comfortable in such foreign lands. John, on the other hand, was—or at least he seemed to me—the original neosuburban cum Big City Kid. He'd done a lot of his growing up in London, England, had known cities the way Langston Hughes's Negro knew rivers; and he had that jaded, seen-it, been-there, done-it glow that Long Island youths exude like radioactivity. His mother and father—whom he referred to as the Rents—were cool with his gayness, supported his pursuit of playwrighting, and seemed the sort of liberal, open-minded parents to envy.

At the same time John Crussell seemed the very quintessence of unpretentiousness. Unlike so many of my other friends, John was not afraid of his own vulnerability, which I later understood as a source of personal strength. He wore his insecurities with the same pride with which a model wears his beauty. People loved John for it; found themselves reaching out to protect him; found themselves enveloped in his web of honesty and kindness and mirth.

In some odd way I came to understand that John Crussell's playful admiration of the iconographic Beach Boy—grudging though it might have been, intellectually, but wholehearted in its open-mouthed passion—was a conundrum he loved toying with, much like a boy scientist with an unknown insect. At once a statement on the superficiality of looks and an admission of his dissatisfaction with his own looks; a brave deconstruction of that thing he most wanted, and was afraid of, yet afraid to live without.

John Crussell.

During that heady summer John was working on what he called The Molly House Play. He had been researching the bordello scenes of seventeenth- and eighteenth-century England and had unearthed some delicious and salacious stories about the bawdy life of men and women in the streets of London during the era of Defoe and Moll Flanders, of Christopher Marlowe and James Boswell; stories of transvestites and man-man lust, of hush money and child prostitution, of aristocratic slumming among the unwashed, of love amid the fetid and the rotten and the despairing. Here was a lode of gold encrusted in filth, hidden so cunningly in wide-open libraries, yet unspoken, feared, and potent—the stuff with which he longed to conjure.

Already John had worked long and hard toward his own personal vision of stagecraft. At Oberlin and later at Brown where he studied with the noted playwright Paula Vogel, he agonized through the annals of drama—from Sophocles to Inge to Beckett to Caryl Churchill. He had little patience for the "been-done" and the "re-done" and the "almost done." He wanted to do the undone. As a Southerner myself, I'd had an outsized love for the poetry of Tennessee Williams, for the Faulknerian whirligigs of Lillian Hellman, for the historical monoliths of O'Neill. John poo-pooed me and suggested I get a real literary life. They all missed the mark, he'd tell me. Luckily we agreed on Beckett and Shepard; and of course on the Greeks.

But John C. Russell was after larger, more dangerous game. The timid be damned; the lackluster be scorned; the facile be shot to death. He was queer; his plays would be queer. He was a child of the pomo generation; his plays would be the epitome of the postmodern theater. He was an admixture of high culture and low culture; his plays would blur the boundaries between Roland Barthes and *Tiger Beat* magazine, between Peter Brook and *Entertainment Tonight*. John saw the immediate contradiction between obsessing over growing his hair shoulder length (and talking about it for a solid hour to anyone who'd indulge him) and debating the validity of postmodern productions of Ionesco or the relevance of existential drama in the Bush era. He knew it and he loved it, cuz it was fun. John C. Russell was a funny man, and fun, and weird, and made of many parts: he defied anyone to dismiss him and nonetheless felt stung when he went misunderstood. Regardless, he wasn't about to change his ways to fit nicely into a prefab box, or trim his conscience to fit the fashion of the day.

To me John was worldly, sophisticated, and possessed of a surety and freedom forever denied me; to John I seemed more disciplined than I was, better connected than I was, and happier and more secure than I was. I watched John with a great deal of admiration and wonderment for I felt in many ways that his path, his way in the world, was far superior to my own— he embraced social danger, trumpeted his political beliefs with a flourish, risked alienation with the verve of a pirate, and had a medieval Jesuit's faith in the primacy of that stingy yet most generous of goddesses: ART. I felt timid by comparison, and woefully conventional, and safe, an elegant little mouse dutifully scampering through a preordained labyrinth. If he was John the Baptist, I was vying to become Cardinal Richelieu's aide-de-camp. Our views of the world, of how the world worked, of what was possible, of what was, forked after a while into many different paths. Yet I could not ever get over the sense that our John Crussell was somehow anointed, even if only in his own mind—his mien seemed blessed.

A long-standing tradition of the MacDowell Colony is that artists at some point share their work with their fellow colonists. I remember John fitfully "stressing" (he was the first person I remember ever using that term) about writing a small play for the group, to be performed one evening in the rustic, stone-floored library. He asked that I be one of the five or six performers. In truth, when he handed me the pages, I was a bit dismayed and disappointed: the work seemed thin, whimsical, even a tad sentimental, involving elves and witches and Christmas. After all our long lunches and late evenings of discussing playwriting, I'd had in my mind something akin to Witold Gombrowicz or Paddy Chayefsky, not *Sesame Street* or *Saturday Night Live*. But I kept my own counsel and arrived at the single rehearsal. I must confess, it was not until we were performing the piece, live and in front of the musicians and photographers and writers and composers who were our audience, that the brilliance of what John had concocted struck me full force. Call it a playwright's sensibility; call it thinking outside of the box; call it magic. But the humor, the metaphor, the tableaux revealed themselves, and the levels, the wheels within wheels, the way he played with "play" and conjured forth something with the grace of Kabuki and the sinew of John Millington Synge, was made manifest. To be sure he considered it a small thing, but the unconventionality of his thinking had shown itself as a dynamic engine, bristling with horsepower to spare. From that point on, I never underestimated my friend's grasp of stagecraft, nor did I question his power as a maker of events, as a wordsmith, and as a serious seeker after art.

John left MacDowell a few weeks before I did, and, as with any such idyllic meeting and summer-camp-like friendship, we promised to stay in touch; but, as Lillian Hellman once wrote of the theater: "People have come together, as much by accident as by design, done the best they can and sometimes the worst, profited or not, gone their way vowing to see each other the next week, mean it, and wave across a room a few years later."

After my seven weeks at the colony I returned to my existence as a New York literary gypsy. Luckily John and I did stay in touch, and we would meet for supper and strolls in my midtown neighborhood, or down where he lived in the East Village, sporadically. In the summer of 1991 I went away from New York for a year, and John Crussell wound up back at Brown University, where he studied fiction writing under Edmund White among others. I remember the phone ringing almost invariably after one A.M., and it would be John. We would talk for hours on the three most important subjects in the world: boys, pop culture, and writing—not in any particular order, and often mixed up, as, at the time, much of John's fiction dealt head-on with his love life and with pop culture icons and the hazy, multilayered meaning of celebrity and youth culture. He sent me some of his fiction, which often took the form of first-person monologues that concerned themselves with the politics of desire, with the codes and language of love and their concomitant frustration, and with the existential maw of individuality. John's work didn't delve into angst—he was a bit too European in sensibility for that—rather, he took his loneliness as a fact of nature, yet longed to remedy it: he dreamt of the boyfriend sent down from Mount Olympus or Valhalla or up from Hades, like everybody else. And while he was at Brown one particular Puerto Rican beauty was taking his heart for a spin around the universe.

To my knowledge John Crussell never wrote about HIV or AIDS during those few years; and after telling me he was HIV-positive the fall after our having left MacDowell, it was not something that he talked about often. Like his queerness it was just there. By and by we discussed it—I remember the evening. We were walking in the Village, somewhere in that no-man's-land between the East and the West best known as NYU territory, and it was evening, past dusk, and the air was mild—and he spoke of how he had no intention of giving the virus any power over him by giving too much voice to it. He did not ignore it, he told me, but he did not fixate on it. By this time the number of my friends who knew they were HIV-positive had begun to mushroom, and each found his own way to deal with the encroachment: denial, hypochondria, sexual mania, utter withdrawal behind closed doors. I, confused and steeped in good intentions, embraced whatever behavior, whatever attitude a given friend had laid out for himself. To me John's attitude felt somehow—again—very European. (What do I mean by "European"? Not American, devoid of Puritanism and neo-Victorian reactionism; as concerned with style and grace as with content; full of bon vivantism and lack of judgment toward anyone else, with perhaps even a touch of amoralism. But that's just an American's view.) Regardless, I stoked the wings of his steely, full-steam-ahead attitude, and dwelt in the Now with him as best I knew how.

I would be telling a bald-faced lie if I said John and I became the closest of friends. Rather our friendship was that easy alliance people in their early and mid-twenties make, willy-nilly, when they first come to the big city: a thirst for camaraderie; a lust after the knowledge of new ways from old places and exotic American narratives in flux; the creeping hunger for a clan, a tribe by which and for which to define one's own self. Over the years some such friendships strengthen, take hold like roots; others fall by the wayside, dying, not of malice or animus, but by sheer neglect, by the inevitable reality that social ties cannot expand exponentially and remain individually sweet. Who can say what might have happened to our friendship, John's and mine; Time never afforded us that luxury.

After his return to New York, after Brown, John began to see his work performed in fits and starts. There was one production of a trilogy of "tiny gothics" called *In the Dark,* put on by the Downtown Art Company in the East Village in 1992. There was a heartrending tale of being young and gay and negotiating the queer meat market performed in Hell's Kitchen. But, by and large, John fretted about the difficulty of negotiating the world of theater and agonized over the understood politicking that had to occur in order to land a play in the larger venues. "I have all sorts of pleasant possibilities," he wrote to me in the spring of 1992, "but the rejections are rolling in—jobs, grants, colonies. I'll be at the Virginia Center for September, and maybe they'll be kind to me at Teachers and Writers and Theater for a New Audience, and dump me into workshops in the public schools after that. But who knows what pleasant and unpleasant upheavals lie before me." He knew his vision was raw and quirky and highly experimental. His fairy godfather had yet to swoop down. He watched as the Fickle Finger of Fate pointed at this play-wright and that one, often missing him by a hair. But he persevered in the way that only New York writers do: rubbing, watching, licking at success, ever around and surrounding, showing itself, brash and bawdy—feeding on the idea of it, the presence of it as if it were ether in the very air, constantly re-newing hope: a latter-day secular faith.

I fell in love with one piece he had written about teenagers in his homeland of Long Island, a play that deconstructed the language of youth with the precision of Margaret Mead and the sagacity of Noam Chomsky and was quite funny and tragic to boot.

And he still worked on the Molly House play now and again, he told me.

Decline struck John Crussell with the rapidity of a spring tornado and with an equal amount of cruelty. Before I noticed that the already thin man had become almost frail, I was visiting him at Cabrini Hospital on the East Side of Manhattan. John met his condition with an admixture of anger and British stiff-upper-lippedness. Often, when he could still get around, he would rage against AIDS, against malady in general, against his cursed luck, but more at the random nature of it all, at the unfairness; more than anything he lamented the vision of time wasted, of projects unfinished, and of the dour possibility that his own might go unfinished. Time became precious to him. And yet, when I would visit him in hospital, he'd insist that I bring along magazines, the fluffier the better: he craved that old celebrity gossip. I figured it was to distract him from his failing body, and it was; but actually, he loved the dish. And for that I loved him even more.

After a few fortnights of what seemed a promising recovery John had to relent to moving in with the Rents. He did not suffer the inconvenience and indignity gladly. He flip-flopped between being a diva and a little boy, exasperating and loveable, trying and generous. The very idea of going home zapped his soul, for, as is true for anyone, such a physical position cannot be ignored or denied. I always found his anger healthy and the state of affairs with his long-suffering family, Tolstoyan in its ultimate love, freighted with melancholy and the foibles of family woe.

A few weeks before he died, John wanted desperately to attend a weekend playwriting seminar at Columbia University. At this point he was wheelchair-bound, accompanied by a number of rolling medical apparatuses, but undaunted by the idea. I offered to let him stay in my apartment not far from the university. I readied myself and my home to help him through what was going to be more of an ordeal than he wanted to admit. The Rents were none too happy about the possibility. When I spoke with his mother she made it very clear that she thought the project far more than foolhardy, but John would not be deterred.

At the very last minute he relented, sullen but resigned.

During his last remaining days he was back in the hospital. A few days before he died I spoke with his mother, as he was unable to speak. She discouraged me from visiting and suggested I write a note which she said she'd read to him. The note I wrote was brief; I tried to make it sunny. What, indeed, do you say? I remain haunted by the idea of such a note. A few days later I got a call from his mother telling me that he had given up the ghost.

I was gratified and saddened to see his obituary in the *New York Times* a day or so later. "Playwright. . . ." "31. . . ." "Award-winning. . . ." Part of me felt he would enjoy the fact that his passing was noted by the national newspaper of record; part of me knew that if he had had a choice that notice would have been delayed by many decades.

A number of days later, in April 1993, a memorial service was held at the theater where his last play had been performed. I realized at that time how many folk John C. Russell had known, how much a part of his theater world he had become, how many friends his blithe spirit had made. Being a church boy from way back, I found the setting odd, the spoken testaments and the reading from his work peculiar, though in their way fitting. The event drove home how different John and I were, ultimately, and how little I'd truly known him; and the service made me wonder how well I knew any of the people I called my friends. The sad truth is that I had known John for only three years. In fact at least two other people I met that summer are now dead, and I have that same sense about them. No matter how many funerals or memorials I attend, or how many times I hear of untimely demise, I experience that same odd feeling—the feeling that I really did not know this person I felt I knew—never knowing quite what to do with that feeling; always critiquing how I felt and feeling that the mere thought of questioning, of not knowing is somehow inappropriate.

I wonder how our John Crussell wore his hair when he died. A silly notion, yes. Definitely superficial. Yet I believe it would have mattered to him. It was his supreme lack of hypocrisy—aided by a keen intellect that dared mix and blur those elements we deem serious with those elements we consider frivolous—that gave his mind verve. He knew there was potential terrorism in elevating something as banal and trite and pointless as appearance to the solemnity of discussions of death. His play was serious; his frivolity a sword.

So I wonder how he wore his hair. And part of me dreams of him capped by a mane worthy of a lion, golden, thick, long and lustrous; *La rubia*, his Dominican lovers would say, *Que lindo muchacho*, in hushed tones; and he would be able to smile with the knowing of the being, and the understanding that the being existed only in their minds, his and theirs, linked through a mishmash of culture and lore and image; and, at that fateful moment, he would have the power to alter the image into his own legend, queer, radical, lethal, de-whitewashed: he'd have achieved some temporal power. But he already had an earthly power, threefold, in the power of his art.

I often think of John and his hair. Of what it represented to John and what it represented to me. The blond boy, the beach boy, the straight boy. Full of entitlement and privilege and sexual desirability. So superficial, and yet so much what we all want. I loved John's honesty in confronting the stereotype and the riddle at its core; and I love him for grappling with his place within that mythology in his everyday, to wrestle with it, to crussell with it. What we desire to be, what we desire, what we desire to desire, what desires us. What?

Unlike stories and novels and poems, somehow the very nature of plays is so much about the Right Now, the moment, the experience. The fragments that Euripides and Ibsen left behind are the mere blueprints for a lived communion of voice and motion and music; so too with John C. Russell's assorted plays and pieces—they are captured footprints from a life, the echoes of a sense and a sound particular to one being. And yet what magnificent shards of life they are. Recently Harold Bloom blamed modern man on William Shakespeare, saying that in his plays Shakespeare wrote us all into existence, "invented the human as we know it." A heady concept. Yet I cannot now look upon John C. Russell's letter ("Someday I'll really write you") and not gasp at the thought that from his pen, from his mind, worlds could be born; that he could create us afresh, that he might have really written us.

Self-Portrait with Rivals
Herbert Muschamp

In "Nothing Personal," James Baldwin describes how your feelings for a city are transformed when someone you love lives there. I've always loved New York, but I wouldn't have stuck around there if I hadn't met Tucker Ashworth in 1973. In late summer of that year, I came to town for what I thought would be a short stay. I had vague plans to catch up with friends in Morocco in December. Tucker was seven years younger than me and had only just moved to the city. We started walking around town. I had the great joy of seeing a familiar place through new eyes. I owe my work as an architecture critic to the moments we shared then and later. Without them, there's no way I could possibly have something resembling a career.

Your feelings for a city can also be radically altered when someone you love dies there. Since Derek Jarman died, I haven't been able to imagine setting foot in London. After Frank Israel died, it took a long time before I felt at home again in Los Angeles. I had complicated relationships with both men, but the two played similar roles in my life. Both of them were guides to the cities they lived in. Since writing about the city is how I've made my way in the world, the two of them live in my heart.

Derek and Frank were both a few years older than me, but all three of us started out in the 1960s. We all wanted to be part of that decade's spirit of change, and possibly thought it would last forever. Inertia would never get us, no sirree, by cricket. Unlike the lives of many of the other people we spent time with in those years, however, our three lives mainly revolved around work. Each of us wanted to make a mark, but how to do that when things are rapidly changing?

In hindsight, I imagine us as three knife-throwers hurling daggers at a round target that is spinning faster and faster. Like a lottery wheel, the target is divided into pie-shaped sections: Movies. Painting. Music. Photography. Writing. Architecture. Modeling. Stage design. Theatrical performance. Fashion. Window dressing. Round and round. More than one knife would be thrown. More than one creative field would be hit. Since we were rivals as well as friends, the knife throwers might even injure one another, deliberately or not. The blindfolds, please.

I met Derek Jarman the day after I got off the plane in London in August of 1969. I was about to start as a third-year student at the Architectural Association School, on Bedford Square. My lottery wheel had come up with the idea of writing about the city. Buildings are pieces of the city, so I would study them. The question was where. It was a weird time to be a student in the United States. I was finding New York oppressive. The A.A. had a reputation for custom-making programs to support the ambitions of its students. And London sounded fun.

A friend in New York had suggested I look up Karl Bowen, another American who was planning to enter the A.A. that fall. I called Karl the morning after my arrival. He invited me to meet him that afternoon in Hyde Park. Karl was extremely handsome, with looks that everyone compared to a Botticelli. His oval face was framed by long, dark, curly hair. We reached an instant and unspoken understanding that we were going to be friends and possibly rivals but not lovers. That would have been incestuous. We were too much alike. Both Americans abroad; both headed to the same school; both more eager to learn from the experience of living in Europe than from formal education; same age; same dark, curly hair.

Karl was keen to be adored. I wasn't, I thought. I'd left New York, in part, to heal a broken heart. I wanted distance. But I looked forward to a new friendship. We smoked a joint together in the park. Karl said I had to meet Derek, a painter and set designer he had met on his arrival a month before. They were having dinner with some other people that night. I should join them. The invitation turned out to be far more generous than I could have known.

Odin's restaurant. Karl, Derek, Patrick Procter, Patrick's Danish friend Ola, Richard Blight, a young photographer, and Brian Robertson, who went outside to smoke a cigarette after the appetizer and didn't return ("He won't be back," Patrick sniffed). Maybe I didn't want adoration, but I did want to adore. I scarcely paid attention to anyone but Richard Blight, who sat across the table. After dinner, we went to Richard's place off the Fulham Road. The next day we went to Paris, stayed for a few days, and remained together for two and a half years after that.

It had rained a lot in England that summer. The country was very green. This is the first thing I remember Derek saying: "There's been so much rain this summer, that's why everything is so green." We were walking through St. James Park. The flowers were bursting, shedding petals. Many more flowers than in an American park. The Queen's Swans. It was so much more exotic that the swans belonged to the queen rather than to nature. Nobody paid that much attention to the queen anymore, but at least she still had her swans.

Derek's London was like the queen's swans. Derek was a poor artist boarding in a house in Islington, but the city belonged to him, nonetheless, because he knew its story. He was fluent in its language. He could turn all of London into a fantastic personal narrative. Some years later, when I was back living in New York, Derek came to visit and filmed some footage of me pointing to different sites in lower Manhattan. In a sense, Derek had cast me as himself, but in my own town. In real life, I could never play this role. I couldn't give myself a walking tour around my own block. I love to walk around with another person, but I prefer to see things through the other's eyes. Still, I could go back to my room and turn the experience into my story. I could make the city my swan.

That's the great thing about writing on buildings and cities. You can do it even if your social skills are impaired. But it helps to be able to penetrate the facades of buildings and check out what's going on behind them. There should be an interplay between outside and inside, between public and private space, and the objective and subjective realms they represent. The membranes should be permeable. Anonymity is one of the greatest pleasures of urban life, but it is enriched by the potential for access. This can be achieved in a number of ways, from learning more about architects' intentions, the temperaments of their clients, and ideas current at the time, to spending time sitting on a sofa in somebody's living room.

Derek's tours around London wove all this information together. At King's College, Derek had studied architecture with Pevsner. As we went walking around London in the weeks after we met, he would keep up a brilliant commentary on buildings, styles, and social history, usually all mixed together, so that, for example, in pointing out the modern building with the

Turkish bath on the ground floor, Derek would name the architect, the date, and also note that this is where he had once met the bachelor prime minister Edward Heath. In and out.

Access can be addictive. If you lose distance and anonymity, you risk losing your grip on time and place. Enough access enlarges freedom. Too much creates dependence. You get tragic, ridiculous, stupid, sad, and second-rate usually without knowing it. I've seen this happen many times. This is why it was wise of Proust to withdraw to his cork-lined bedroom. He preserved his independence. Unlike Truman Capote, for instance. I couldn't afford cork, much less a maid to bring in coffee, but I had my depression to keep me at a safe remove. Much later, I came to realize that I'd been operating from what Winnicott called "the depressive position" for virtually all my life. In London, I kept falling into gloom. At the time, I couldn't understand it. I'd made lots of new friends very quickly. I had a nice boyfriend. He lived in Paris most of the time, which helped keep romance alive. I'd found a nice studio on the Chelsea Embankment. It faced onto the gardens of the Royal Hospital, a terrific view, and when I left the house in the morning I saw the Thames, with the Battersea power station, across the river, often bathed in smoky gray, white, and yellow light. This was heaven.

Why all the hell? Because my main motivation in going there was to escape here. Here and there aren't the same. Going and being aren't the same. It had been exciting to say, I'm getting out of New York, I'm going to London. Just thinking about it was escape enough. Once there, I had to cope with life in a strange city, the awfulness of English people, the familiar horror of myself. My father had died just weeks before I got on the plane. This was a temporary relief, but the relief was self-deceptive, because I'd long ago internalized that monstrous ogre, always judging and condemning me; had long ago transformed it into judgmentalism toward others. Eventually, I started to put this fatal quality to what I hope is constructive use in writing criticism. Meanwhile, the cost of using it as a psychological defense was horrendous. At the slightest provocation, my judgmentalism would turn on me.

I was thinking the other day about Leonard Whiting, for example. He was a friend of Richard's because he was living with Cathy Dahman, a model Richard had befriended when he was working in New York for Antonio Lopez, the great fashion illustrator. The night we arrived in Paris, we went a restaurant and Leonard and Cathy were having dinner there, too. The sight of him sent me into shock. In New York, among other places, Leonard was that year's fantasy love object because of his starring role in Franco Zeffirelli's movie version of *Romeo and Juliet*. And here he was, dressed in a beautiful velvet suit, behaving in the most open, warmest, way. There was I, brimming over with low self-esteem.

Later, I ran into Leonard a few times on the King's Road. He was always friendly, always suggested we get together sometime for coffee. Even at the time, I could imagine that he meant it. What I couldn't imagine was making my tongue work long enough to have a conversation without Richard present. Later, I heard that some consider depression a form of protection that evolved to encourage the less powerful ones to withdraw from risk situations. What was the risk here? Looking stupid, literally dumb. I'd based what self-esteem I had on a completely untested belief in my intelligence. I couldn't imagine that Leonard, or others like Leonard, had much use for that card. Just to look at this gorgeous, friendly, confident movie star was to feel inadequate. I regret that, but in a way I can't say that I regret my depression. Something self-protective was going on.

Sex must be another device that evolved for more than reproductive purposes. I admired the way Karl used his looks as a form of passive assertion. But I didn't want to be a muse. I wanted to have one. I needed someone to do things for.

With Derek I felt safe. He was a perfect older brother. We shared a bed for about a week, but nothing physical happened. Karl told me that Derek would say, "Maybe tonight will be the night!" Actually, I think this was said more to irritate Karl than to admit to an attraction to me. Derek was in love with Karl. I was like the "second American student" in the summer of 1969, and I should have appreciated this more. On the other hand, who really likes being the less cute, less rich one? For, in addition to looking like a Botticelli youth, Karl was a trust fund baby, the descendent of some extremely rich family from Buffalo. I never knew which, though someone once said it was rumored to be Kellogg, the breakfast food manufacturers. Karl's trust fund wasn't huge, but the income enabled him to treat himself well: trips to Venice; a nice flat; superior narcotics; the best art supplies; frequent dinners at Wheeler's, the fish restaurant in Victoria. Most of the money, however, went for psychiatry, and I could never tell if Karl was truly disturbed or whether he indulged in therapy as a status symbol, a necessary accoutrement of the artist he hoped to become.

Derek was bursting with confidence. That spring, the Royal Ballet had staged a new dance by Frederick Ashton, "Jazz Calendar," for which Derek had designed the sets and costumes, his first for the company. The critics had applauded his designs, and the ballet, starring Nureyev, Wayne Sleep, and other Royal stars, was a popular success. But Derek's confidence enabled him to deal with failure, too. The previous year, both critics and the public had hated his designs and John Gielgud's staging of Mozart's *Don Giovanni* for the English National Opera, but Derek had managed to turn this rejection into proof of his genius. The opera had been staged at the Coliseum Theater, formerly the Alhambra, where Diaghilev's Ballets Russes used to play their London seasons, and Derek used to stress this connection, as if somehow, in his mind, the booing of his *Don* had been equivalent to the pandemonium that broke out in the audience at the Paris premiere of "The Rite of Spring."

I envied this confidence enormously. And envied the group of pals that helped Derek sustain it. More likely, it was the other way around: the pals fed off Derek's self-confidence, were entertained and stimulated by it, and in exchange they agreed to suspend judgment on his work. It was my loss, but I couldn't be part of this arrangement. I wanted to like Derek's work, but I couldn't see that he had a great booming talent. He clearly was creative, and he did have an eye for design, and there was a group of paintings he'd made of Majorca or somewhere—stylized cliffs rising from a black horizon line meant to represent the sea, some green color and marbleized plastic—that were pleasing to look at. But they were awfully polite, like the voices of English people on holiday in Latin countries that come tinkling through the air and completely ruin your dinner.

In the fall of 1969, Derek moved to a factory building on the south bank of the river. There was no heating or hot water. He would go over to friends' houses to take a shower, and every day or so he went to a gas station to buy oil for portable heaters. He had no money and except when a friend would treat him to a meal he lived entirely on tea, yogurt, and Sainsbury's fruit jam tarts. "Quite good, these fruit tarts." No, they weren't. They were terrible fruit tarts, from the cheapest supermarket in Great Britain. But Derek had given himself permission to claim that they were quite good. After all, he was quite good friends with the Sainsburys. And the Sainsburys had the good taste to use Helvetica typeface on their cellophane packaging. This talent extended to every facet of his life. Every day at low tide Derek would go down to the river and collect junk, mostly small pieces of rusted metal. These he began to incorporate into large bishops' capes of transparent plastic, to be worn or hung on the wall like paintings. One of his girlfriends sewed the pieces together.

I didn't think much of the capes, but Derek's resourcefulness was awesome. Poor? Become a beachcomber. Make garments that evoke ecclesiastical splendor. Become the Pope of Upper Ground. Lonesome? Throw a party. On November 28, my birthday, Derek, Karl, Ingo Thouret, a German student at the Royal College of Art, and I gave a big party at Derek's place, which I recall as amazing but otherwise remember little about, except that Francis Rose was there. Gertrude Stein wrote that a second bell rang in her head when she met Francis Rose, the first having rung when she met Picasso. In 1969 Rose was living in a basement bed-sitter in Chelsea and was considered proof that Stein's bell was cracked.

At the end of the year, I went to Paris to stay with Richard for a month, thinking that this would cheer me up, but things got worse. I had to force myself to get out of bed, leave the house, or see Richard's friends. The streets were wintry. Paris then was still a poor place, full of anger and resentment toward Americans, part of the fury that had welled up in May of the previous year. Still, if you bought a simple bunch of anemones at a neighborhood flower shop, they would tie them together with ribbon, encircle them with a doily, and wrap the bouquet in glistening plastic. In the shop windows, there were Christmas log cakes frosted with chocolate, vanilla, or mocha butter cream, and beautiful boxes of candied chestnuts, a crystallized violet atop each one, set out on pedestals with their lids off.

For the first time, I had a glimpse of my own mortality: one day, I would close my eyes, as if to sleep, but for the last time. It seems ridiculous to write it down now, but in 1969 the realization genuinely frightened me. It would take me a long time to make the connections between this fear, my isolation, and my anger. Meanwhile, at some point during that month in Paris, a story came out in *Time* magazine claiming that in twenty-five years scientists would have a drug that would halt the aging process and twenty-five years after that another drug that would reverse it. This brightened my mood in time for New Year's and the start of a new decade.

I had invited Derek to spend New Year's Eve in Paris with Richard and me. Derek arrived in Paris with a new boyfriend named Kevin in tow. The two were out of the house to go sightseeing early each morning. Tony Kent's parrots spoke more than Kevin did, though Richard claimed that Kevin had a lot of soul. Many profound spiritual experiences, the boy must have had. Right after New Year's, Derek dropped Kevin, who then called up Richard and asked if he could come to Paris. I only found out about this later. I thought it was rude, but meanwhile I was a having a fling with Ingo Thouret. Ingo was being kept in grand style—townhouse in Kensington, etc.—by a filmmaker who lived in Cologne. Every morning I woke up to the horrible sound of Ingo conversing in German with this person. Otherwise, our affair was very light.

Derek had asked if he could bring a madwoman named Blake to Paris also. Blake was devoted to Derek in an utterly masochistic way, which must have appealed to Derek's narcissism. I think Derek had dreams of becoming a British Andy Warhol, complete with entourage. David Hockney already had this role, but Hockney had demonstrated major talent. Derek was prepared to settle for the entourage before making his artistic mark, but there was no way I was going to spend New Year's with this lunatic. Nonetheless, shortly before midnight she appeared at La Coupole, where we'd gathered for supper, Derek ordering the cheapest dish on the menu: mushrooms à la grècque.

Blake was a creature out of one of Truman Capote's early, Gothic stories. Her madwoman radar locked onto my depression immediately. At my birthday party, we'd played a current hit song with the refrain, "One is the Loneliest Number." Blake came over, stuck her face in mine, and repeated the refrain several times. I dreaded the stunt she might try to pull at La Coupole and decided not to stick around. When the lights went out at midnight, I ran out of the restaurant and went home.

Derek and Kevin left two days later. On the boat-train back to London, Derek struck up a conversation with a woman who worked for Ken Russell. Russell needed a set designer for *The Devils*, a movie starring Vanessa Redgrave and Oliver Reed that was about to go into production at Pinewood Studios. And that's how Derek was discovered. The woman arranged an interview with Russell, and Derek got the job. No more showers at other people's houses. "It's the biggest film set since Cleopatra!" Derek exclaimed when we met up again in London a few weeks later.

Derek taught me to contract the distance between cause and effect. Between learning and realization, ambition and achievement. Act before you think that conditions are ripe. Make the cause, and start practicing the art of realization. Get ambition and realization within shouting distance of each other. The result is bound to be crappy, but that's how you learn the difference between being and becoming.

Two other friends in London helped out with this education. David Usborne, a young graduate of the A.A., had recently been made a trustee of the school. I met David about a week before school started. Over dinner, he said that the A.A. only worked if you showed up with an idea of what you wanted to do there. This was a shocking idea for an American student, but it forced me to realize that there was neither reason nor excuse to delay further what I wanted to do: write stories about the city. David said I should get Colin Fournier as my tutor and promised to call him.

Colin Fournier had graduated before I'd arrived and then been hired by Peter Cook to work on Archigram's famous Monte Carlo project, an amusement, media, and convention center that, for a time, promised to become the visionary group's first realized building. In fact, it hastened Archigram's demise. Colin helped me put David's advice into practice. If I wanted to write, then I had to write. With Colin's guidance, and the school's flexibility, I took the plunge. Instead of trying to design buildings, a task for which I had no talent, I would practice using language. The school agreed to accept written pieces in lieu of architectural plans.

Architects typically practice postponement. This was true even of David and Colin. Derek helped break me out of that, in a way no architect could. His example encouraged me to make the psychological leap to the immediacy of writing. I also learned from him a variation on Fitzgerald's theme that action is character. It goes, Action is sensibility. At any time, you can push against external factors—of craft, of acceptance—and in that process of assertion a distinctive way of looking at things evolves.

Derek's sensibility initially derived from the group of artists and writers Martin Green called the Children of the Sun. The solar children, many of them gay men, started out in the 1920s, the era of the Bright Young Things. They included Harold Acton, Brian Howard, the Sitwells, Rupert Brooke, and the young Auden, to an extent. They were ardent fans of the Ballets Russes and preoccupied with the figure of Harlequin, the trickster. They were adepts in a cult of youth and beauty, especially young male beauty.

In their own time, and later, these people were often scorned, branded as dilettantes, dandies, exhibitionists, lightweights. They lacked "the wound," so to speak. At times I was scornful of Derek and some of his pals. After the violent edge of New York, London's sweetness, its balletic decorousness, its generic, second-hand avant-gardism seemed remarkably tame. By the late 1960s, the cultural transformation of Britain was essentially over. In movies, music, fashion, photography, theater, and architecture, the big oppositional statements against the country's staid traditions had all been made. The nails in the coffin of Empire had all been hammered.

With one exception, perhaps. We'll call it gay rights, of which the greatest may have been the right to use the word gay. In Britain, gay rights was a relative issue: it is universally acknowledged that all English men are gay. This is what the Profumo and other scandals were essentially about. A few nongay men were at loose in the land. When their heterosexuality was un-masked by the press, there was hell to pay. When word of the Stonewall riots reached England, there was further consternation. What to do about gay rights in a country where everyone is gay? Homosexual acts had only recently been decriminalized, which in itself was shocking, since British men had long found it impossible to get an erection unless they were breaking a taboo. Without regarding sex in general as taboo, the English would not have been able to procreate.

One night in 1970, Derek and I went to a gay lib meeting, a first for both of us. I remember thinking that this meeting was the ideal British form of gay sex. I never went back a second time, but Derek did, and became quite ostentatious about his activism. The taboo only peripherally concerned be-ing gay. David Hockney had mooted this point for most of us. The taboo had to do with taste. It had to do with having the poor taste to become politically engaged. Sun Children are not supposed to be political. They are expected to be epicene. Attending rallies, making overtly political statements, wearing buttons, etc.: such things weren't done. But Derek's art began to gain sub-

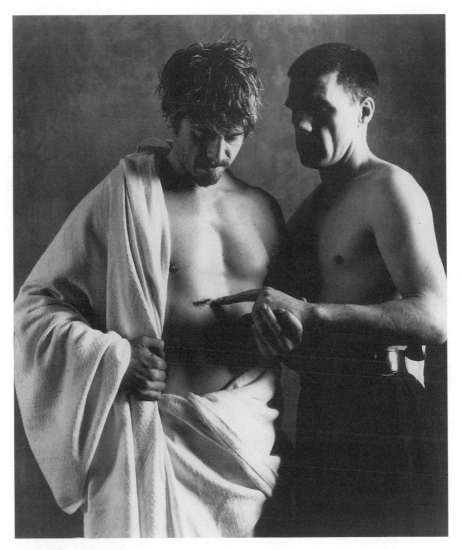

Nigel Terry as Caravaggio from Caravaggio.

stance when he became an activist. British social complacency gave him a means to get beyond his own. And also to get beyond the cultural transformations that had already occurred in the 1950s and 1960s in music, movies, theater, photography, architecture, and dance. He needed the politics to give his work an oppositional quality.

I can't say that I'm a big fan of Derek's movies. I consider the diaries

Tilda Swinton from Caravaggio.

his most valuable work. It was, however, excellent to follow his progress from a distance. We didn't see each other often. After the mid-1970s, we had no contact at all. But Derek's movies and his activism made the news. He'd made the world accept him on his own terms. When those terms included being sick, he made the world deal with it. Because of that, I can't think of another English artist of my generation who did more to regenerate the image of London in the eyes of the world.

Until Almodovar's *All about My Mother* came out, I didn't understand the Spanish preoccupation with blood. I was put off by the imagery of death, machismo, grand operatic passion, morbid obsession, kinship pride and feuding: power struggling, in short. But the way Almodovar presented it, the power struggle was not for domination over others. It was just the struggle to survive. The fight to live in a harsh environment. Nature is harsh and culture is harsh. The blood business is just about keeping in mind the distinction between living things and stuff.

The movie is made of stuff, but it's also what's called life-affirming art. A city is made of stuff, but people can make a life-affirming city. Architecture can contribute to this city. It accomplishes this not just, or even mainly, by creating new buildings, but by revealing the stories buildings have to tell, the stories behind the forms and the stories behind the walls. Derek Jarman could have made a movie about his relationship to London and called it *All about My Mother.* The city had nurtured him, and he gave a lot back in return. Frank Israel could have made a movie about Los Angeles and given it the same title. Both of them were part of a story that transcended their individual careers: the transformation of the city during our lifetimes, and the major role played by gay people in that process.

In her 1961 book *The Death and Life of Great American Cities,* Jane Jacobs talks about how modern city planning has ruined one of downtown Philadelphia's historic squares. It has become, Jacobs writes, "a pervert park." Some things have changed in the past forty years. A pervert park! How quaint! Today, it almost goes without saying that the survival of cities like Philadelphia had already come to depend on the denizens of that pervert park, and many other pervert parks, and on the contributions of people who, forty years ago, were meant to see themselves as socially undesirable. Us perverts served the city and saved the city. We were nurtured by it, and we gave something back. Along with other minority groups, we recast the urban condition following the suburban exodus of the postwar decades.

A few weeks ago, I went with Steven Shortridge to visit Frank Israel's grave at Westwood Memorial Park. People had told me that Frank's ashes had been buried next to Burt Lancaster's. They hadn't said how close the two are parked. These guys are practically on top of each other. Then, if you raise your eyes and look straight ahead, you see a crypt where fingerprints have turned the white marble casing to smudge gray: Marilyn Monroe. Burt and Frank are in the ground, while Marilyn hovers slightly above, like an angel. If you knew Frank, you have good reason to think he must be in heaven. And Burt and Marilyn are both well housed.

Dozing on the plane back to New York, I thought, now there's someone I can call up in the middle of the night and talk about what it's like to be dead. This thought woke me up with a smile on my face. Frank was my favorite three-hour-difference West Coast telephone partner. When he answered the phone, his voice had a grave-like solemnity. "Hul-lo." When he called me, at the same hour, the voice was wide awake. "Herbert, it's Frank." For years, the message on his answering machine started out, "Yeah, I can't come to the phone right now." Yeah? Who was that message intended for?

I met Frank in 1973 at a bar in Murray Hill called the Barefoot Boy. Marc Balet, a mutual friend, had given Frank a manuscript copy of my first book, because I was desperate for feedback and Marc thought Frank could give me some. I'd started this book at the A.A. in 1971, moved around while I was working on it, and eventually finished it in California two years later. It had found a publisher but wasn't yet in print.

At that point Frank was working for the shah of Iran on a vast city planning project in Tehran. Frank could be a fabulist, but I choose to think that this story was true. Frank had helped design a huge rose garden for Farah Dibah, Iran's empress. At the opening ceremony, this empress pressed a button to release hundreds of doves that had been kept in cages in the hills above the city. The birds were supposed to come soaring down from the hills and fly into huge, ornamental aviaries that had been placed around the garden. Some of the birds had been trained to lead the others. Everything went well until two of the leaders got into a fight. The rest soon followed. Within min-utes, the cages had filled up with hundreds of dead, bloody doves.

The point is, Frank was Farah Dibah. He was also a dove, free, air-borne, flying to his doom, and a director organizing a spectacle inside his head. He wasn't as colorful a figure as Derek, nor as voluble a talker. Frank tended toward the taciturn, and wasn't big on hand gesticulations. Even on a disco dance floor, he didn't move much. But he did have the capacity to put on a time and place, as if the moment were a magic cape.

After the fall of the shah, Frank decided to move to Los Angeles. He had no desire to join a large New York firm. He wasn't even sure he was go-ing to stick with architecture. It didn't feel like a great moment for architec-ture. Richard Weinstein, head of UCLA's architecture school, offered Frank a teaching job. Frank saw this partly as a stepping stone to Hollywood. He'd try to design movie sets.

When my first book was published, I hoped it would lead to a journalism ca-reer. It took years for this to happen. By the mid-1970s, the architecture mag-azines had more or less purged critical writing from their pages. The writers and editors thought of themselves as journalists. In reality, they were flaks for the architectural profession. They were careerists, with no particular interest in ideas. And that was the way things were going throughout the culture.

The mid-1970s brought mounting pressure on members of my generation to succeed. To get somewhere, be someone, collect an identity in the world, be part of some approaching wave, become a rising star. It was a time of panic, that is to say. Intentions were not good enough, even talent was not good enough unless it was recognized with the reward of a well-paying job. We were supposed to pull ourselves out of the carefree indulgence and idealism of the 1960s and become pragmatic grown-ups. At the same time, we were supposed to keep some kind of distance from the suburban herd mentality many of us had grown up with. From these competing goals, irony was born.

People like myself, who weren't able to pull off this trick, were to be scorned, pitied, and feared, even by themselves. Our failure might be conta-gious, or could even be interpreted as integrity by those who sensed that they were losing theirs. I was frightened, for instance, by what had happened to

Karl. He'd moved back to New York around 1980. He still looked good, but his mind had checked out. His references were stale. He would talk about the architects people had talked about fifteen years before, when he was a student at Cornell. His art talk was even less current. While in England, he'd been inducted into the Sun Children's mentality—everything was beautiful at the ballet—but you couldn't import that kind of preciousness into the United States, not unless you were willing to try an extreme version of it, like Gilbert and George, or MacDermott and McGough.

You would go to Karl's little loft on Sixth Avenue, and he'd be trying to duplicate some kind of Patrick Procter tea party, and it just seemed terribly sad. Worse was to come. The trust fund ran out. Overnight, Karl came to think that he had a Messianic message to deliver to the world and that it was my job to transcribe it. He sent me notebooks full of insane ramblings. Then he was evicted from his loft, so that the building could be torn down. He started living in a series of SRO hotels, in between stays at Belleview. I would go visit and bring him cigarettes. When he was out, he worked as a bicycle messenger. He would stop by the school where I was teaching and leave urgent messages with the receptionist. Eventually, I couldn't take Karl's problems any more.

In 1992 or 1993, I was walking home and saw him sitting in Washington Square Park. He was smoking a cigarette and still looked handsome. He was showing his profile to the pedestrians from Fifth Avenue, in fact. I was too scared to say hello. About a year later, Marc Balet told me that Karl had killed himself. It's painful to think of all that memory being wiped away. But the truth is that, long before he died, Karl's memories had become more accessible to me than they were to him. Visiting him in Belleview, or in an SRO hotel in Hoboken, I mourned him.

This was twenty years after the time I'm talking about. But I'm telling this story to make a point. It's hard enough to be an artist under any circumstances, but I don't see how it's possible to do it unless you have defined yourself at a very young age as an acting subject. Wilde was onto this idea when he wrote that you should either make a work of art or be a work of art. Wilde wasn't unattractive in his younger days, and he deluded himself into thinking that Alfred Douglas was an artist. But of course this was never in the cards. Karl had defined himself as a passive object and that was that.

Derek, Frank, and I saw ourselves as acting subjects. We envied the great beauties of the world. We certainly envied the attention and the access it gained them. But there was nothing we could do about it. Even if we'd had plastic surgery to turn ourselves into major Adonises, we couldn't have tolerated objecthood. We had our bursts of self-esteem when strangers admired us, and then we fled back into our work. (If there's a difference between being an acting subject and being a control freak, I have yet to discover it.)

This is worth talking about because of the importance played by youth and looks in the gay male world. Younger, cuter, younger, cuter, younger, cuter. It can be a cruel economy, no matter which side of the age-beauty line you happen to be standing on. Young gay men are often cruelly misled by older gay men into thinking they have artistic talent. Or, if they are talented, the younger ones find the attention so pleasant that they put off practicing their craft until it's too late. Though this has been going on for thousands of years, there's still a conspiracy of silence about it. The glare is unflattering to everyone involved. The young men don't want to see themselves as prostitutes, and the old ones don't want to see themselves as Uggoes, to use the aptly ugly term for anyone who doesn't resemble a Bruce Weber model.

There are, of course, equivalent economies in the straight world, but there is also this difference. At the time I'm talking about, women were developing the social, political, and psychological skills to overcome such power relationships. That never occurred among gay men, at least not to a comparable degree. I wish that this story could be a beautiful tale of love and solidarity between three men of a certain age. Since none of us wanted to live in San Francisco, however, this was not the case. I don't blame Frank or myself for the rivalry that existed between us, and I don't hold the gay community responsible for not fostering more powerful bonds of brotherhood. Our energies were better directed toward struggles against intolerance and fear. But society benefited enormously when women began to talk about sexual power struggles. It opened everyone's eyes to the dangers of exploitation.

When I met Tucker Ashworth, I was twenty-four and had a contract for my first book. By the time the book came out, however, I was twenty-six, the book wasn't well received, except by students, and it actually made it harder for me to break into journalism. I had no mentor, and my thinking was out of step with that of the journalists I knew. Postmodernism was On the Move!

The magazine writers were expected to fall in line with the new dispension of cribbing from period styles.

This was anathema to me. To me, postmodernism represented a suburban rear attack on urban values. I think I was right about that. In any case, I had fled the suburbs while in my teens and resented this incursion of conformity, of nostalgia posing as history and tradition. I still do. But the truth is that if someone had offered me the opportunity to sell out, I would have, in a minute. Fortunately, no one was buying.

Like Frank, I loved Los Angeles, in part because the urban and the suburban were mixed up with one another and somehow held together, as if in colloidal suspension. No matter how suburban the individual pieces might be, the whole added up to a new, raw urban condition. It still does. You can't walk around Manhattan now, like J. J. Hunsecker, the evil gossip columnist in *The Sweet Smell of Success,* and say, "I love this dirty town." Most of the dirt's been scrubbed away. Not in Los Angeles, however. The place is too big to keep clean. Earthquakes, floods, and brush fires are constantly making messes even in the loveliest parts of town.

Frank and I didn't develop a close friendship until years after we met. But we kept tabs on each other. He was supportive of my first book, but the support was compromised by the friendships he needed to maintain with those who were in a position to publish his work. At this juncture, Frank began to develop the reputation as someone whose friends all hated each other. This wasn't true. I liked the few friends of his that I met in those years. But I naturally resented those who'd succeeded in journalism, and would have resented them even if I'd liked the architecture they were promoting.

Frank, for his part, wasn't sure what kind of architecture he should be designing. Since he was precocious, it naturally made sense for him to jump aboard the postmodern bandwagon, even though its avatars were a generation and more older than him. For guidance, he looked a lot to Charles Moore. Then, in California, he became aware that something else was going on, mainly involving Frank Gehry, but also Eric Moss, Thom Mayne, and Lewicky, Frank's contemporaries, who were having none of this postmodern business at all, at all. Eventually, Frank settled into a kind of updated Art Deco style, which drew on Richard Neutra, Rudolf Schindler, Charles and Ray Eames, and other California modernists. In other words, he made a kind of postmodernism out of modernism itself. This was something. But not enough to endear him to those who wanted to make more radical work.

Even in the early nineties, after the term deconstruction came into use, I remember having these conversations in which Frank would say that post-modernism had really changed things but decon showed no signs of catching on with the public. Later, Frank would design houses that could easily be described as decon, by those who enjoy using such terms. I couldn't see what difference it made whether or not something was catching on with the public. What matters is finding your voice, figuring out what you want to say, and getting the freedom to say it, not necessarily in that order.

Meanwhile, I was plugging along with struggling writer jobs. I suspected that the kind of mind that wondered about things like whether or not or not a style was catching on with the public would have at most peripheral interest in my writing. Occasionally, I got little moments of recognition. Grants helped keep me going. A second book appeared in 1983. But I didn't get a real journalism gig until 1984, when Ingrid Sischy offered me a monthly column on architecture in *Artforum*. In 1987, I became architecture critic for the *New Republic*, and added a third column, in 1989, for *Seven Days*, a weekly that shut down about four months after I started.

Tucker and I had a personal crisis around 1980. I was spending a lot of time in the Berkshires, working on a book about Frank Lloyd Wright. I came down periodically for long weekends. One time, Frank called and said, "someone's really interested in you." The someone was a movie producer I'd never met. I'll call this person Dick Head. He was part of the so-called Velvet Mafia, the group of gay men who exercised power in Hollywood. The next day, I was talking on the phone to another friend, who lived in New York, and she said, "I didn't know Tucker was friends with Dick Head." The day after that, a Sunday, I had brunch with a friend, and she started asking these weird questions about Tucker's and my relationship. The questions seemed designed to suggest that our relationship wasn't all that solid and perhaps had no future. This gave me the creeps. She didn't mention Dick Head, but I figured that he was behind these questions. She had aspirations to writing screenplays. It was horrible to realize that she was capable of betraying our friendship for the price of a movie treatment.

Tucker had always been sexually active outside our relationship. I wasn't, but not for any moral reason. The desire just wasn't there. Tucker was seven years younger. When we met, this struck me as a wide gulf. As I saw it, it would have been unnatural if he hadn't played around. I had, at his age. But there was a boundary around my life that was not to be crossed. And now it had been. My feelings toward three people had been affected.

I don't know whether one of them had been tempted with the lure of a screenplay. I don't know if Frank had been tempted with the prospect of a set design job. I do know that Frank envied my relationship to Tucker. I know that he had social aspirations toward membership in the Velvet Mafia. Months later, he told me that this ambition had been thwarted. I never confronted him with the suspicion that he'd been acting selfishly. There was, I suppose, an erosion of trust. This tested my relationship to Frank but didn't undermine it, perhaps because, from the start, the relationship had been built as much on rivalry as on trust.

Needless to say, the rivalry didn't cease when I started working at the *New York Times* in the summer of 1994. But, of course, I had the luxury of not having to think about it any more. Whoever has the job of the paper's architecture critic has the power to affect the careers of architects around the world. That person becomes the most widely read narrator of what's going on in the field. I use the third person because the power of that position has nothing whatever to do with me personally.

For some months before I was hired, Frank would call up and offer the inside scoop on the likely contenders. It was this one, it was that one. I never volunteered the information that I was being considered, and it was a relief to know I wasn't in Frank's incessantly grinding gossip mill. After the announcement was made, Frank was embarrassed that it came as a surprise. "I just wonder whether you'll be able to handle all the pressure," was all he said.

Frank was stingy with praise. In fact, I can't remember a single time when he called up to say he liked a story. Once, when I'd been at the paper about six months, he said, "People seem to like it." I think that, like many others, he was surprised that the editors were giving me considerable leeway to develop new ways to write about cities. Actually, the top editors wanted this to happen. They didn't want architecture to be seen as free-floating objects in space. They wanted more of the connective tissue. I took this to mean that a building could be treated as a piece of the city, part of the social as well as the artistic weave.

By then, Frank Israel was someone I'd known for twenty years. I might have recused myself from writing about him, but in 1995 there was a gallery show of objects made by California architects called *Angels and Franciscans* that included several pieces by Frank, and I decided to write about it. He'd taken drawings, inscribed them on cobalt blue steel plates, and surrounded them with glass frames. In my review, I described them as looking like Art Deco wall sconces. Frank called up in a white rage. "A lot of us spent a lot of money on those projects," he screeched. I don't think the anger was really over my fairly innocuous remarks about those pieces. It was about having the freedom to say what I wanted to say, without fear or favor.

No architect has that freedom. If they are artists, they will find a way to feel independent within themselves. They will find a way to turn the constraints of the medium, like the budget, or the wishes of their clients, into creative challenges. In the last years of his life, Frank managed to do this. He moved away from the Art Moderne mode and began to soar. One day a package arrived containing plans of a design he'd made for an art center at the University of California, Riverside, campus. I put it to one side of my desk and didn't look at it for a few weeks. When I did, I knew I had to write a story on it right away. It was such a departure: looser, more attuned with the landscape, unafraid to look awkward. It took risks. So did the remaining work Frank produced.

Writing about the Riverside project helped to change my work in turn. People have talked about the subjectivity of my criticism, or the narcissism, the empathy, the emotion. These were always present in my writing, but they began to become more pronounced with the Riverside story and another review I wrote about that time, on an Alberti show in Mantua. The subjectivity was partly a response to the surrealist strain I was seeing in the work I was writing about—like that of Frank Gehry, Rem Koolhaas, and Phillippe Starck. It was also provoked by my involvement with a person I'll call Tom Ripley. Frank was part of this story, too.

Tom had briefly worked in Frank's office. He was one of the most extreme narcissists I've ever met, a total puer eternus type, in Jungian parlance. That type can be very attractive. Tom got into some kind of financial trouble in 1995 and decided to move back to New York. I met him just in passing around that time. This was the first time I'd been attracted to somebody since Tucker died. Nothing came of it, however, until about two years later, when Tom asked a mutual friend to arrange a dinner between us. He wasn't the same person I'd met. He was full of fear, and, at age thirty-five, had reason to be. He'd spent the previous two years drifting on a more or less permanent vacation, drinking heavily, and it showed, physically and emotionally.

In our relationship, Tom fell into the classic behavior of fighting the last war. By seducing and then attacking me, he tried to regain the dignity and integrity that he'd lost during his long vacation. While this was going on, I sometimes felt anger toward Frank for not introducing us sooner. In truth, it wouldn't have made any difference. Tom had been fighting the last war all his life. He hadn't figured out that the conflict was within him. (At the time, I didn't, either.) He had constructed a worldview around depression and disappointment, and the only relief he could get from this isolation involved gaining other people's attention and then lashing out at them for giving it.

Many of my friends disapproved of this relationship, and with good reason. But I suspect that Frank's disapproval was complicated by the fact that he'd never sustained a passionate relationship with anyone. For a long time, he carried a torch for a young designer who specialized in painting fake marble walls. But the designer himself was made of genuine stone. He was phlegmatic to the point of system shutdown. Later, Frank formed a relationship with a really excellent person, a jewelry designer. This relationship continued almost until Frank's death, but there was never passion on either side. They were more like brothers, which would have been fine, except that toward the end of his life, Frank became acutely aware that the passion had been missing.

A few months before he died, Frank met another designer, very young and introverted, and it was as if at last he'd found The Real Thing. The Real Thing for a person nearing the end of his life, at least. That was how it appeared to Frank's friends. The guy was unbelievably devoted, and defiantly territorial. When he accompanied Frank to dinner, he tuned the rest of us completely out of the picture. It was obvious that Frank enjoyed the attention, and that, because of his sickness, he felt entitled to ignore the bad impression it made on others. As indeed he was.

In the summer of 1997, Sylvia Lavin, dean of UCLA's architecture school, organized a symposium in honor of Frank's fiftieth birthday. The event coin-cided with a retrospective of Frank's work at the Museum of Contemporary Art in downtown Los Angeles. These events were both in the nature of rallies. At the symposium, no one wanted to speak openly about Frank's illness, but that was the unspoken reason for the gathering: Let's do it right this time. Let's not wait until someone's gone before we say publicly what we think. Frank, sitting in the audience, must have known this.

I started my presentation with that chilling quote from Gore Vidal: "It is not enough to succeed. One's friends must fail." Very few people in the audience knew much about the rivalry between Frank and me, and I didn't talk about it on that occasion. I went on to talk about ambition, the ruthlessness of art, and Frank's self-dissatisfaction. But I wanted Frank to hear the personal meaning in that opening quote: he'd used me and others in the room as barometers to gauge his place in life.

There was a light side to reckoning with Frank's illness, his friends found. Frank was always a hypochondriac. He'd died a thousand deaths before we'd known each other five years. When he got sick, some of us comforted ourselves with the thought that hypochondriacs outlive us all. And Frank's descriptions of his illness were somehow comforting. Illness hadn't robbed him of the power to complain, and this somehow seemed like an expression of the life force. It would have been more upsetting if he'd decided to be stoic.

I didn't feel imposed upon by Frank's descriptions of symptoms and treatments. Having lived through Tucker's sickness, I was prepared to handle the full litany of horrors that this disease can bring. But I'd also given myself the choice not to get involved. This is a survivor's prerogative. If you've survived the loss of a partner, you have the right to refuse to go through it with someone else without feeling guilt. But Frank wasn't just someone else. We'd been witnesses to each others' lives for many years. And we'd lived through a time, and reached an age, when witnessing came to be one of the most valuable things in life.

In the spirit of Sylvia's symposium, I'd already decided to write a cover story on Frank for the Arts and Leisure section of the Sunday *Times*. It's rare for architecture to get this privileged spot in the paper, but I had no doubt that Frank was entitled to it. He'd achieved breakthroughs in his work. He represented something special to the architectural community in Los Angeles. His New York connections mattered, and his appetite for glamour mattered. They caused some to look askance at him, but provoking that kind of

"Dan House." Courtesy of the American Academy in Rome, Franklin D. Israel, FAAR '75, Archives.

regard is itself a contribution, particularly when the provocation comes from someone with talent. In the catalog for the show, Frank talked publicly about having AIDS for the first time. He hadn't talked about it before, because he'd never come out to his parents. But in the catalog, he let his anger come out, his sense of urgency, his impatience with architects who fail to respond to the imperatives of their time. I would have written my story even if Frank hadn't spoken out, but I was inspired by his decision to do so.

The cover page had a fantastic picture of the Dan House, the last project Frank completed before his death. Steven Shortridge helped design it. The house replaced an earlier one that had burned down in a brush fire not long before. In the foreground of the picture, you could see the battered remains of the house's concrete foundations, some charred landscape, and new grass

Out of Order exhibition. Courtesy of the American Academy in Rome, Franklin D. Israel, FAAR '75, Archives.

coming up. I used the site to represent the instability of Los Angeles—the earthquakes, riots, floods—and also the unpredictability of life. How did we get from the Barefoot Boy to this place where I was essentially writing an obituary for an old friend, to be read by him only weeks before his ashes went into the ground?

To be a survivor, it is not enough to live. One's friends must die. If I've em- phasized the rivalry in my friendships with Derek and Frank, that's partly a defense against the pain of losing them. The anger, too. How dare they die. And leave us alone to deal with all this shit. With no one to complain to. The tenderer moments in these friendships are harder to talk about. They're private. Saying good-bye to Frank when he'd dropped me at LAX and not wanting to look back because I couldn't stand that it might be the last time. But looking back anyhow. Trying to describe how modest Frank could be about the support he gave me. Taking me to meet Frank Gehry for the first time, as if it were no big deal. Thinking about the moments that won't happen is hard, too. A reunion with Derek after so many years. Whatever happened to Blake? I hear Richard Blight is living in Hong Kong and frequently flies off to the Philippines for cheap eye jobs. Can I be in a movie again? I want to play a critic who kills people. I'm thinking about how smart Virginia Woolf was to avoid sentimentality in *Jacob's Room*. How smart even to avoid developing Jacob's character. He's a child and his mother is calling, "Jacob!" Then he's a dead soldier and someone is looking at his shoes.

It's a privilege to make a contribution to the culture. Not everyone wants to, not everyone knows how to, not everyone is willing to make the sacrifices it involves. Derek and Frank were artists. They were not politicians. The word art stands for something in relationship to cities. Cities are places that produce. They're not just for consuming. Artists don't just slither through their time and place, nibbling here, tasting there. They don't have silicone minds. They produce objects, ideas, spaces, sensibilities. Above all, they produce the contemporary city itself, a place where they and others can live more comfortably, more fully, with greater dignity, a city more deeply aware of its contemporaneity, of its responsibility to the present. AIDS deprived my friends of the right to enjoy long life in the cities they helped to reinvent. It deprived them of their right to demand that society acknowledge this achievement. But their contributions live on.

Before we went to the cemetery, Steven took me by the office to look at some of his recent work. Along with Barbara Callis, who handles the business end of things, Steven took over Frank's office after he died. To my surprise, the two have not only kept the office going but increased the volume of work. In 1999, they dropped Frank's name from the firm and began to look for new office space. Frank's portrait, commissioned for the MOCA show, is still on display in the old office. It hangs in the lunchroom, so that the architects can have lunch with Frank. I expect they'll take it with them when they move.

Frank would have been proud of Steven's work. And perhaps a bit jealous. It took Frank a long time to find his voice, but Steven has been able to use Frank's vocabulary as a departure for his own work. It's a lot more assured than Frank's. Steven is working on a group of houses now that are very fine. They don't look like Frank's, but clearly they spring from Frank's example. I'm looking forward to writing about them. Frank's children—his city—will want some looking after.

Corpses Dancing, Dancing Ghosts

David Gere

Over the course of my life, I have enjoyed ample interchange with both corpses and ghosts. As a child, I witnessed my first human corpse when my great aunt Louella was laid out in the parlor of her creaky old house in the Pennsylvania town where she had been born, raised, taught school, grew old, and died while waiting for a friend to pick her up to go shopping. She lay carefully groomed in the casket—the upper half of which gaped open on its hinges—her skin smooth and waxy, almost but not quite as if she had simply gone to sleep. For all her lifelikeness, however, the illusion was not sufficient for some close family members. My father, who was Lou's nephew, and his sister-in-law Mary were disturbed that Lou's hair had been combed in an uncharacteristic fashion and that she lacked her bifocals. So, before the arrival of the larger family brood, they took out a brush and restyled Lou's reddened hair, sweeping it back the way she always had done and replacing the wire-rimmed eyeglasses carefully on her nose. Upon finishing, they stepped back to appreciate their work: there she was, just as they had remembered her in life. The adults seemed reassured by this. As a seven-year-old, I was terrified and clung to my mother's skirts.

Twenty-five years later I would bathe the dead bodies of my friends and lovers with the same ease and familiarity my father had brought to the coifing of his dead aunt. Joah Lowe died in 1988 in a Longview, Texas, hospital, his once handsome torso swollen with the *Pneumocystis carinii* pneumonia that had drowned him, his smooth face distorted by the tube that had connected him for the last week of his life to a ventilator. (In his last days, I sat by Joah's bedside, transfixed by this unstoppable machine with its aggressive rhythm, force-feeding him air.) Through his last night, as it became clear that Joah was beyond the assistance of doctors or their technologies, the machine nonetheless wheezed on. Bubbles formed at his lips and extruded from his nose. His ribs continued to expand and contract, but this movement became dully mechanical, a response to outside forces rather than a more complex dialogue between human will and medical intervention. Technically speaking, Joah's body remained alive, even after the precipitous drop in blood pressure that triggered the emergency room staff to "code" him, to shock his chest with a jolt I could feel through his hospital room door. But by that point Joah's body was no more than a corpse, a life-size puppet animated by the doctors and the machines like some postmodern Frankenstein. When, as the sun rose the next morning, the machines were finally turned off, it took less than a minute for Joah's spasmodic breathing to subside and for the last stirrings of his body to cease. Now he was officially a corpse.

In the fresh quiet of his room with birds singing outside his window, we bathed his corpse—his nurse Cindy, his friend Mary, and I. We ran warm soapy cloths over the length and breadth of him, tracing the line of his thighs—repositories of countless falls and recoveries that had once belonged to Doris Humphrey, before she passed them on to José Limón and he to Lucas Hoving and Pauline Koner who, in turn, had taught them to Joah. We massaged the muscles of his face, intent on erasing the tension and strain caused by foreign tubes and labored breathing. We rubbed along the length and breadth of his arms, allowing the inward inclination of his hands to mirror the cupping of our own fingers, as if sharing a last class in harmonious port de bras. We soothed the callused feet, chronically blistered ever since Joah began dancing as a teenager, first at the North Carolina School of the Arts, later at Connecticut College, later still in San Francisco where he taught classes in "The Art of Flying" and was making his way as a choreographer. And then I bathed his penis, as I had before as he lay in that hospital bed—one last time, this penis that would never be hard again. When we finished, we unfurled a clean white sheet over his body and left him alone. From down the hall, I watched as the attendants rolled him away to the hospital morgue in a body bag.

Throughout this time, in fact, throughout the night following his dramatic drop in blood pressure, I imagined Joah outside his body, floating, watching the drama unfolding at his bedside. I could not fathom him remaining inside his skin, amid the wreck of drowning lungs and proliferating infection. Yet I couldn't imagine him simply disappearing either. His indomitable personality and this thing we blithely, without proof, deem "spirit" seemed too durable for that, as evidenced by the last clear-headed notes he had scrawled to me in pencil on a pad of paper, notes I have kept to this day. How could he be so present one moment and altogether gone the next? How could a life so strong be simply annihilated? But if not annihilated, what form might that life take?

Back in my little studio apartment in San Francisco two days after Joah's death, his ashes resting in a cardboard box on a table, I was taking a shower when I became aware of a gentle, high-pitched sound keening at regular intervals, every second-and-a-half. At first, I thought this was the distinctive warning note emitted by a truck in reverse gear. But something about its timbre seemed strange, unfamiliar. Wrapping myself in a towel, I hurried to the front window to look for the expected service vehicle down on the street. To my surprise, however, the sound wasn't coming from the street at all, but rather from the room behind me, from inside my apartment. My heart began to pound as I searched for its source. Almost immediately, I determined that it was emanating from inside the wooden mantle over the fireplace. I began to feel along the oak surface with my hands, trying to discern exactly where the sound was coming from and thinking all the while of Joah.

I had said to Joah in the silence of my mind, in the hours after his death, as I bathed him and watched the attendants roll his body away, that if he could manage it, I'd like a sign. Nothing scary. Nothing too big. Just a simple indication that he had endured, that he was "safe." I was thinking of this as I moved along the mantle, feeling the vibration of the high, repeated tone, and wondering what was causing it.

In a matter of moments, my hand was drawn to a place on the mantle where a Christmas card was propped up. I picked up the card, and as I did so the gentle, rhythmic tone metamorphosed into the first note of the melody of a holiday song, "Chestnuts Roasting on an Open Fire." The electronic music box built into the card had somehow become stuck on its first hypnotic note, like a broken record. Realizing what had happened, I fell down on the couch, still wrapped in my towel, and let loose a great sob, not because this phenomenon of the repeating sound was suddenly explained— as if by science—but because, for me, at least, there was no other way to interpret this than as Joah's "sign." He had come back to me, cheerful as Bing Crosby, as a ghost.

In the bodily syntax of AIDS and dance, the transformation from healthy, sexy body to sick, emaciated body to inert corpse to meat in cold storage to ashes and, finally, to ghost is repeated every day. Each stage of the bodily process subsumes the one that came before, obliterating its predecessor and taking its place. At the end of the cycle, this series of replacements allows for a double formation at its terminus: when ashes and ghost coexist. On the table lies Joah's body, in a box. His ghost, meanwhile, speaks to me from a greeting card on the fireplace mantle. Neither is equivalent to his body as it had been in life. The ashes represent his corporeal presence in a "purified" post-contagion state, burned down to a concentrated form of carbon, all other elements virtually expunged. Since his death, portions of Joah's ashes have been divided and planted along with a memorial cypress tree, floated out to sea on a makeshift boat, and, by the whimsy of one of his friends, preserved in an amulet and worn around the neck as a talisman of memory and good luck. These ashes remain inert, stable, lifeless, functioning solely as fetishes of memory and devotion. The ghost, however, appears in numerous guises, transmuting easily from one slippery form to another. Initially, in my studio apartment, Joah's ghost manifested itself as invisible and mute, just efficacious enough in worldly terms to be capable of nudging open that greeting card. Thereafter, the ghost appeared in my dreams, wafted a trail of familiar scent through my living room one late evening, and, according to his mother, returned at significant moments over the years to proffer a sort of ethereal hug. And yet, for all its initial activity, this ghostly form of Joah gradually faded away. I half expected it to return to me on the tenth anniversary of his death. I lit a candle. I held him closely in mind. But the ghost did not visit me in any of its previously discernible forms. Instead, ten years after his bifurcation into corpse and ghost, all I have of Joah is a photograph that I keep in my daily diary, a photograph that stands for a set of memories which, like his spectral form, seem gradually to be fading away.

Donald Alan Lowe was born August 1, 1953, in Henderson, Texas, the son of working-class parents who had made good in a watermelon merchandising business. Lowe was small and temperamentally unsuited to sports, so he delved into books and became a trainer and masseur for the football and basketball teams instead. An outstanding student, he served as a page in the Texas State Legislature, was elected president of his senior class, and planned to pursue law after enrolling at the University of Texas at Austin in 1971. A

Joah Lowe. Courtesy of the estate of Joah Lowe.

scant year later, however, he was inaugurating his dancing career at Antioch College in Ohio—in the nude, no less—in a piece by Harry Sheppard titled *Field Event*. One local reviewer called it "about the best-managed bacchanal-in-the-buff" he had ever seen. (In 1987, a piece titled *Theiresias* earned Lowe the colorful *San Francisco Chronicle* headline, "Joah Lowe Bares All for Art.")

The unlikely switch of careers came about as the result of his seeing the Alvin Ailey company perform *Revelations*. "I want to be able to do this," he explained to a hometown reporter. So, after a brief sojourn at Antioch, he continued on his way to New York, where he studied on partial scholarship at the American Ballet Theatre School until it was discovered he had misrepresented himself as a sixteen-year-old when he was in fact nearly twenty. Entranced by images of former Limón dancer Pauline Koner, based on an article he had read in the Dance Collection of the New York Public Library (where he worked part-time), Lowe shifted immediately to the North Carolina School of the Arts to study with his new "spiritual and artistic mentor." After three years, during which he frequently followed Koner to the American Dance Festival at Connecticut College, he enrolled at "Conn" as a degree student, graduating with honors in 1977.

The seeds of a serious dance career were sown in Connecticut. Lowe debuted in Koner's Dance Consort there; tried out a raft of stage names such as "Donovan" before settling on the elegant "Don Austin Lowe"; forged a profound student/mentor relationship with Martha Myers, Connecticut College professor and dean of the American Dance Festival; and was deeply influenced by movement teachers Daniel Nagrin and Lucas Hoving, with whom he later reconnected in San Francisco. Even more significant for his future direction, Lowe applied for and won a prestigious Watson Fellowship to study dance and theater abroad for one year. According to the initial Watson proposal, he was to study with the Royal Shakespeare Company in London, with Marcel Marceau in Paris, and with new masters of the avant-garde theater in Poland. But in an unexplained turn of events, he was directed to discuss his plans with the great Asia specialist Porter McCray, director of the John D. Rockefeller III Fund, and traveled to the Far East instead.

This was a felicitous and momentous shift, for Asia—particularly the cultures of Japan and Bali—would become the major personal and choreographic touchstone of his life. Upon his return, Lowe began making dances based on the themes that had inspired him on his journey. *Blood Remember-*

ing (1980), a large group work for dancers at the University of Wisconsin–Milwaukee, where he taught from 1978 to 1980, was concerned with "modern man's loss of personal myth" and with his alienation from his body. *Tendered Voices* (1982) continued to probe the revelations of his travels with sections titled "A Sandbox in Texas, 1957," "A Bamboo Hut in Bali, 1977," and "A Studio in San Francisco, 1982." (He had moved to the Bay Area in 1980.) *Churinga* (1983) explored even more sharply the contrast of his Texas upbringing with his experiences in Asia, the Asia segments being mistaken by critics as a Vietnam chronicle. (Curiously, Lowe—who was too young to be involved in that war—referred to his final days in the hospital as his "Nam.") His 1988 project was to have been a further working out of the ideas embedded in *Churinga*, using a mask that a friend had procured especially for him in Bali.

Lowe did not conceive of Asia as some sort of mystical Shangri-la. Though deeply affected by his journey there, he had spent much of it in mental and physical consternation, finally forced to return to a New York hospital for a long convalescence from hepatitis (which, not inconsequentially, added enormously to his distrust of Western medical practice). Perhaps as a result, his choreographic borrowings never appeared shallow. Even *Savage Gestures for Charm's Sake* (1985), in which he performed as a Japanese geisha in the tradition of the male *onnagata*, was a treatment of utter seriousness and respect. Joah was not a "disciple" of the East as much as an admirer of its cultural riches, which he strove to understand through readings, choreographic explorations with masks, and self-identification as a healer.

In 1980, after changing his name to Joah (the name was "given" to him in a dream, he said, but one friend claims it was a self-consciously creative act), Lowe moved to the Bay Area to study Aston-Patterning, a system of movement education and bodywork developed by Judith Aston, an associate of Ida Rolf. Joah integrated the therapeutic technique into his work as assistant director at the Drama Studio in Berkeley from 1981 to 1983 and as movement therapist at the alternative medical clinic run by Dr. Judith Northrup on Capp Street in San Francisco's Mission District. He taught his "Lessons in the Art of Flying" there, mixing daytime clients from the clinic with professional dancers who were attracted to his alternative approach. After Northrup's death from pancreatic cancer in 1984, the clinic practitioners remained closely associated with one another under the rubric Somacare.

Bowling Lesson no. 1: Letting Go of the Ball. *Courtesy of the estate of Joah Lowe.*

Lowe also worked at the San Francisco Orthopaedic and Athletic Rehabilitation Center and developed a private practice.

In the last months of his life, prior to his diagnosis with AIDS in December 1987, Lowe contemplated new choreographic ideas, touring possibilities, more frequent "flying" lessons, and the strategy of financing his art with commercial and television work. (He was studying with acting teachers Gregg Snazelle and Ann Brebner at the time of his death.) Besides his considerable acting gift, the nerdy kid from Texas had cultivated a sturdy and marketable all-American look. More than fame, though, Lowe desired the quixotic life of the choreographer.

Joah performed publicly for the last time on November 15, 1987, at Oakland's Laney College Theatre in a solo he had commissioned from Lucas Hoving, the esteemed teacher and choreographer he had first met at the American Dance Festival. It was called *Forgotten Song*, a strangely apt title, seems to me, now that both Joah and Lucas are gone—Joah on January 7, 1988, at the age of 34, Lucas on January 5, 2000, at the age of 87. I try but cannot quite conjure the particular elasticity of Joah's thighs, the remarkable radiance of his eyes, the humored seriousness of his dancing. Our first date comes back to me as a series of flash frames that disappear almost before they register in the brain. The lovemaking, the struggles, the breakup, the AIDS tests, the fevered sweats, the last sharing of Christmas gifts—all of which filled to overflowing the latter half of 1987—are now nothing more than disconnected threads pulled from a once-rich fabric. Decontextualized puffs of smoke. Ephemerality itself.

Still, one image from Joah's final days in the hospital remains vivid, nearly as well formed in memory as if it were a photograph. It is New Year's Eve, and Joah's cheerful sister conveys some Latin beat music to his hospital room. I remove a cassette of Bach's Brandenburg Concerti from the boom box and replace it with this new musical offering. A party hat magically appears on Joah's head. Catching the beat, his eyes begin to lurch and arch with a knowing insouciance. The tube in his throat, the catheter, the feeding lines have rendered him nearly immobile. And yet the effect of the rhythm remains unstoppable. It travels up his spine and he begins to sway. His arms float upward, the fingers of his hands caressing the air. He is funny and sexy again. And I realize that the dying man before me is dancing the merengue. Beautifully.

Joah Lowe's personal papers are housed at the San Francisco Performing Arts Library and Museum.

Who Turned Out the Limelight?
The Tragi-Comedy of Mark Morrisroe
Ramsey McPhillips

Mark Morrisroe loved ice cream. We ate it a lot. In fact, we started our relationship in 1987 by having ice cream in the East Village of New York right after he lured me into an art gallery to look at his photographs. He mesmerized me with his artistic talent, then took me to an ice cream parlor and with french vanilla dripping down his chin asked me to take him home and screw him. Later on in our relationship, we shared a banana split in Boston (at Friendly's) when the two of us went back to his hometown to find the link that might prove the Boston Strangler was his father. And near the end of his life, I was with him when he scored a bag of heroin and a scoop of rocky road ice cream in an effort to soften the blow that afternoon of his diagnosis of AIDS.

A lot has been written about Mark Morrisroe . . . that he was a Rimbaudian genius, a *poète maudit,* a chronic liar, the bad-boy ringleader of the art movement Boston School, the illegitimate son of the Boston Strangler, and the teenage concubine for a gang of gay Mafia hit men (my favorite). To me, however, Mark was just a brilliant child in the body of a thirty-year-old man. Mark really didn't have much of a childhood (unless you consider that childhood is pretending John Waters and Divine are your father and mother), and yet when we came together, which ironically was the last eighteen months of his life, we had a relationship based on making up for his lost boyhood.

When I first met Mark, I lived with a rabbit in my apartment in New York City. His name was Dennis Hopper. He was brown and small, more like a guinea pig. When Mark slept over, which was a lot, we all slept together—

the boys and the bunny. Dennis Hopper was actually quite ferocious; he bit your fingers if you weren't careful. Mark and I used to compare bunny bite scars—the bigger the better. Sometimes, Dennis couldn't help but mess the bed and I would wake up to Mark lining little raisin-like rabbit turds along my stomach. I let him do it. I grew up on a farm. It was all the scatological kinkiness I could muster. Mark would call me every day and ask about Dennis Hopper. I think he saw him as the puppy he never had as a child.

Mark did have a cat in college however; a black and white pussy named Lefty. Lefty was a movie star . . . in a snuff film. Lefty became deathly sick and Mark decided to take him to be put to sleep at the Boston Humane Society. But when he arrived they demanded a fifteen-dollar fee fee. Mark was broke. He had just spent his last dollar on penicillin for an outbreak of gonorrhea. So, Mark took his kitty cat home and killed it himself. His friend Steve Stain filmed the execution. At first, Mark was shown injecting the cat with a syringe full of house paint, which didn't work, so then he tried to strangle the cat with his hands. The camera jumped all over the place making the film all the more authentic and horrifying. After all his attempts failed, with the cat obviously suffering terribly, Mark limped into the bathroom and threw the cat's head in the toilet. The drowning took forever. Finally, Mark dabbed paint onto the dripping wet cat cadaver as though it were canvas. After Mark and Steve processed the film they gave it to their friend, and later Mark's art dealer, Pat Hearn, to screen on her Boston television program, the Pat Hearn Show. Pat's show was one of the first live cable television programs in the country. Pat didn't review the film before she showed it and was mortified when it aired. Pat had gained a reputation for having sensationalist topics on her show—nudity, ear-piercing industrial music, discussions of pornography as art. But nothing prepared her, or her viewing audience, for this. It caused an immediate uproar. The phones to MIT were ringing off the hook and Pat was called into the dean's office where she was informed her show was canceled. She was told that the Boston ASPCA was suing her and the university for animal cruelty. The dean demanded to know where she got the film. She refused to acknowledge its authorship. She knew Mark wouldn't be able to handle the pressure of being labeled a fiend. Although much of his life was based on igniting the fires of controversy, this particular act was too hot for even Mark to defend. He knew he had stepped over the bounds of artistic freedom. Many of his friends stopped speaking to him. Steve Stain was so upset that he fled to the West Coast to hide. Pat went to court represented by the MIT lawyers and apologized for showing the film. The case was dropped. Pat Hearn was Mark Morrisroe's guardian angel; Mark her diabolical son.

Pat Hearn fulfilled Mark's Madonna/whore complex. Extraordinarily regal, enigmatic, intellectually savvy, entirely unpredictable and prone to periodic bouts of the coquette, she was . . . his artistic patron saint, his fantasy dominatrix, the Jackie-O doll he reviled, the Combat Zone stripper he created, the mother he always wanted but never had. When the world branded Mark a monster, Pat extended her apron strings. When Mark questioned his self-worth, she took out his portfolio and examined it in his presence with the reverence she would give her most prized intellectual possession. When Mark was driven to do something vicious, dangerously salacious, or destructive, she stood by without judgment. She understood that Mark created his best art when tempting the onslaught of death, like a sadomasochist exploring and enjoying the thresholds of pain. No one was more shocked by Mark's death than Pat Hearn. To her, he was invincible. Pat's own mortality has recently come to an end . . . she died from liver cancer this past summer. She was only 45 years old. I wish Mark could have lived to have seen how Pat handled her immortality. Like Mark she treated it with tenacity and exploration. I was with her the day she was told her internal pains were "just an ulcer." She confided in me that she intuitively knew that it was much worse. She was so frightened and instantly turned to the subject of Mark as if he would be able to guide her through it. Towards the end of her illness, after living well beyond that which is humanly possible under her condition, she told me that it was Mark who taught her how to fight for her life. She told me her only regret was that Mark didn't experience the same universal love from the extended art community that had rallied around her need for financial and emotional support. Mark died with a few friends at his side, Rafael Sanchez, Gail Thacker, and me, but Pat died under the watchful eye of an entire art kingdom that exalted her one of it's queens. Her life was truly a lightning rod for all that has been creative about the visual and conceptual arts during the 80s and 90s, and in the end she took the cues for her truly aristocratic swan song from the creative magic Mark wrought by living an entire lifetime just a membrane away from the final unknown. Pat was Mark's Madonna and in a strange twist of fate, Mark's effigy had become her Holy Ghost. For me, they will have always died together.

I've never met Mark's real mother. Ironically, her first name is also . . . Pat. I wonder if she is still alive. I wonder if she knows Mark is dead. I am forbidden to *ever* contact her; one of Mark's many dying wishes. He told me she was a "whore" who would bring home young boys and tricks to fuck while he was sleeping in the same room. She was a real Budweiser mom. He told me that she made the rent by fucking Albert De Salvo, the Boston Strangler, and that Mark was his illegitimate son. De Salvo and Mark do look an awful lot alike, and the fact remains that Mark and his mother were his next-door-neighbors in Malden, Massachusetts. Mark had the reputation of lying and many people stopped believing his outrageous stories. Especially this one. I, however, believed everything he said. Mark had the uncanny ability to spin facts into unbelievable truths. It was a gift. Presenting the truth as an ambiguity was just the device Mark used to infuse beauty and romanticism into his truly tragic life. This manipulation of his own personalized reality is what made Mark bigger than life . . . it is what made his otherwise benign genius artistic and notorious. His photographs manifested this same charade of ambiguity—the human body captured through the lens as recordings of light saturated with layers of muted color so beautiful as to become ethereal . . . in essence, unreal. In essence, beautiful lies.

Mark kept the book *Confessions of the Boston Strangler* next to his bed and loved to tell anyone that his father, De Salvo, was also a photographer who used a camera as a guise, telling women that he was a model scout to worm his way into their apartments to strangle them. Mark gave me the Boston Strangler biography as a birthday present. Written on the inside cover next to a picture of Albert De Salvo is the inscription:

> To Ramsey,
> My father and I have the same hands
> Love, Mark

Kids usually aren't very ambitious. Not like Mark. He did have one very ambitious childhood friend, however, Lynelle White. Back then, Lynelle was half Chelsea Girl, half Mona Lisa. She turned Mark on to Divine and the movie *Pink Flamingoes*. She made him read philosophy books about the Symbolists. She colored his hair. They met in Catholic high school and started a photocopied magazine called *Dirt* that contained made-up vicious gossip about celebrities and local Boston people. Her writing and Mark's photographs made the magazine a cult hit. At fourteen they were trying to pass themselves off as punk versions of Elizabeth Taylor and Richard Burton in *Who's Afraid of Virginia Woolf.* Lynelle loved Mark. She was supportive of his creative experimentation with sex and drugs, even though she wasn't into it. She made Mark intellectualize it all. Lynelle encouraged Mark to romanticize his out-of-control-ness beyond pure documentation and into the realm of artificial beauty. More than anyone she nurtured into full bloom the brilliant narcissism that is Mark Morrisroe. She and Mark entered the summer program of the School of the Museum of Fine Arts in Boston and made it their mission to cause as much controversy as they could. Mark painted a swastika across school property while Lynelle photocopied a picture of Joan Crawford with the words "DRINK PEPSI" written across her face and turned it in as her homework over and over again. Mark ended up staying at the Museum School but Lynelle was not asked to return after the summer program. I guess they found Joan Crawford more threatening than Hitler. It didn't matter. Lynelle went to Harvard. After Mark died, Lynelle came to live on my farm. Mark is buried there, his ashes scattered in the fields and in the river along with my grandfather, father, and brother. Lynelle needed to resolve his death by moving to Oregon. She brought her beautiful new boyfriend, and I gave them my great-great-grandfather's little hillbilly house to live in. Life is funny. One minute you're growing up too fast and too brilliant in suburban Boston, and the next minute you're buried in rural Oregon with your best childhood friend making daily pilgrimages to your grave to finally say good-bye. Recently, Lynelle and her boyfriend got married. They seem very happy. They moved away. Life goes on.

Mark learned early that he could get ahead by making himself appear bigger than life. That's why his early photographs were not the photographs of a typical boy but more the work of a promiscuous sensationalist (Dirty Old Man). Boys take photographs of sports, and fishing trips, and their families. Mark's earliest photos were of suicide, sex, and a lot of himself with no clothes on. Not many boys do that. Eventually, Mark mastered the power of sensuous art—sensuous as artistic as opposed to sex as provocation. Once, in New York, he made me put on a suit and posed me on top of the Empire State Building for a photo shoot. I had just won The Best Nose in New York City Contest, which landed me on a couple of TV shows and news programs, and Mark was trying to convince me that I was going to be a *huge* star. We stopped at Penn Station before the shoot, and he demanded that I cut all my hippie/glamour-rock hair off. The barber accidentally nicked my ear, and I was bleeding everywhere. It was at the height of the AIDS media paranoia and the barber freaked out. I remember him backing away while throwing me a towel. I remember all the mirrors, and the blood dripping on a pile of multicolored shorn hair on the tile floor—and Mark dragging me out of the shop because he thought I was going to beat the barber to a pulp. I've never felt sexier. Believe me, it was the only time I out-dramatized Mark Morrisroe. We finally made it to the Empire State Building and I pranced around posing for the photos like I was James Bond. I used the blood from my ear as mascara. Mark developed the photographs and they were awful. They made me look like a late-in-life baby of Queen Elizabeth. I've got those hideous flapping ears of the royal family. Eventually, Mark did take some nice pictures of me on my Oregon farm, when we were swimming and just lying in the sun.

Mark loved to swim, and we spent most of the time he was in Oregon on the river that runs through my farm. It is shallow and meandering in the summer—perfect for Mark and his paralyzed leg. He wore his boxer shorts as swimming trunks, and you could see his huge balls swinging around inside them when they got wet. Mark liked to pick blackberries along the river while I swam stark naked with a horse up and down the river. I was showing off. That is, until the horse reared and I took a nosedive into a muddy bank, me under its stomach and pinned underwater on the muddy bottom. I barely came out alive. Mark loved it. He stood watching me thrashing around under the horse's belly while stuffing berries into his mouth like popcorn at the cinema. When I finally escaped and came up vomiting mud, he screamed in his strongest Boston accent that I was a "Wicked Fucking Idiot." We both agreed that both of us could have been famous if he had only had his movie camera.

Mark left the farm and went back to New York City without me. He had decided that art was moving in the direction of fashion and he wanted to do High Fashion Photography. He arranged appointments at some of the big fashion-model agencies where he did test shoots. The photographs came out blurry and muted in color. They were gorgeous. Yet, the agencies and models said that his photography was juvenile. They said it lacked professionalism. He was really hurt and went back to taking pictures of himself. Of course, his old friends, Nan Goldin and Jack Pierson, are now doing huge Matsuda and Gucci fashion ad campaigns in their own unique offbeat styles. And now, it seems as though every Nike, Armani, and Dolce & Gabbana ad campaign looks like it was art-directed by the "juvenile" Mark Morrisroe.

Mark was no stranger to artistic criticism. His first review in art school read:

In my opinion, this student should never have been admitted. The faculty of this school are not prepared to deal with a disturbed student of this sort. . . . I find it difficult to discuss his work because I find it shallow. The few pieces that show promise (in my opinion) he feels are garbage. I am not in favor of giving this student any credit. . . . I request this student not be re-admitted the second semester.

Mark was devastated by this review, feeling he had worked harder than any other student. He responded with this heartfelt reply:

I need a place where I can do what I want and have it criticized—not me. I want to be told how to make it better—not me. I do put forth a lot of effort and I try very hard and I don't get it because people are repulsed by images. People want to see cheery things which I can not produce.

Mark's letter didn't go unnoticed and he was re-reviewed by his professorial champion, Jeff Hudson, who wrote:

Mark is very talented with a wide style of graphics and languages. He prints a magazine, and does silk-screen, lithographs, drawings, and sculpture. He is a strong imageist but should work in some other mediums of a less throw-away nature. He's off to a fine start at the school and seems excited and committed.

Mark went on to graduate with honors and was presented the prestigious Museum School Fifth Year Award.

Mark was a true alchemist. His real artistic drive was to discover new ways to make beautiful photographs. He was always experimenting with chemicals and made weekly pilgrimages to local thrift shops in hopes of finding aged photo chemicals that might produce mutant effects in the darkroom. The Polaroid Company realized his genius early on in his career and would ship him free products that they were developing. They knew that if anyone would find interesting ways to use them, it would be Mark Morrisroe. His relationship with Polaroid was really quite amazing considering that he was so open and cavalier about depicting his prostitution. Polaroid and the man in charge of their collection, Elco Wolfe, played a crucial role in Mark's progress as an artist. Mark's most famous process, which he is credited with inventing, was to take a color photograph first, re-photograph the same image again in black-and-white, and then sandwich the two negatives together during the enlargement process. Each of the resulting prints was unique by virtue of his printing process and became unmistakably "his" by the addition of fingerprints, intentional smudges, and off-color retouching and spotting. It made for a very foggy color, muted image, more like a painting then a traditional photograph. When this process was personalized with his romantic, albeit melancholy imagery, it made Mark's art stand out from that of the group of his friends who were also making photographs—artists such as Nan Goldin, the Starn Twins, Jack Pierson, and David Armstrong.

Each of these artists had a dramatic effect on Mark's life. David Armstrong was on the admissions committee at the Museum School in Boston and insisted that Mark be admitted over the protests of the other admissions officers. I often wonder what would have happened to Mark if he hadn't gone to the Museum School. Mark was making a living as a prostitute at the time and had already suffered the gunshot wound that paralyzed his left leg. Mark said that back then David was a gap-toothed beauty drinking loads of cheap booze while parading around the Provincetown beach in drag. Mark could relate. David reeked of budding fame. He was the first artist Mark knew who moved to New York to make a go at the art world. David's photographs are very beautiful. Straight-on photos of his friends looking right into the camera lens as unadorned human souls. No smiles, no tears, no irony. Just sexy black-and-white truth.

David Armstrong's best friend, Nan Goldin, also had a huge effect on Mark's life. She was the most ambitious of the Museum School group and her early success, with her first book *The Ballad of Sexual Dependency*, quickly became an achievement for Mark to beat. Mark is seen in the book looking especially pathetic holding a pint of Jim Beam whiskey. One of Mark's most prized possessions was Nan's bloody tattoo bandage. When asked why he became a photographer, his answer was NAN GOLDIN. Nan taught Mark how to use the Museum School darkroom, which is ironic, because Nan wasn't re-

Untitled, Double Self-Portrait in Drag. *Courtesy of Pat Hearn Gallery, New York.*

ally interested in the darkroom—she was interested primarily in the subject matter of her work and often sent her negatives out to a lab to be processed. In his cattiest moments Mark scorned Nan's lack of interest in darkroom technique and wondered why Nan bothered taking photos at all. He thought her vision, which he called "vital," would have been better served in writing. He disagreed with those who found Nan's work raw, candid, and impromptu. He found her work "calculated." He believed that the complicated subtext of her work, the full "scope" of her life behind the photos, was where her genius ruminated. "Nan is driven to take photos because she suffers from a deeply broken heart," he once told me. "She is the unrequited love photographer of our age, and no matter how hard she tries, no photograph will ever really show or take away her pain."

Nan has gone on to be one of the most celebrated iconographers of our time, maternally wielding her show-it-all camera to capture a variety of marginalized cultural groups from which she derives her love. Mark was very jealous of Nan, envious of her art-career fortitude. He was very upset when she didn't come around to see him when he lay dying. He repeatedly uttered her name in his morphine delirium. She was fighting her own battles in a detox program at the time. It was an era in which death was in control. When she recovered, Mark and many of her friends had died, and she included them in the infamous 1989 NEA-censored show she curated at Artists Space (Witnesses Against Our Vanishing). I know, to this day, she talks about him as one of her true artistic soulmates. His love for her is unrequited by death.

The Starn Twins, two handsome younger classmates of Mark, also became hugely famous shortly after graduating from the Museum School. They took many of their cues from Mark, such as skipping class and then showing up for their semester reviews with an amazing amount of completed artwork. They would spy on Mark and his friend Stephen Tashjon and fantasize that they were vampires. They were especially inspired by Stephen's eclectic messy collages and less so by Mark's calculated careless handling of the photo image. The Starns took the limelight away from Mark during an exhibition in Boston called *Boston Now, Photography* by showing large photographs that had been ripped and then taped back together. Many thought that they had stolen the idea from Mark. Mark never thought so. He was just furious that they had taken the limelight away from him and that he was being usurped by not one, but two beautiful men. In reality, he really liked the Starns and saw their work as quite different from his own. Their strongest images were appropriated from the classical world: Jesus foreshortened, marble horses, architecture. Mark, on the other hand, was capturing the images of his personal objects, close friends, lovers, and himself. Mark's artistic locus was the negative while the Starns concentrated on manipulating the photo paper. Mark and the Starns took turns posing for each other, an act at the Museum School that would be synonymous with becoming blood-brothers. The Starns really worshipped Mark, and in their beautifully quiet and sensitive way, provided for him as he lay dying.

And then there was Jonathan, or as he is known these days, Jack Pierson. Jack changed his name about the same time that he and Mark ended their love affair. Taking a new name was Jack's way of finally having his own identity outside of Mark's circus sideshow. Mark had a huge ego and during the end of their relationship, Jack was his whipping boy. He thought Jack had enormous talent as a graphic artist but warned him not to take photographs. "Don't even try to be a photographer," he told Jack, "because you'll fail— there's room for only one genius photographer in the art world, and that genius is Mark Morrisroe!"

Of course, Jack was amassing a portfolio of artwork unbeknownst to Mark and has since become a major art star. He is very respected. His work is saturated with a sad come-hither mystique, filled with color-coded pheromones found in the sublimity of sex. In a word, it is Advertising. Jack was Mark's own personal red-haired super-model boyfriend, always looking sexy in Mark's intimate photographs. He looks especially great in Mark's Andy Warholesque Super-8 movies, where he could be seen dressed as a gay-bashing hillbilly or a Spanish contessa. Had Mark lived, their feud would have undoubtedly been one of the most colorful battles in the art world. They measured their love for one another in increments of artistically based psychological torment. Theirs was a case of competition fueling brilliance. Had Mark lived, he would have been a huge art star too. He wanted fame at any cost.

July 13, 1985: I Mark Morrisroe swear to coldly use and manipulate everyone who can help my career no matter how much I hate them. I will pretend that I love them. I will fuck anyone who can help me no matter how aesthetically unpleasing they are to me.

Mark's dramatized life was exacerbated by his HIV. Death was his biggest leading role and his home an appropriate stage for his last performance. It was a railroad apartment in Jersey City handed down to him by the painter Philip Taaffe, who had moved into the city and eventually the Chelsea Hotel. Mark had been living in the apartment for the last several years by the time he became sick, and coincidentally, the building had been sold to a developer who had removed the other tenants in anticipation of renovating the building into fancy condominiums. The law prevented the landlord from removing Mark, however, because of his disability from HIV. Mark's continued occupancy prevented the landlord from realizing his pot of gold. The landlord was an older fat man from Eastern Europe, named Walter Piacowski, who smelled of fried food, rancid talcum powder, and poodle urine. He reviled Mark and tried everything to evict him. He even gutted the entire building—walls, windows, staircases, everything. You could see clear through the building to the alley behind. However, Mark's apartment was left intact. Four small rooms suspended in the sky like a single-wide trailer house. All the exposed wires and plumbing ran up the core of the vacant building into Mark's apartment on the fourth floor. It was a big life-support bubble not unlike the one he would shortly be connected to at Jersey City Medical Center.

Mark didn't want to leave his home because he feared the landlord would somehow prevent him from returning. But I had to get him to the hospital . . . he was a veritable talking cadaver. We tried to sneak out but the landlord appeared out of nowhere escorted by his tiny chocolate-colored poodle. I had Mark draped over my shoulder; he only weighed ninety-five pounds then. The landlord saw how sick he really was and tried to block us from getting down the four flights of stairs. He stopped us to tell us what he thought. "You faggots are all going to die of AIDS. . . . You'll be much more comfortable in the hospital, where you will finally fucking die. . . . Make sure he never comes back to my apartment building." He was shoving at me with his fat belly. I was defending us by using Mark's limp legs as battering rams. It was futile. Then I suddenly heard Mark laughing. He giggled in my ear, "Pull my pants down." I didn't wonder why, I just reached up and yanked them down and Mark swung his ass around on my shoulder and sprayed a stream of runny shit right onto the wife beater T-shirt of the landlord. Mark screamed "I just gave you AIDS and now you're going to die just like me!" I started to laugh so hard that I almost dropped Mark, but somehow I slid past the landlord who had fallen onto his knees wailing and in shock. The last thing I heard was the sound of a yelping poodle that the landlord had kicked away from licking Mark's shit off the floor. I rushed down the freestanding flight of stairs and onto the street. I cleaned Mark's ass off with my shirt, threw the shirt over some cyclone fencing, then carried him several blocks to a cab. We arrived at the hospital, me bare-chested and Mark still bragging about his aim-and-shoot victory. It was his tenth time in the hospital.

When Mark was in the hospital, my friend Lisa Morgan went to visit him. She helped him continue to make art in his electric bed. Once the doctor showed Mark his X rays revealing that he had pneumonia. Mark's response was, "THAT'S A MASTERPIECE!" He took it, added some of his concocted color photo chemicals, and made the X rays into beautiful images. Mark made art every hour of every day his entire life. Even on his deathbed.

Mark and Lisa made sculptures by sewing his X rays together with really thick yarn. I remember them sitting around singing "the thigh bone is connected to the hip bone, and the hip bone is connected to. . . ." The X rays also showed the bullet that was lodged behind his heart. Mark was shot when he was sixteen by one of his "johns" while negotiating the payment for a twenty-dollar blow job. He had picked up a stranger off the street on Beacon Hill to get money to buy his mother a Christmas gift. The bullet left him paralyzed. The doctors gave him little hope to ever walk again. But they didn't know Mark. He came out of his coma a born-again monster and refused to accept the possibility of having the stigma associated with being wheelchair bound. Apparently, it was not a very pleasant convalescence for the hospital staff. The doctor's report read:

Mark refuses to use Lofstrand crutches and continues to be a behavioral problem. . . . he is manipulative and demanding. His *psychopathic* behavior continues to be a problem on the ward.

Eventually, Mark walked without even a cane. Half your job as his friend was to watch that he didn't fall on his face. He was always falling on the ground. I got so I could break his fall like a father catching a toddler.

Mark liked me because I wasn't part of his East Coast world. It was my destiny to be an Oregon farmer. I never posed a threat. He listened to me. I always told him to act like a lady whenever he started to get vicious about someone. I'd say, "You're going to be famous no matter what, Mark, so why not do it with class, a little style?" It would make him laugh. It calmed him down. Inevitably, he would say all he really wanted was to live on my farm and cook for all the big strong cowboys that he fantasized I employed.

Mark did make it back to my farm one last time, but not as the cook.

∾ ∾ ∾ ∾

"Sir, your flight is leaving in five minutes!"

"Yes, I know, but they won't let me on the plane."

"Why?" she said.

I showed her the box of Mark's cremated ashes. Suddenly there appeared a huge action-hero security guard with coiffed blond hair and a badge at the counter saying,

"May I please see the death certificate?"

"I don't have a death certificate," I said.

"And, your letter from the airlines granting you permission for your travel with the Remains of a Loved One."

"I don't have that either."

"Then, I'm afraid you will not be able to board your flight."

"Look," I said as I tapped the small black box containing Mark. "This is not a VCR, it didn't come with operating instructions. This is a dead man whose ashes I am taking to be buried on my farm in Oregon."

"How do I know these ashes aren't really—A BOMB?" the security guard sneered.

"A bomb? You think I'm carrying a bomb?"

"You could be, and I'm not risking the other passengers on your flight. I have no way of really knowing what is in that box."

"Then, take a look inside," I snapped. He took a long time to decide, then opened up the plastic box and peered inside.

"I still can't tell what is in here."

"Take the contents out," I suggested. The ashes were contained in a plastic bag, with a bright red metal bread tie keeping it closed. He pulled the bag out, and a thin stream of Mark's ashes started falling out a small hole in the bottom of the bag. Without thinking, he reached for some Scotch tape and closed the hole. He swiped the ashes off the counter onto the floor as if they were crumbs, then fondled the plastic bag like an evil kid squeezing a water balloon.

"I still cannot be sure there isn't something explosive in here."

"How about if you open the top a little and force the ashes up into the flute of the plastic bag," I said. He grunted and once again complied.

"The only way you're getting on that plane is if I can take the ashes out of this bag!"

"Be my guest." He reached for five small white plastic trays, you know, like the ones you put your change and keys on before going through the security arch, and began pouring Mark Morrisroe (aka THE LOVED ONE) onto the counter. I turned around to look at the line of people waiting to take late night flights to Seattle, Phoenix, and Boise. They all looked like Edvard Munch's painting *The Scream*. The original reservation clerk was further down the counter softly crying as mound after mound of Mark's ashes were emptied out onto the trays. Finally, we watched a clump of metal fall out onto the last tray.

"Ah ha," said the security guard. "What is this?" Pointing to the glob.

"It's the bullet," I yelled. "It's the bullet that was lodged in my friend's chest, next to his heart. You see, he was shot when he was a prostitute when he was sixteen years old, it's why he limped. He died of AIDS and his father was the Boston Strangler. I'm writing a book about the New York art world, you know, about him and his friends—they're all going to be really famous some day." I reached over and picked the bullet out of Mark's ashes as the security guard leaned into my face and said,

"I have had enough! Get these piles of your friend back into that bag. I'm going to escort you down to the gate, and you're going to leave. NOW!" I did as I was told and we ran down the concourse, me swinging the taped-up plastic bag that contained Mark, the security guard shaking his head in total disbelief. He'll never forget that day, but then few people did forget the bigger than life genius Mark Morrisroe after they first met him . . . whether it was as a pile of ash, as a photograph of a naked teenage prostitute, or as a brilliant child in a man's body about to change your life forever while licking ice cream off his chin in New York City.

Robert Ferro
Felice Picano

"To Lou-Lou," minuets the dedicatory handwriting across the title page of Robert Ferro's novella, *The Others*, "with love, across the ages!"

He gave me the book several years after we'd become friends. Published in 1977 by Scribner, it was already out of print by then, and we were playing with the possibility of the SeaHorse Press, which I owned and operated, reprinting the book. That never happened, for several reasons (his current publisher expressed interest in the novella, we couldn't agree on a format, etc.). But throughout my many moves from residence to residence in the years since, whenever—packing or unpacking—I've come across the slender, handsome little book, I've always stopped and opened it up to the dedication and I've always found myself rooted to the spot.

Seldom has an inscription been so revealing of a person—and to a certain extent—of a relationship. So revealing, and at the same time, so cryptic. Now that a decade has passed since his death from Kaposi's sarcoma, I've only begun to appreciate that paradox was the domain of Robert Ferro's life, of his work and possibly also of whatever influence he may in the future wield: to have been the most confidential of strangers, the most arcane of explicators. Luckily, much of this quality was caught in his writing and so it is still communicable to those who never knew him personally.

A bit of explication about that inscription is needed: Lou-Lou is myself. It was a pet name for me of Robert's—and of Michael Grumley's, his lover and, in the truest sense, life-partner. But how does one get from Felice to Lou-Lou? Follow the permutations for a glimpse into the Ferro sensibility. The year is 1982, several years after we all had met and formed a short-lived but ultimately momentous writing group called the Violet Quill Club. One member of the seven, George Whitmore, had fallen away completely. A second, Christopher Cox, had ended his relationship with a third Quillian, Edmund White, and only I would continue to see Cox much socially. Edmund seemed already mentally, if not yet physically, in Paris. But the remaining four—Andrew Holleran, Robert and Michael, and myself—had somehow grown closer after the Violet Quill meetings had ended, and we saw each other often. The four of us were spending a late autumn weekend at Gaywyck, my nickname for the Ferro family's beach house (taken from Vincent Virga's novel of the same name, and blithely appropriated by Robert), sited on an estuary of the New Jersey shore, between the "Irish Riviera" town of Spring Lake (its Grand Hotel used in the movie *Ragtime*) and the newer, yuppie shore town of Sea Girt. We were seated outside, on the ocean-facing roofed porch, in the midst of a typical Ferro-Grumley ritual, tea and muffins, and I uttered something by way of explaining a particular career move. Robert laid a hand over mine and his large bittersweet chocolate eyes almost melted as he said, "That settles it. You are darker and deeper than Lake Louise. No one has ever sounded the bottom of Lake Louise. It is reported to be the deepest freshwater lake not only in Canada but in all North America."

For the rest of that stay I was "Louise" rather than Felice. And a month or so later, when *Christopher Street* magazine published a portfolio of authors' photos, with Robert Ferro's captions, my photo—of me seeming to touch up with a paintbrush a mirror in which I was reflected—was captioned "Poor Louise—mad at last." From "Louise" to its foreshortened "Lou" required barely a year. And was probably due to the fact that among the Ferro-Grumley retinue, I was insufficiently femme (perhaps also insufficiently "grand") to merit a full-fledged drag name. The doubling to "Lou-Lou" took place a few months later and was clearly an affectionate augmentation, an indisputable sign that I had entered the magic circle of the most inner of their cronies. For months afterward I tried to discover what had so suddenly endeared me, and when I couldn't, I asked Robert. He assured me it had nothing to do with anything directly beneficial to them, but to the fact that I'd written a dismissive review in the *New York Native* of the stories of David Leavitt, an author whose work Robert wholeheartedly loathed.

And so I unearthed another aspect of Robert Ferro: what I would come to call his Commendatore persona. For if Robert could be the most delightful of one-on-one personal and cerebral communicators, he also possessed another, more forbidding, persona equally critical to who he was and how he wrote: social and intellectual arbitrator, nay, despot, whose judgment was as good as an edict: instant and immutable.

So I put up with a nickname I didn't care for, though there were times I fled from it, such as when Robert shouted across the half-acre width of a New Jersey garden supply center where he was purchasing gigantic flower pots. "Where were you?" he stamped his six-hundred-dollar, silver-tipped, Florentine boot heels at me when I finally deigned to appear, "I was calling you!" He was so irate, I wasn't about to tell him that I'd been busy flirting with one of the employees and would have eaten glass shards before answering to the name Lou-Lou.

Both the Italian boots and the enormous ceramic pots I just mentioned are further aspects of what were by that time intrinsic facets of his character. Robert's family, he told me, derived from Calabria, the area around Bari known as the boot of Italy, and from Sicily, the ball the boot is kicking— far from my own father's Roman background. Robert was born October 21, 1941, in the New Jersey town of Cranford, and grew up in the tony suburbs of Morris County. After he'd graduated from Rutgers University in 1962, he immediately moved to Florence, Italy. Robert would write several times about this brief era of efflorescence and of his life amid the far more evolved personalities of the tiny, family-like Florentine pensione, testimony to how climacteric it had been to his life and thought. The first time was while at the Iowa Writers' Workshop, the second in a never completed heterosexual novel he was writing at the time he and Michael went in search of Atlantis, and the third, most successfully, in the gay-themed, first sixty-seven pages—titled "The Bardolini"—of his second published novel, *The Blue Star*, which some readers consider Ferro's best writing.

Robert remained in Florence until late 1965 when he began a two-year program leading to an M.A. and M.F.A. at the University of Iowa Writers' Workshop. It was there, in the Midwest, that he met Michael Grumley. Originally from nearby Davenport, Iowa, Michael had by then already been to Hollywood where he'd taken a few small film roles and sufficient body modeling work to live on and had returned home unsure what career to follow: film actor or writer. At Iowa, Robert and Michael studied with Kurt Vonnegut and Chilean novelist José Donoso; among their classmates were the novelists John Irving, Gail Godwin, and Andrew Holleran—a stellar group. After they left Iowa, there were some months in which the two young men moved about and tried to solidify their lives together. They finally did so only by leaving the country and going to Italy. This time their destination was Rome, which in the mid-sixties was the center of a flourishing, international movie business at Cinecittà. I myself was in and around Rome during this same time, and later on we would reminisce about people and places and events we'd shared in ignorance during those carefree days.

For myself, however, my visits and finally my stay in Rome—all of Europe for that matter—was a detour, a way to recognize how unchangeably American I and my destiny actually were. After I left in 1967, it would be decades before I went back. For Robert and Michael, Rome became home, and in later years, their second home and haven. At the time, it was a perfect place for Michael to find studio work and for Robert to become reacculturated to Europe. They remained expatriates for another five years, by which time the Italian film business had begun to flounder, taking with it Michael's hopes for a screen acting career. When they returned, it was to New York City. They first lived in a small, loft-like apartment downtown, then moved to what would thereafter become their permanent base of operations in the United States: a large, sunny, prewar apartment on West 95th Street, off Central Park. But most of the time I knew the Ferro-Grumleys, i.e. from 1978 to their deaths in 1988, they spent spring and early summers in an apartment high above the Piazza di Spagna in central Rome. It was only following the nuclear accident at Chernobyl, Ukraine, with the venting of atomic radiation all over Europe, that the pair ceased their annual three-month-long Roman sabbaticals.

Even in New York, their art, their furnishings, their clothing, their jewelry, and their accessories all spoke of their life in Italy. For Robert, the most beautifully made example of anything could be found within a few miles delimited by the Via Corso and the Piazza della Repubblica, except for leather goods—better in Florence—and cloth—superior if from around Turin. Once prices in Europe began to rise, and Robert and Michael found themselves more involved in the New York gay literary scene they helped create, Italy slowly began to lose its attractions and become more retrospectively appealing, grist for essays and novels. At the same time, it became a great treasure house for Robert to rummage through as he delightedly took on the large task of repairing and updating the Ferro family beach house.

I recall the first time I became aware of both the magnitude of this labor and also Robert's commitment to it. The large first-floor living room/ dining room area encircled one end of the house, as a bowrail semicircumnavigates a seagoing vessel, debouching onto side and back terraces, enclosed porches, foyers, and subsidiary corridors. It boasted nearly two dozen windows in need of new curtains. At one point, I—and every other guest in Gaywyck—was asked to offer opinions on the swatch book of favored chintzes. Later on, when a pattern had been selected and work begun, Robert proudly offered this update: "There isn't enough fabric left for the whole place. They're having to reprint it at the Italian factory!"

The enormous pots—ten were needed, it turned out—were for a small forest of trees to grace the numerous outdoor sitting areas, and at long last they were discovered, with befitting silhouette and appropriate ornamentation, some of them two-thirds as tall as Robert. A tractor trailer with electronic loading gate was needed to deliver them. By then, Robert had redecorated the three upstairs bedrooms (mine, aquatically done up in tones of white and green, instantly dubbed the Princess Louise sur Mer Suite), the two basement ones, the halls, and the maid's room downstairs. He had the entire driveway moved ten feet to curve more incisively into the property, nearly redefining it as a porte-cochere. When a Madison Avenue tycoon moved into the adjoining acreage, Robert panicked, fearful privacy would be compromised, and had an enormous earthen rampart raised between the houses, upon which he installed pine trees, once boasting that it was large enough to be seen from outer space. When the neighbor complained to the village that he was losing any view of the water, the pine trees were removed and the berm itself whittled down a bit.

Robert's mother, née Gaetana Panzera, had died in that beach house, not many years before, in the very front bedroom Robert and Michael subsequently slept in. When she'd been healthier she'd governed two houses: the newer, larger one upstate, which was a home and entertainment center for her husband, president of his own generic cosmetics firm, and this shoreline abode, originally named Eagle's Nest by its builders and first residents in honor of the largest of the seabirds that occupied the estuary, as well as for its unobstructed site.

Intensely invested both in his mother's death—a major element of his first published novel, *The Family of Max Desir*—and in keeping her memory alive in the beach house he came to see as her embodiment, Robert in effect turned himself into a new family matriarch. Quillians and other big city visitors were welcome, but only off-season. In the summer, Robert's large family—his two sisters, his brother, and their spouses and children, as well as his father and the father's lady friend—would stay there. Robert seldom wrote during these times; he was too busy cooking, cleaning, keeping house and order. But even off-season, he'd hold parties of women—sisters, aunts, his niece—varied with parties of men—his brother, uncles, brothers-in-law and their sons—at the house for weekend card parties that might have come out of the pages of *Max Desir*.

Robert wasn't at all deceived, he told me, about the reasons behind his father's largesse in allowing him such artistic freedom during the renovation: the expensive beach house was to be tarted-up only to be sold. Gaetana's four children would share the proceeds. Robert's stratagem was to do all the work necessary and then stall for time, possibly until his father died and he would be able to lay total or partial claim to the house with one other sibling—easily manipulated, he hoped—since the rest of the estate was otherwise divided. Another example of Commendatore Ferro putting Machiavellian precepts into action.

Via George Stambolian, who remained in contact with the Ferro sisters after Robert's death, I followed for several more years the history of Gay-wyck. Evidently, early postmortem plans to sell it dissolved on several occasions for unexplainable reasons—which seemed to belie what Robert's sister Camille Ferro-Burns told me after his death: "If there was any trouble in this family, Robert was invariably its source. It's been so quiet since he's gone!"

Once the decision to sell had been made by the three surviving siblings, the house was quietly acknowledged to be haunted. One of Robert's nieces claimed her boyfriend was literally stopped from ascending to the master bedroom floor, pushed back down by some unseen force. Bizarre noises and flickering light fixtures became commonplace occurrences. Vases dropped off deep shelves and dinner plates self-ejected out of closed cabinets; the eerie become the everyday, all events easily attributed to Robert's revenant, since no one could deny the selection of destroyed objects seemed to so precisely fit his often stated preferences and dislikes.

An exorcism of the house was contemplated and discussed, but before that extreme step another plan emerged: three of Robert's friends, myself, Stambolian, and Steven Greco, were delegated to visit Robert and Michael's grave high above the Hudson Palisades to entreat him to desist. We made an early June social call, brought flowers, engaged in literary shoptalk and gossip, picnicked rather well, sunned a bit, and, before leaving, danced upon the grave in a ring—three not very lissome Graces—whether to divert or to mollify Robert's refractory spirit was never made clear to me. But possibly in response, or to avoid any further cemetery visitations by the oafish living, the haunting of Gaywyck abruptly ceased. After Stambolian also died in early 1992, I lost track of the Ferro family and have no idea whether the beach house remains in their hands, continues to be frequented by Robert's phantom, or is merely family—secondarily Violet Quill—history.

If the above reads rather dottily like something out of a Shirley Jackson novel, still, it is more than apropos. For while in life (and in the one book they wrote together) Robert played the rational, skeptical, Renaissance man to Michael's greater credulity, in truth he allowed the occult, the arcane, the not quite visible or material a larger than ordinary place in his life, crediting to it much that otherwise seemed inexplicable. His meeting with Michael, for example, fit into the category Robert called "karmic connections." He told Andrew Holleran, whom he first met in the Iowa writing program and with whom he remained lifelong friends, that until his final book tour for *Second Son* in 1988, he and Michael had been apart only six days in the intervening twenty-two years. And, going back to his dedication to me in his novella, that phrase "across the ages" spoke of Robert's conviction that when he and I first met at a preview screening of Helen Whitney's pathbreaking television documentary of gay life in America in the autumn of 1978, we had already known each other in former lives and would meet again in future existences.

I'd already noticed both Robert and Michael within Manhattan's gay underground a few years before our formal introduction. At private dance clubs like the Loft and an earlier incarnation of the Flamingo on Duane Street, Robert's equinely handsome dark bearded face, his aristocratic, erect bearing, his slender, well-muscled quattrocento physique and long straight mane of brown hair made him an immediate standout in an era of what in retrospect seems to have been a stunning number of natural, distinctly beautiful men. At that time, I recall him being referred to as "Max" by my artist friend David Martin, who had already painted Robert, and later—fittingly—drew him as a centaur for an invitation to a Black and White Men Together Party. More solidly built and less aloof than his partner, Michael was then known as

"Mickey." At that time, the mid-seventies, both were deemed prize catches for the night among the mixed crowd of whites, African Americans, and Cubans among whom they danced, and with whom they had love affairs.

Although Robert only insinuated but never really wrote about it in *Max Desir*, while Michael did write about it a bit in his posthumous novel, *Life Drawing*, if only as something that had happened in his youth, by the time I met them, the Ferro-Grumleys were confirmed "black hawks," meaning the only men they ever saw outside their relationship were African American. More than once, Robert insisted I join them at "mixed" parties and get-togethers. During one such party, I met a fellow I'll call Clem, who seemed by far the least interesting of all the intelligent, handsome men present. In fact, with his facial scar and brightly colored clothing, his aggressiveness, and annoying, loud, interruptions of anyone speaking, he seemed more like a "street person" and totally out of place. Mentioning him to a pal later on I said he acted like a pimp just out of prison (which it turned out he was). So, naturally, when he put the make on me, I was appalled and rejected him almost reflexively. Shortly afterward I left the party; and it turned out, so did Clem. The following morning Robert was on the phone, furious, demanding to know how I dared betray him by "stealing" Clem. I was thunderstruck— not only by the accusation but also by the realization that what so turned me off about Clem was paradoxically exactly what made him the most attractive man at the party to Robert and Michael.

When we first did become friendly, Robert and I, he was already trailing years of glory behind himself. For one thing he was several years older, for another he'd lived in Europe on and off for years and still did. His first book had been published almost a decade before and was still in print, albeit from a discount reprint house. His second book, the novella, had received admiring reviews in the mainstream media. He and Michael had a substantial history together, which included months on a yacht sailing the eastern intercoastal waters and the Caribbean in an allegedly successful search for a newly arisen section of the mythical lost continent. Among their circle of friends were men and women of all ages and occupations, from jazz singer Susannah McCorkle and novelist Julia Markus to landscape designers/gardeners for the affluent, Parke-Bernet appraisers who resided in eccentricity on upper Fifth Avenue, and a smattering of acquaintances who never worked at all, but who occasionally sold some small thing they'd inherited at auction or had a travel book published or lived on "incomes"—fast food heiresses, dilatory scribblers of columns on interior decor in hardcover, coffee table bound, quarterly magazines only eleven people in the world actually read. Even for someone like myself who'd by then lived in Greenwich Village a decade, it all seemed epicene and soigné.

At those first, elegant, upper West Side "teas," after everyone else had left and Michael had withdrawn to his studio to sketch or nap, Robert would keep me by his side plying me with Milanese nougat and Pinhead tea while we discussed the crop of awful novels and the teachings of I Ching, current publishing and problematic Tarot readings, the niceties of Mahayana Buddhism and manners in the most au courant downtown sex club. Robert was witty—of a short story writer whose quite bad novel had been trumpeted on the front page of the *New York Times Book Review* he said, "She's gone directly from mud huts to the cathedral stage without a single intervening era!"

He too was writing a new novel, the one that eventually became *The Family of Max Desir*, his first openly gay-themed book, and he was frankly desirous of having it make a splash. Among the members of the Violet Quill, when we seven first gathered to read and discuss our work, two of us, Andrew Holleran with *Dancer from the Dance*, in 1978, and myself with *The Lure*, in 1979, had "hit the big time" in Robert's words: i.e., published unquestionably "out" gay novels with major publishers that had generated publicity, reviews, word of mouth, and especially sales. Robert was candidly curious how it happened. Although he'd known Holleran for years and exchanged letters with him whenever they'd been apart, Ferro found his old pal too flummoxed by success to talk about it; Robert thought for fear of jinxing the next project. I had no such fear, having readied my next, very different novel, *Late in the Season*, for publication, and already looking to short fiction and a memoir to outline an even more wayward course.

I ended up reading much of Robert's novel in manuscript and it was at his urging that I consented to put together what now appears to be the first gay and lesbian literary anthology, *A True Likeness*, which I then published through my own small press in 1981. The high standard of fiction, poetry, and drama in the book, and the contributors involved—including most of the Violet Quill members, Bertha Harris, Jane Rule, and Jane DeLynn—guaranteed the book would get attention. It did, including a handful of reviews, an American Library Association citation, and a small grant to SeaHorse from the New York State Council on the Arts. Within its pages were excerpts from two books that subsequently rocketed into prominence, Edmund White's *A Boy's Own Story* (1982) and Robert Ferro's *Max Desir,* published the following year. Also in its pages was the fragment of a never completed autobiographical novel by Michael Grumley set in Rome, a piece that, aside from whatever intrinsic merits it possessed, signaled a sea change within Robert and Michael's relationship to each other and to the world that the rest of us, no matter how close, wouldn't become aware of until years later—and that continues to haunt and intrigue me a decade after their death.

Here I have to retrace steps a little, back to the Ferro-Grumleys first production, *Atlantis: Autobiography of a Search.* In that book, still a remarkably readable, personable volume thirty years after it first came out, Robert and Michael alternate narrating how they became interested in, then ended up actually looking for, "Poseidia" not far from the mouth of the western inlet separating two islands of Bimini in the Bahamas. It devolved as a result of an Edgar Cayce prediction years earlier that Michael had come across, Michael's own dreams, the loan of the thirty-five-foot boat by Robert's father as an enticement to woo Robert back to the United States, and, finally, the predictions of a *strego,* or male witch, the two had come across in Rome.

Yaria is what they call the witch in the book, but I recall Robert telling me his actual name, something more like Hieronimo. Months before it had become anything more than a notion, he'd assured the two Americans they would take the boat journey and fulfill Cayce's prediction of a 1968–1969 Atlantean "discovery." What they—and their teammates—discovered was a to-this-day ambiguous archaeological find, an unexplainable series of huge, regularly shaped stone slabs, forming what resembles an underwater causeway. Later finds by a scientist who'd accompanied them included other underwater walls set at right angles to the first, along with nonrandomly spaced columnar fragments, all deemed to be composed of material found only in the Andes Mountains and dating back over twelve thousand years. In the book, Michael concentrates mostly on the "mumbo-jumbo" aspects, while Robert's sections deal more directly and straightforwardly with the "action," i.e. problems of handling the yacht, geography, meteorology, the people they met, and how the thing got—and almost didn't get—accomplished.

Whatever else besides the book accumulated once the adventure was over, the Ferro-Grumleys' conviction in the strego was consolidated. When I first met them, they continued to consult him and to receive *auguri* every year in Rome. Thus I learned that he had foretold their deaths, "together, around the age of forty-seven, from some kind of new cancer." A prediction that unfortunately came true, but which a decade earlier seemed implausible.

Robert's first solo publication, *The Others*, begins with the narrator speaking of surviving a greatly debilitating illness "which changed me." He then goes on to say he wasn't certain whether it was "of the mind or the body," and some have read the entire short, often baffling, book as an allegorical charting of the transition between life and death. *The Family of Max Desir*, published six years later, opens with the protagonist's uncle suffering a fatal stroke while driving a car, and quickly segues into the subsequent cerebral seizures of Marie Desir, Max's mother, whose slow death from an inoperable brain tumor forms one well-investigated center of the impressive debut novel. In *Second Son*, published five years later, the illness that comes upon the narrator and then dominates the book is an undefined one, an obvious correlative of AIDS; the then-inevitable death is transmogrified into a fantasy ascent to a gay planet of complete health. Of Robert's work, only his third novel, *The Blue Star*, escapes thanatological subject matter, and even that book seems to contain the theme embedded in his elaborate reverie on the hidden Masonic temple beneath the Obelisk in Manhattan's Central Park. By now, we're used to reading about death and dying whether in self-help books, memoirs, or novels, but Robert was one of the first to address the subject with candor, unflinching stoicism, and all the abhorrence it deserves, both in his books and later on in his life.

Another motif that insistently appears in Robert's writing is that of the seagoing vessel. It's the very setting of the novella, and its layout and decor are described with the lapidary disillusionment of a Kafka fable. In Atlantis, again a boat dominates: this time Ferro Senior's *Tana* is the milieu of most of the book's action. *The Blue Star* is titled after another luxury yacht sailing up the Nile, first helping to cement, then aiding to drive apart the book's two male characters. In *Second Son*, the vessel appears in two forms—first, the canoe in which the two desperate heroes row across the vacation lake that has become their final refuge and thus the physical gauge of the progress of their declining health; second, the fondly desired spaceship and its promised escape, which they eagerly await.

The third most salient of Robert's topics, and the one most crucial to his success as a writer in the mid-eighties, is the relationship of gay men to their birth families, an issue Robert grappled with in his life and in his writing as fiercely as the biblical Jacob wrestled the angel. As the third child, second son, of a large, affluent, ambitious, second-generation Italian immigrant family, Robert had from birth a predetermined place and position. Traditionally, the first son received all the attention and the bulk of the material bounty but was then forced to bear the complex burden of continuing the lineage, enriching the household coffers, and upholding the family name. Decades ago, in the "old country," the second son—automatically bereft of power and status—typically accepted his situation, becoming a priest or professor, sometimes a doctor or lawyer, i.e., someone "helpful" to others. When, that is, he didn't instead turn into a wastrel. The same basic problem held true for myself, born into the exact same family position, but where Robert and I—vocally, sometimes angrily—differed was that he accepted the fundamental rightness of the system and only sought a greater place within it. Certain of his intellectual and moral superiority, Robert rebelled early and in varied ways, trying to usurp his brother, although he'd never dream of taking the elder's position as active second-in-command of the family firm or raising a family, as was also required.

By being a homosexual and by becoming an artist, Robert—like myself—doubly betrayed his origins. If the first was acceptable only by a stretch of doctrine, in that it might be innate—if not precisely "natural," at least not solicited, not chosen (who would be mad enough?)—the second was both unnatural and overtly sought after. To decide to be a writer, painter, composer, in the face of the likelihood of poverty, defeat, and most significantly a built-in lack of stability inimical to family structure, was equal to spitting in one's parents' faces, denying them the fruit of their years of care and sustenance. As an example of this attitude: even when my second published novel was on national bestseller lists, and I barely thirty-two years old with a presumably long career ahead, my mother could only comment, "Your father and I still preferred if you were an attorney." I could ignore their preferences since by then I'd already supported myself since the age of sixteen and sent myself through college.

Robert's parents were far more materially supportive of him during the decades when he wasn't yet published and self-supporting. For one thing, they had more resources than my family to do so. Then too Robert never abandoned them as I did my kin, but remained a major player in their intricate familial rivalries. Thirdly, they expected him to fail as an author, and then to fall in line with their rules and wishes. It took Robert an interval to prosper. I recall some hand-to-mouth years for him after the money from home had ceased, when all prospect of other loans had been used up, when he worked as a waiter for a gay catering service—years he endured, even enjoyed, with a certain noblesse oblige, a well-disposed slumming, but which he afterwards shuddered over whenever they were alluded to.

Beyond our differing experience, however, Robert and I disagreed on the role of the family in gay life on a far more essential level. When I'd discovered I was gay, it had been with joy, providing me another potent arrow in the quiver I'd amassed for my attack on all that was rigidly established. I embraced homosexuality with the goal of tearing down society and starting all over again. While Robert claimed to admire the revolutionary in me, he secretly desired an accommodation in which he eventually shared in what had been amassed. It was only natural that his tenets would prove more agreeable to reviewers and critics than my more subversive ones. It's equally comprehensible that his books would continue to win favor and be read by a younger generation of gay people who seek the same ends Robert wanted— to marry, to have families, to serve in the military, to be just like all the rest of the dreary straight world. At the moment that faction continues in the ascendant, under the preposterous sobriquet of Post-Gay, but I (perhaps illusorily) believe that my way will ultimately be seen as the more successful one.

I could be fanciful and call these years of striving Robert's "lost years." The truth is less glamorous and rather more interesting. The time between when Robert and Michael left Iowa and the publication of *Atlantis* was a mere three years. It was another seven years between the publication of *Atlantis* and Robert's novella, *The Others*. It would be another six years to the publication of his next book, *The Family of Max Desir*.

Meanwhile Michael went on to write and publish: in 1974, *There Are Giants in the Earth,* a book about sightings of mysterious man-ape creatures around the world; in 1977, *Hard Corps,* a study of the American leather S/M subculture; and in 1979, *After Midnight,* portraits of night people, folks who slept during the day and worked during the night, a book both well reviewed and commercially successful. In other words, Robert's partner seemed to have made (or had made for him) the right career decision: he was moving ahead full steam, with more nonfiction tomes in preparation: one about beaches, another about lighthouses, a third concerning Alexander VI, known as the Borgia pope, who presided over Counter Reformation Italy in its great mannerist period.

Robert appeared to be dragging his feet, content to play spouse and mainstay. He seemed to have been working at *Max Desir* in one form or another several years before the Violet Quill began meeting. Another two and a half years would pass before it was ready in manuscript form. At the time, this was understandable, especially given Robert's stratospheric aspirations and incredibly high standards.

Then something strange happened. No sooner had Bill Whitehead, senior editor at Dutton—then an independent company—accepted his first novel, than Robert began writing *The Blue Star*. That book was nearly finished by the time *Max Desir* was receiving its last reviews. Robert barely could wait for his first novel to come out in paperback before issuing the second in hardcover, in 1985, again through Dutton. He'd barely completed that book when he began laying out the outline for *Second Son*. He wrote that volume faster than any previous book, and the only reason this third novel had to wait till early 1988 to come out was because in the meanwhile Whitehead had sickened and died of AIDS. Robert's agent took the book to Crown Books—also then an independent company—otherwise it would have come out in the spring of 1986.

Suddenly Robert Ferro's work was everywhere. Putting into service his recent friendship with *Newsweek* book critic Walter Clemons (whom all of us knew was gaga over Robert), he managed to get Walter to write a cover piece for the influential national magazine on gay books and literature, with of course a special emphasis on his own work. The Commendatore had reappeared in full regalia, and Robert arranged to call in every favor, cash in on each flirtation, play off every connection he'd made in previous years to ensure getting his books reviewed as widely as possible. Sales weren't at all bad, either: *Max Desir* in paperback especially sold well.

Yet during those same years, 1983 to 1988, Michael Grumley's writing career virtually dried up. Although he worked as energetically as ever on various projects and several seemed quite promising, none was ever completed as a book, received a publication offer, or saw publication. Stymied, Michael turned to fiction. First, back to the Italian based novel he'd titled "A World of

Men," that I'd excerpted in *A True Likeness*. Then, when that book was deemed by their agent to contain material too similar to what was already in Robert's works, Michael moved to an autobiographical novel set in earlier years, in the Midwest, in Hollywood, and in New Orleans. He gave readings from this work in progress from 1983 on, and several friends, myself included, encouraged him, as it felt both authentic and distinctive. What we couldn't help him with was the blatant fact that not too long ago he'd had a writing career and now suddenly he didn't; while Robert hadn't had a writing career and now suddenly he did. Their friends naturally wondered what this might signify. Were we witnessing some species of psychological vampirism, similar to that depicted in several late Henry James novels, where after being together so long, a couple involuntarily exchanged power, energy, even destiny? Or was it all less rarefied and far more haphazard than that?

These intangibles were soon swept away in the growing reality of first Robert and then Michael becoming symptomatic for HIV infection. As early as 1984, when Robert and Michael came to stay at my beach house at Fire Island Pines, I was sworn to secrecy about the already noticeable Kaposi's sarcoma lesions on Robert's legs and arms. They only visited me during the week and were careful who saw them out on the beach, spending most of their time there on my private house decks. The following year, Michael had a large skin tumor removed from his forehead, but assured us it was nonmalignant. The next year was calmer and Robert's lesions had been lasered off, seemingly with no lasting effects. But during the spring of 1986 in Rome, Michael began to suffer from severe headaches, which he attributed to the Chernobyl radiation leak. Europe was abandoned, and that summer and the following year, they rented a small lakefront house outside the village of Tully, in Orange-Athol country in north-central Massachusetts, a place they'd happened upon due to the good offices of my longtime friend Allen Young.

I visited Allen during the summer and so had a chance to see Robert and Michael in their new domicile. Both were writing—Robert completing *Second Son*, and Michael working toward a draft of *Life Drawing*. They were unusually antisocial, seeing no one locally but Allen—and then rarely. The afternoon I spent with them was cut short by their need to nap. The dinner we made together at Allen's octagon house at nearby Butterfield Farm was marred by Robert's being restless and criticizing everything. They left early.

My partners and I at Gay Presses of New York were anticipating reading Michael's finished book and putting it out the following year through the SeaHorse imprint. But when the manuscript arrived that autumn, it led to an abyss opening beneath my feet. The manuscript was a jumble, both physically and in structure and organization. Some pages had been typed over others, some had been done with nearly invisible typewriter ribbon. Entire sections were missing or misplaced. Pagination was erratic. Characters kept changing names. I persisted, I read the whole thing, then gave it to my partner, Larry Mitchell to read, without any prejudicial comment. His response a week later was "My god! we can't publish this mess!" Getting Michael to even recognize the unserviceable condition of the manuscript proved impossible: my first, and only, exploratory phone call to him on the subject was met with by cries of betrayal, effusions of paranoia, and an adamant refusal to in any way amend the thing, followed by curses and imprecations. Thereafter, and until his death, Michael referred to me as "that former person" and refused to speak to me.

What had happened is in retrospect obvious: the HIV virus had proliferated, passed the brain-blood barrier, and begun to damage Michael's mind: what is known as dementia. Ever loyal, Robert also cut me out of his life, tried to get the book published elsewhere, and began nursing Michael through awful bouts of headache and pneumocystis. This went on for several months. By early 1988 Michael was so ill, Robert had to place him in a hospice they would share, something like a hotel room, next to a hospital in East Side Manhattan.

As his partner declined to total invalidism, Robert began reaching out to friends. We became close again and remained so. Michael was feverish and raving anytime I went to the hospital to visit. So I mostly visited Robert. We walked around the neighborhood, checked out antique stores, drank tea in little shops, rearranged the furniture in the tiny elevator landing outside their new domicile. Robert was clearly exhausted, much thinner, and his Kaposi's lesions had returned, this time internally as well. He spoke with controlled anger of what it was like to have the bad luck to become a medical patient: the numbing horror of being trundled about and anti-individualized he compared to being a numbered prisoner at Auschwitz.

I urged him to write about it. But Robert astounded me by saying that he was now and forever done with writing: he'd recently completed an lecture on gay literature to be delivered at the University of Michigan, and he'd laid his pen aside. He had done so much excellent writing in such a short time, I can't be blamed for disbelieving him. Thereafter we argued about the decision. I couldn't help but think that besides depression Robert was in shock, and in terror. I'd been involved with AIDS from the very beginning of its time in America. The first two infected men on the East Coast had been friends and former Fire Island Pines housemates of mine: Nick Rock and Rick Wellikopf. I was subsequently immersed one way or another with the progress of the disease and attempts to discover its source, define it, and help solve it. Besides many, many friends and acquaintances, my straight younger brother—a weekend drug abuser—died of it in 1985. His wife was later diagnosed. As was my business partner at Gay Presses of New York, Terry Helbing, my bisexual older brother, and finally my closest friend and life partner. Meanwhile among Violet Quill members and colleagues, Chris Cox, George Whitmore, Vito Russo, George Stambolian, and later Edmund White would all test positive for the virus. All of the people above but Edmund succumbed to it. Naturally, every day I expected myself to become symptomatic and to test positive. Around me, loved one's illnesses doubled and trebled. Sometimes I would walk into a hospital ward to see one person and end up visiting a half dozen people I knew. Like everyone around me I became expert in the disease, its manifestations, and, because of my connection with various AIDS organizations, with the newest treatments. Following a complex discussion of steroids as treatment for one series of symptoms—virtually a consultation—over a patient I'd visited, one hospital resident asked where I'd gotten my medical degree. "Here, and on the street," I replied.

But as deeply submerged as I'd been, Robert and Michael had been equally remote from it. They'd never even allowed a discussion of AIDS in their presence. I continue to wonder how much that ignorance and the concomitant ice water bath of reality that followed contributed to Robert's utter demoralization over Michael, with natural reference to his own future

Michael died in May of 1988. After his large memorial service there was a gathering of friends held at the upper Fifth Avenue home of a friend. There Robert cornered me and George Stambolian, who'd also been shown the manuscript, and asked us what we thought had to be done to get Michael's last manuscript in publishable shape. As it had already been retyped and physically cleaned up, it was a mere matter of restructuring with bits and ends added and removed. Could he do it? Robert asked. We thought yes:

he knew as much about Michael's life as Michael himself. Thereafter Robert worked on *Life Drawing* nonstop, with phone calls back and forth, checking on this and that aspect of the book. He had a completed manuscript in mid-July. Stambolian and I rapidly read it, approved it, and, upon Robert's insistence, swore to him our oath that we would see it to publication. (It was published in 1991 by Grove Weidenfeld.) A day later, Robert left his apartment and moved back to his father's home in New Jersey. By then, the Kaposi's sarcoma had spread throughout his legs, his lungs, his stomach, and other internal organs. We spoke every day by phone. As I'd been his gadfly from the onset of our friendship, I continued to try to goad Robert back to health, frightening him with scenarios in which I alone survived to tell the world about him: then I would paint the blackest possible picture. Robert appreciated what I was trying to do, but it was too late. He died at his father's home, in his bedroom, awaiting a cup of soup, not ten weeks after Michael.

It has come to me anyway to write about Robert. I could say I've been circumspect here because I expect to meet him again in my next lifetime, as he believed, and I've already had tastes of his temper. But the truth is I cannot write anything but the truth. I loved Robert—we loved each other—in a way that only siblings ever do, and problematical as our relationship was, it was more than worth it: it was a privilege to have known him. So having to write this has meant having to relive that friendship, which I did again, with pleasure and sadness. Having to read Robert's work again I'm pleased to declare that it holds up well, and the best of it—his three novels—richly and accurately convey his voice, his mind, and his life. For years after he was gone, I heard Robert's voice in my mind, prepping me, beginning with "Lou-Lou!" then going on to laugh or threaten or invite, and I now realize I've left out many anecdotes illustrating his sophistication, his vanity, his wit, his generosity. So I'll leave Robert Ferro with one moment I can never forget: it was on the top deck outside his bedroom at Gaywyck, before AIDS was even a shadow—and he turned to me and repeated Blanche DuBois's line, "Someday, I shall die—of an unwashed grape!" And Robert's smile after he said those words was amazingly enigmatic.

Warren Sonbert
Phillip Lopate

Until complications from AIDS claimed him in 1995 at forty-seven, the avant-garde filmmaker Warren Sonbert was the picture of robust health. Tall, curly hair kept trim, with a triangular mustache that extended from a strong nose, and warm, often ironically amused eyes, his lank, tanned physique toned from regular workouts at the gym, he looked remarkably consistent from decade to decade. Warren exuded a nonchalant, burnished vitality, and seemed never to tire, however overstuffed his schedule. He was fully *present*, whether at work or play (which, in his case, seemed an almost meaningless distinction, since each fed the other so relentlessly), driven by inner discipline. On the one hand the most sociable human being I've ever met; on the other, by his own cheerful admission, a solitary. "I just follow my own needs and wants and desires. Do I sound too megalomaniacal?" he told an interviewer. "Well, I am. I think all artists have to be solipsistic, very exclusive."

I first met Warren around 1967; we were introduced by our mutual friend, Jimmy Stoller, who saw Warren at a distance. He was leaning back in his chair in an outdoor café in Lincoln Center plaza on a perfect summer day. He looked bronzed, worldlier than his nineteen years. He was wearing a brown velvet tie and a shirt with subtle tan and yellow stripes. I searched for years for such a shirt and never found one. It's funny to think that, long before we became friends, Warren was my sartorial model on the basis of this one fleeting encounter, since, in later years, I became the clotheshorse, and he pared his wardrobe down to lumberjack red flannel shirts and jeans. In any event, that first time I projected onto him an air of gilded youth, as he sipped white wine.

Warren Sonbert had already been celebrated in underground cinema circles as a post-Godardian wunderkind. Curious what his films might be like, I took in a one-man screening at the Filmmakers Cinematheque, then housed in the basement of the Wurlitzer Building on 42nd Street. I was very impressed. In two years, 1966–1967, he had made eight short films

(*Amphetamine, Where Did Our Love Go, Hall of Mirrors, Tenth Legion, Truth Serum, Connection, The Bad and the Beautiful, Ted and Jessica*), an explosion of wry, electric imagery. Each like a roller-coaster ride: you just hung on and followed.

The venerable filmmaker Rudy Burckhardt, himself a master of the collage/diary film, wrote about this work: "What first attracted me to Warren Sonbert's films in the sixties was their easy elegance of moving among beautiful people. Maybe I was feeling old at that time. In one scene the camera circled completely around a handsome young couple in Gramercy Park, in another fashion models flitted by, then you could get lost deliciously in Lucas Samaras's room of mirrors. The movement seemed more sensuous and relaxed than Brakhage, and up-to-date rock music added excitement." It was the world of sixties urban chic: boutiques and discos and art openings, Andy Warhol and Henry Geldzahler. But these fashionable subjects were not photographed as in *Vogue*. Instead, Sonbert gave us the private, often lonely moments of the beautiful people. We saw both their scarlet silk blouses unbuttoned *and* their pimples and eye-bags, and they were filmed in context, in their East Village apartments or on their street or relaxing with friends. His *Bad and the Beautiful* consisted of several portraits of couples edited in the camera, showing the tenderness, horsing-around, clinging to each other. Someone would be lying on a bed, waiting for his lover to return from the other room. Sonbert already had the knack of creating an intensely elegiac mood about the present, as though he knew how quickly these sixties costumes and postures would fade. Even his titles and song choices ("Where Did Our Love Go?") accentuated the anticipated loss, as much as the haunting tracking shots which seemed to be searching for the separated lover.

I did not see Warren Sonbert for several years, until 1974, when we bumped into each other again in the Lincoln Center area: this time at a bar after a New York Film Festival screening of Fassbinder's *Fox and His Friends*. I was with my girlfriend at the time, a poet named Kay, and I remember Warren entering with a loud group. I went up to tell him how much I had enjoyed his films, and he, in friendly response, detached himself from his coterie and sat at our table. He was drawn to writers, especially from the St. Mark's poetry scene; we had friends in common. This time we hit it off immediately: I sensed the chance for a serious friendship. I also recall him flirting with Kay, who was much taken with him, that evening and afterward. Kay, from Mississippi, was an accomplished flirt. Warren, for his part, was good at befriending both halves of a couple, and remaining loyal to each (much to my chagrin), long after, as often happened, they had split up.

We discussed the Fassbinder film, which I liked, and which he did too, up to a point, but also disparaged. He found its class analysis of the gay world heavy-handed. Odd that this particular film should have been the occasion of our reunion. Kay, I think, assumed from the first that Warren was gay, whereas I—tabled the question. He and I exchanged phone numbers, vowed to stay in touch, and (New York rarity) actually did.

In the formation phase of friendship, usually one person feels he is making more of the overtures; but the advances between Warren and me seemed equally distributed. We were both men-about-town, though he was certainly more in demand; he was devoted to the punctilio of popularity, the duty not to give offense. We would meet twice a month or so for dinner, talk for hours about movies, books, life, the people we knew. I found Warren wonderfully discriminating and sympathetic. He had a way of taking your side in any recounted dispute, while leavening his response with just enough humor to permit you to laugh at yourself.

Each time we parted, no matter how gossipy or light the conversation had been, he would produce this leave-taking look, his eyes liquid from the pleasure of your company and regret at its imminent removal, his voice velvety with promise: Till next time. Even if he did this with everyone, I was pleased with the effort—part of his courtly manners, from which I (who rarely modulated the abruptness of my exits) could well afford to learn.

The question of his sexual orientation did not arise, strangely, in first few months. For one thing, Warren never spoke, acted, or gestured effeminately; that was not his style. For another, he had the uncanny ability, like most socially gifted people, to mirror the person he was with. Too, he may have kept back that information, leaving pronouns vague, while figuring out just how deep my homophobia ran. Perhaps "homophobia" is too strong a term: certainly in our hip, liberal-artistic circle, it was assumed everyone would feel comfortable with homosexuality and have many friends and acquaintances who were gay. Both assumptions valid, in my case. And yet I had had my moments of bitchy overgeneralizing about gays. At the very least, the novelist in me was ever on the lookout to interpret individual behavior as an extension of tribal or sociological patterns, and the gay life provided abundant material for such speculations. (To give an example: once I knew that Warren was gay, I began to interpret his velvety, throaty vocal tone, and a certain constriction in the larynx, as a possible "gay reflex." My thinking went something like this: gay men were often choking back a good deal of rage in their determination to be nice, which tightened up the vocal cords.)

What complicated the sexual-definition issue was that Warren managed to let me know he'd been sleeping with a female student at Bard, where he was teaching film. Though his primary sexual identity had always been gay, he was up for the occasional tryst with a woman, especially in this period. At the time, I think, he was testing his sexual magnetism on everyone. His friends used to joke about how Warren would go into, say, a record store: in less than two minutes he would have made eye contact and the next thing you knew, Warren had disappeared into the men's room. I never saw this pickup routine myself, but once I realized he was gay (not from any coming-out scene: I think Warren was genuinely surprised I hadn't known all along), he found ways of sharing less obliquely with me this part of his life.

I often think about the night he took me to an all-male bash of balletomanes somewhere near Lincoln Center. It was a small apartment, a brownstone walk-up, and we got jammed behind the kitchen table with the booze. Some corpulent, red-faced man accosted Warren with what seemed to me belligerent lust. "Well, where have *you* been hiding out?" he demanded, and dove his hand into Warren's shirt, squeezing one bosom. Warren took it good-naturedly, looking tolerant and amused. He was the favorite that night, discouraging no one, giving none consent. I stood by his side, for safety's sake, playing the part of his date. I was the only straight man there.

Later, I drifted into the living room, with its exposed brick wall. I wanted to give Warren a chance to operate alone. The men at the party were either cruising each other or making out on the couch; that didn't faze me, they were not my friends. I also remember the circling men's cropped beards and their fierce eye contact, first intensely hungry, then dismissive, when they realized I wasn't in the game. After that they looked through me, as if annoyed that I was taking up space. Nowhere felt safe to stand, until David, Warren's film critic friend, came up to rescue me by talking film theory. He said he had been reading Noël Burch. Burch claimed we Westerners misread Japanese movies; we thought we grasped their core, but we were being "universalist," falling into ethnocentric bias, deceived by our bourgeois-hegemonist-humanist codes. His words grew more abstract, the more the scene around us heated up; and for one paranoid moment I even suspected him of speaking in code for my benefit, as though to say: Just as the Japanese subtexts elude you, so you misperceive the meanings here.

I kept insisting that it *was* possible for a "round-eye" like me to get Ozu. The argument went in circles but I clung to it, for lack of anything else, until from the corner of my eye I caught Warren's leather jacket and red flannel shirt. He whispered, mustache warmly tickling my ear: "Had enough?" I said I was ready to go, and we left. Warren started laughing as soon as we hit the stairs: "What an obnoxious party!" he said. "Had I known what assholes would be there, I'd never have wasted your time and mine."

He was generously bonding with me as friends, above the gay-straight divide; but I wanted to confess—or complain—to him how strained and alienating the whole experience had been. Why had he put me through this? Straight men and gays seemed suddenly like ancient enemies, each mocking the other's desires. But before I could deliver this harangue, I admitted to myself that the party hadn't been all that bizarre; I was exaggerating its off-putting nature to distance myself as fast as possible from the potential queer in me. When I was a teenager going to an all-male college, I had what might be called crushes on classmates and worried about it. My therapist at the time asked me: "What are you most afraid of? Quick, first thing that comes into your mind!" I blurted out: "That I'll become a homosexual." As it happened I didn't, and Warren did. Friends live the lives we don't have talent for, or taste, or courage. It hardly matters, so long as they live something other than one's own life.

Warren moved to San Francisco, a city for which he became an avid booster. He would give *"Vertigo* tours" to visitors, taking them around to Ernie's and Coit Tower and other locations used in Hitchcock's film. But he would always schedule annual visits to New York, timed to coincide with screenings of his films or that part of the opera season that most interested him. Over the years, Warren had become a classical music aficionado. Sometimes, on these fortnight visits to New York, he would stay in my flat, which was small and musty but close to the Metropolitan Opera.

Warren had a curious habit of keeping a small piece of unlined white paper in his back pocket (I assumed he did not use a pocket calendar because it would have broken the trouser line), on which would be written his day's schedule hour by hour, from eight A.M. until midnight. He tried to accommodate all his old friends, new acquaintances, and business associates on these whirlwind visits: breakfast with J, watching a morning rehearsal of the opera (he knew one of the ushers and for a while he dated Jerome Robbins), lunch with K, some business at the film lab, then tea with L, maybe a quick screening, then dash to the opera, after which dinner with M, N, and O, followed by late drinks with P and Q . . . and perhaps after that, some catting around. A few nights, he did not return to my place at all, but showed up in the morning, with an abashed "Don't ask" smile, followed by some morsels of gossip about our mutual friends to throw me off the scent, then a shower, and morning phone calls. Eavesdropping, I would hear him gathering information about the condition of the opera singers' throats ("Tatiana has a cold, she may not even go on!") Tatiana Troyanos was his favorite for many years: there is a lovely shot of her in one of his movies, taking a bow and receiving bouquets. Warren was a passionate missionary for opera among his more philistine movie and poet friends. I tried to learn from him: waited in line once for hours to buy a ticket for the Paris Opera's production of Verdi's *Otello*, with Margaret Price, sets by August Everding, which Warren assured me it would be unthinkable to miss. I liked it, but the sublime upper registers of the opera experience escaped me. I would be thrilled beyond measure for the first hour or so, settle in, then get a little antsy. Two hours of richness seemed enough, though I didn't dare tell Warren that. Once, he and I saw Mozart's *The Marriage of Figaro* together, in a production he highly approved of. During the third act, some of the Met's season-ticket patrons, elderly businessmen and their begowned wives, started leaving. Warren said scathingly under his breath: "Some people would walk out of heaven."

Warren's film style had changed from the sixties. He had abandoned the Downtown-Motown beat for a more severe succession of composed shots, projected absolutely silently. On the one hand, aesthetic austerity; on the other, a much broader social and geographical focus. Warren's suppression of the sound track had a good deal to do with his love for music and his desire to give his visuals a "musical" form. As he explained once, in a lecture: "In very much the same sense as one hears a series of notes, chords, or tone clus-

Warren Sonbert. Courtesy of Ascension Serrano.

ters, one sees a progression of a series of shots. . . . to purely watch the images is a much freer, broader experience than any track would add. The film can truly breathe this way—go many more places than it can anchored to sound." (Yet he returned to musical sound tracks on his last few films.)

The first of his films in this silent manner, *Carriage Trade* (1967–71), had an ambitious global range, and that Sonbertian knack of framing an anecdote in three seconds; but it also taxed viewers with its lengthy stream of silent images. I like what Jonas Mekas, then champion of underground movies for the *Village Voice*, wrote about it:

What it is, it's a canto on people and places. It's the first canto film I know. Sonbert keeps splicing together, one bit after another (each bit about the same length, not very long and not too short), bits of footage from his journeys in Europe, Africa, India, and the United States. He cuts these pieces in such a way that places and time are completely jumbled together. A shot taken in Tangiers is followed by a shot from India, and then by a shot in New York (maybe from a year ago) and another shot from India, etc.—and it's amazing how it all works together. . . . It is a little bit tourist footage, only more splendorous, with a kind of special Sonbert touch. In between these impersonal or touristic shots the very real faces and bits of action of some of his New York friends appear. It was a pleasant and new experience to sit through this film—a collage of the world, a world which seems to be the same everywhere. I don't know if there are any lessons to be learned from this film, and I have overheard some people complaining that there is nothing new in Sonbert's footage, no new information is given. Nevertheless, as I sat through these eighty minutes, I felt there was a completely different information being passed to me, something that wasn't in the shots; something that came from the fact that the totality of the film, the sum total of the shots, became more than the content or value or information of the individual shots. Something begins to happen, after ten or twenty minutes; the information is changed by time, by the ever repeating rhythms of places and people, and a new kind of information and form is born.

The eighty-minute version Mekas saw was eventually edited down to sixty-one minutes; and thereafter Warren—as though sensing that, glories of time element aside, there were limits to an audience's patience—settled into roughly a half-hour format for his films. In his next, *Rude Awakening*, Warren imposed a strict conceptual grid on the material. As he described it in an interview: "It's very much influenced by what I would call 'directional pulls,' where either the composition within the shot, or the camera movement itself, would be going either right-to-left or left-to-right. . . . But I would never have a moment in *Rude Awakening* where a figurative shot would be followed by another figurative shot, or close-up followed by close-up and so on. In other words, it would be a close-up, wide angle, movement vs. still, abstract vs. figurative." It was as though Warren were seeking the cinematic equivalent of Schoenberg's twelve-tone row.

The problem is that filmed images (except for the most abstract) are not as neutral as musical notes; they cannot help but carry certain meanings, narrative possibilities. You watch two children playing in snowsuits in the park on-screen for three seconds and are immediately plunged back into your own childhood, while wondering about this specific pair (one seems more aggressive, self-assured, the other one more tentative). Depending upon how you feel about childhood (sentimental, repelled, uneasy), you project your own affective baggage onto the fleeting image. Now, Warren was well aware that each person "read" his shots in a subjective manner, and even exulted in this semantic libertinism: in a sense, he wanted to be the detached impresario of the spectacle, without taking a moral position himself. On the other hand, he kept being drawn to "loaded" images or shot combinations, whose meaning seemed all too obvious. He flirted with cliché—only to undercut it (in his mind, at least) by further shots.

To give a much-discussed example: in *Divided Loyalties,* he shows shirtless guys embracing in a Gay Pride parade, followed by a shot of a graveyard. This would, on the face of it, appear to be a sardonic commentary on the gay lifestyle; and Warren was certainly not averse to taking an ironic distance from any group propaganda, including gays'. But we also know that Warren was increasingly gay-identified from the time he moved to San Francisco; so we wonder what to make of the juxtaposition. He told an interviewer: "Well, in one sense it may be obvious. You know, 'All is vanity.' These beautiful bodies will eventually be dust. But what follows after that—you just can't take it from A to B without including C as well. It changes with all the things that are surrounding them. There is a shot of sheep getting clipped and another of sitting ducks on ice. It's people being exploited and not really knowing it. It's both embracing everything and being unbelievably critical of it at the same time."

Looking at this explanation purely on the technical, cinematic level, I would say that it sounds like wishful thinking—having one's cake and eating it too. Sonbert disliked Eisenstein for his didactic "dialectical" equations (shot of plutocrat, followed by shot of crowing rooster, means the rich guy is a silly braggart). But Sonbert was a montage filmmaker, like Eisenstein: so how do you keep the audience from drawing its own simplistic moral conclusions based on the collision of X + Y images? To say that later images, further on in the filmic stream, will complicate the equation, still cannot keep the viewer from glib causal reactions induced by two shots. One way Sonbert tried to evade these links was to separate two potentially narrative-making images with what he called "palate-cleansing shots," usually of something in nature, and filmed so close-up as to verge on the abstract. This device seems to me both mechanical and overly optimistic, in that it doesn't really defuse the satiric editorializing of individual shots.

Just as Warren was a nonnarrative film artist who loved classic Hollywood movies (Ford, Hitchcock, Sirk), so his challenge was that he was an avant-garde filmmaker (though he disliked the terms avant-garde or underground) dedicated to "difficulty" and ambiguity, who also happened to have strong political and moral sentiments. He qualified his own content by saying: "Usually works are mirrors of what is contained already in the viewer, and it is the role of the creator to 'place' or qualify these reactions. Lead the viewer down one road only to diverge onto another, upset inbred expectations at the same time as exploiting these very clichés." I wonder if I am entitled to ask at this point: To what extent is this desire to keep things morally ambiguous and multivalent as long as possible—this subversive urge to "upset inbred expectations"—connected to being gay? Is it part of a gay aesthetic? Of course this subject has been worried by many more theoretical or empathetic minds, in queer studies and elsewhere, and I realize I sound naïve by raising it this baldly. But I am trying to convey how, from a heterosexual (i.e., hopelessly naïve) vantage point, one tries to puzzle out one's gay friends' inner lives, particularly if they are artists.

The paradox of Warren's films, it seems to me, is that they are both sensual and punitive, with ravishing images which add up to a sense of futility. And this paradox is not only aesthetic, but goes to the very heart of Warren's personality. He had killer charm and a core of anger. Perhaps he was angry at straight society for having stigmatized him as a gay male; perhaps he was angry that his mother had died. He was alone in the world—except for a million friends. Somewhere this bitterness and urge to lash back, in contrast to his seductive, all-embracing public persona, had to emerge, and it came out, albeit still masked, in his art.

He seemed quite aware of the provocation latent in his film method: "Some people are disturbed by the brevity of some of the images—particularly those that one might label 'beautiful' or 'ecstatic.' They are over before one has a chance to barely luxuriate in them, they are taken away before one can nestle and coo and cuddle in the velveteen sheen of it all, so that feelings of deprivation, expectations dissolved, even sadomasochism arise. Very often a cut occurs before an action is complete. This becomes both metaphor of frustration, hopes dashed, and yet of serenity if you like—that perhaps all of this activity has been going on, is going on, will be going on, and even all at the same time. That we are privileged viewers of many sectors of humanity. . . ."

Warren loved to have it both ways. On the one hand, admitting to a certain sadomasochistic impulse to undercut expectations; on the other hand, expressing a healing wisdom by offering us the solace of the ever-ongoing material stream. It was in the tension between these impulses that he operated, creating a body of work which assured him a solid place in the history of American experimental film.

When I was visiting San Francisco, I would sometimes stay with Warren, who lived just off Castro Street, in the heart of the gay district. Warren shared a beautiful Victorian with bay windows and wooden steps leading from the sidewalk to the first floor. I slept on a couch in the outer parlor, which had a large piano and a theatrical arrangement of tall orange irises in a vase, and a kitschy statue of two men embracing.

Warren, solicitous of my comfort as a guest in the Castro district, took me around the first night and pointed out which coffee shops and bars catered to straight men as well as gays—adding with a laugh that I would have no trouble picking up women. He had a mocking irreverence toward many aspects of gay style, the conformity of "Castro Street clones" and the fussy decor of his own house, which he blamed on his roommate, a *Gone with the Wind* fanatic. (The parlor bookcase was filled with foreign editions of Margaret Mitchell's novel and every possible publication related to the film.) At the same time Warren seemed proud to show off the Castro as an international gay magnet.

He was dating, he said, four, five, six, or seven people at the moment. One of his regulars arrived while I was reading a book in the back porch: I heard him go into Warren's bedroom and leave some twenty minutes later, about the length of one chapter. I kept planning to put down my book and mosey up front to introduce myself; but the man was gone before I even had a chance to see him.

The next day, Warren showed me what he called "the playroom," a little secret addition put in by the homeowner just above the basement. The house, located on a steep San Francisco hill, was actually built on stilts, and the playroom had been tucked down underneath the back porch steps. Warren informed me that it was the fashion for many of these Victorians to have their own playrooms. This one was small and dark: black walls, black curtains, one naked green light bulb, and a harness floating in the center, suspended from the ceiling. It was some sort of torture device, which he assured me was "actually quite comfortable, I understand," accompanying this statement with a nervous laugh trapped in the throat, rapid hand movements dishing out dissociation, and underneath, the complicitous pleasure of offering a tasty tidbit for my file of social manners.

I examined the other paraphernalia: a black executioner's hood, chains on the floor, and a row of shiny balls on a string. "What are these for?"

"Oh, those come from Japan. Japanese prostitutes would put them in the anus of the man and pull them out one by one, to induce a bigger orgasm. As I say, I never use this place myself, though we do put up guests here!" he added wickedly.

My eyes kept returning to the Super-8 projector on the night table, cocked at an upward angle to throw an image onto the wall screen just beyond the bed. The mattress was bare except for one creased black sheet. The projector was already threaded and had been stopped at mid-reel (under what circumstances I could imagine). I had my old cinephile's temptation to watch the film—any film.

The playroom felt essentially comic, like a spook house; but what did threaten me was the extent of Warren's sexual activity. Not because of AIDS—this was before we'd even heard the deadly acronym. No, it was that I envied his hedonism, while mistrusting the way it mocked my sense of the consequential difficulty of life. If I encountered in his films an emptiness, underneath the pleasure-seeking spectacle, this was only partly because he had intended it there. (He described *Rude Awakening* as "things not working out, things not materializing, people having certain expectations, plans, input, and those *dissolving.*") The other part was that I *wanted* to find "sterility"— that harsh judgment which heterosexuals, even one like myself who had no children at the time, are eager to level at gays—as the price to be paid for Warren's sexual freedom.

But I do not want to belabor the point: after all, I never saw Warren engaged in sex, except in my imagination, but I saw him plenty of times preoccupied with his art. When Warren was filming, usually with a spring-wound 16-mm Bolex, he did it in a relaxed, unobtrusive manner, his camera a natural, dance-like extension of his height and coiled bearing. Once, he came to the public school where I was working and shot the kids and me, getting down on the gym mat with us: the shot turned up in *Divided Loyalties*. When he edited, there was that same blend of casualness and concentration: a bagel and cream cheese might lie dangerously close to the splicer, on which two celluloid strips were about to be joined. Warren defied the usual precautions by cutting the original, instead of making a work print first. I think he relished the whole primitive, artisan setup of physically cutting film with a safety blade, scraping off the emulsion, applying glue, and watching the results through a flickering monitor, guiding them by turning the take-up reel's hand-crank

He knew there was little financial reward for his kind of filmmaking— as little as there usually is for writing poetry, which may explain why he felt so close to poets. I used to wonder how he supported himself. The answer was, partly from a trust fund, and partly from fees earned showing his films, or selling prints to archives, or getting grants, or teaching. Within the limited remunerative constraints of his genre, he was successful, hustling, networking, cultivating friendships with festival organizers and film curators all over the world. He also began writing lively, acerbic movie reviews for the *Bay Area Reporter.*

Though still gallant, the omni-appreciative persona of the younger Sonbert had given way to a more jaundiced tone, a dislike of stupidity, as he approached middle age. Warren said it this way: "There's so much junk around, there's so much crap. Webern talked about this—about how there's so *much* junk, why not produce *less,* something really scaled down and perfected. A small contained body, that really says it all."

Recently, Paul Arthur in *Film Comment* made a strong case for Sonbert's artistic variety, pointing out not only the different thematic emphases of each film, but shifts in technique from movie to movie. Arthur warns of the mistake many viewers make when they "conclude that Sonbert's films are more or less the same in tone and ideas. . . ." And yet I must admit that sometimes it seemed to me he *was* making the same film over and over. He had perfected a form which suited him, and which yielded quality results, even though it did not quite express the full brio and range of the man.

I once chided him publicly about this. Contributing in *Film Culture* to a special Warren Sonbert section (1983), I wrote a piece which both praised and found fault with his movies. (I told myself that he was so surrounded by admiring friends, and that avant-garde film in general is so resistant to self-criticism, that it was up to me to prod him toward taking up new challenges. We won't talk about my own unconscious hostility in doing this, or the ethics of criticizing a friend in print.) Among other things, I questioned his repetition of certain motifs, such as parades, elevated trains, car trips, be-ins, air-plane wings, which made one film begin to look like the outtakes of the other.

Warren replied in the same issue. Though he bristled at the term "diary-films," believing it was too suggestive of an accidental, anything-goes mode of composition, he still relied on the materials of his daily life: "There are certain things that interest me, and that's what I film. People think that when they see new work of mine that I'm using out-takes from past films, things from seven, eight years ago. But I'll always go to the circus during a given period of film-making, or a parade, things that are out there on public display. But at the same time, the opposite of that—private, intimate things with friends, what they'll do at home, leisure, etc."

In truth, he did have larger ambitions. He wrote a screenplay for a feature film set in Nazi Germany, built around the premiere of Richard Strauss's *Capriccio*; but it was a complicated schema with a dozen characters, and would have cost millions. In the absence of such backing, he continued working on his self-contained, jewel-like "cantos."

A stabilizing force had come into Warren's love-life: a somewhat older man, Ray. Immensely cultivated and kind, securely employed, silver-mustached and rail-thin, Ray became the protector, nurturer, devoted partner, and champion whom Warren had long sought. They moved in to Ray's Victorian near Castro Street, which soon became a gathering-place for their circle. Ray and Warren loved to entertain and give lavishly prepared dinner parties. Over the years, they developed into as secure a couple as can be imagined, gay or straight. Living with Ray, Warren became much more domestic. They also traveled together, Ray shepherding Warren to his screenings in foreign cities, Warren indulging Ray's scholarly passion for Renaissance painting. They had over ten happy years. In the best of all possible worlds, they would have grown old together. But Ray came down with AIDS, and died.

Warren was bereft. Ray had been his lover, older brother, advisor, and guardian angel. As he said to one friend, honestly if a bit self-centeredly: "Who's going to take care of me now?" In the year after Ray's death, Warren's friends, comparing impressions, began to notice that he was becoming rather imperious and irritable, his temper flaring more readily than normal. I started to hear reports of his storming into projection booths and complaining about some technical flaw in the screening of his film. He was starting to act more like a prima donna. We had our own little falling-out: it involved my being on the selection committee of the New York Film Festival when Warren submitted his latest film. In past years when I was on the committee, the NYFF had been very kind to Warren: we had almost automatically included him in our Avant-Garde program. But this time, the committee, myself included, felt that the new film was a little too much like his earlier ones; it did not seem to mark an advance. So we passed on it. Warren was stung, outraged, the more so because he regarded everyone on the committee as his personal friend. He was too proud to chew us out directly, but I heard of his displeasure in the usual roundabout way.

The next year, I rotated off the committee, and, sure enough, Warren resubmitted the film. The second time around, it *was* accepted. Either Warren had guilt-tripped the committee members, or they had come to their senses and realized what a gem they had insufficiently appreciated the year before.

Their decision may have been affected by the news that Warren was suffering from a mysterious illness. He insisted it was not AIDS, but some sort of baffling brain disease which eluded the diagnoses of his physicians. He described to me episodes of passing out and being taken to the hospital, going through grueling tests, and finally being released. Knowing how Ray had perished, I suspected from the start that Warren was HIV-positive. A mutual friend, who lived on the West Coast and was very close to Warren, confirmed my suspicions: she had noticed certain medications on his bureau, and asked her father, who was a doctor, about them. He told her they were treatments for AIDS. She confronted Warren with this information; Warren, still denying his condition, added angrily, "Well, given the fact I'm gay and the life I've led, it wouldn't be surprising if I *were* suffering from AIDS!" This was classic Warren, wanting to have it both ways, to tell and not tell. Perhaps it was too much for his pride that he should have been afflicted with the common scourge, rather than some exotic ailment. Or perhaps he resisted appearing before friends in a pitiable light. Regardless, I can't help wishing he had trusted me enough to tell me; but then, he stonewalled everyone, till near the end.

The last few times I saw Warren, we got along well. He seemed to have forgiven me my treachery on the New York Film Festival committee, or at least controlled the urge to allude to it. He had hooked up with a young man named Ascension, who was looking after Warren and whom Warren, in turn, was educating in the finer things in life. They were running from appointment to appointment, seeing everyone and everything there was to see in New York.

One day in early October, I got together with Warren for what turned out to be the last time. His speech sounded slurred either from the drugs he was taking or, more likely, from the toxoplasmosis that had attacked his brain. It was hard for him to stay on a subject; his attention wandered. I remember he was looking forward most to the opera that night. He was wearing shorts with the ends rolled up, and he bragged about how he'd still been going to the gym and how great his body looked, all things considered (it did); how he was unafraid to walk around in shorts in October, when most New Yorkers had already started bundling up. I thought to myself, "All is vanity, indeed! He's a step away from death, and it's still so important for him to show off his muscle tone?" In retrospect, I should have more properly appreciated the bravado, or seen it more intuitively as a species of courage.

There were some screenings of Warren's films at the Museum of Modern Art, which he had to introduce, so he excused himself at five P.M. After that, there would be the opera to go to. "Ciao," he said amicably, walking up 53rd Street to meet up with one of MOMA's film curators, who was waiting for him in the museum lobby.

It will always seem too short, Warren's last good-bye, like a clumsy essay which ends abruptly and you turn the page, thinking there must be another page missing. He who taught me the value of a gentle leave-taking was forced to make his own exit from life an overly hasty one. We can stare at photographs of him, marveling at his jaunty presence, vital as a superstar, yet detached, *contrapposto*, his torso turned away from the head, away from us, and try to grapple with the paradox that someone can still be so alive to us and yet—gone. It is like one of those cruel oxymorons he alluded to with his titles, *Rude Awakening, Friendly Witness, Divided Loyalties, Honor and Obey*, something he was trying to tell us all along. Now that we are rudely awakened to our loss of him, we must turn to his art for vestiges of his insouciant plenitude.

There is a traveling retrospective in the year 2000 of Warren Sonbert's work, originating at the Guggenheim Museum under the curatorship of Jon Gartenberg, with newly struck prints of everything, including rediscovered films thought to be lost, such as *The Tenth Legion* and *Ted and Jessica*.

Prodigal Son
Benjamin Taylor

We thought it the funniest thing to phone up some fleabag hotel of the red-light district and attempt, in elevated language, to make a reservation. Or else we'd sit in his mother's Cadillac and be a couple of stars driving from Fort Worth to New York to open in a Broadway show. While others were outside playing ball, Robby and I would lie around his house or mine listening to Sophie Tucker, last of the red-hot mamas, sing, "Who wants 'em tall, dark, and handsome? Who needs glamorous guys?" We loved the great indoors. One Saturday afternoon, in a corner of my bedroom, we opened an expensive Polynesian restaurant. On a sleep-over at his house, draped in afghans and turbanned in bath towels, we lip-synched all of *Pelléas et Mélisande*. Ordinary boys we were not. We adored theater and ceremony and pomp and pretense of every kind. We especially loved funerals. One time we put on a funeral for a bookmark.

While there has been life for me after Robby, sixteen years of it, there was none at all before. His parents were the closest friends of my own—you rarely saw Shirley and Charlie without Sol and Annette—and so it happened quite naturally that Robby, three years older than I, became my first friend. It is a piece of luck I'll marvel at till I die: to have been granted, from earliest childhood, the company of a genius.

As recollection probably can't go back much farther than when I was five, my earliest memory of Robby must be when he was about eight—an eight-year-old man in the spell of a calling, hard at work on his art, which was puppetry. He had a stage his parents had brought back from F. A. O. Schwarz (I wept till my own got me one just like it) with a box of hand puppets: an alligator, a glow worm, a cockatoo, a muscle man, a bearded lady, a heavy-lidded ostrich, a monkey with a violet maw, and so on. And how, with his God-given theatricality, Robby stirred it all to life! After a few attempts to emulate him at home on my own bare stage, longed-for to the point of tears, I folded it up and put it away. Under my tutelage the dramatis personae had refused to live. With glass eyes they reproached me.

Yes, I was a flop who decided, like flops before me, that reflected glory would be better than none at all. So I made myself Robby's factotum, taking up the slack backstage, operating the lights out front, etcetera. Our audience? Our squirming and beneficent parents. And occasionally our guffawing older brothers. (About them the less said the better.)

It was with puppets that Robby began, and with puppets that he ended. That he became in the last decade of his brief life the greatest puppeteer the world has ever known is not contested by those who saw his work of the late seventies and early eighties. This time he made from scratch the cast of endlessly protean characters, literally breathtaking to watch in their changes. Here was a single-handed mythology, outside of all creeds and yet systematic, in which tiny finger puppets broached the darkness, made alchemical discoveries, suffered, and were metamorphosed from their illusions. Robby told a tale embodied in characters original to his vision. William Blake comes to mind as an artist of comparable impulse and power. Robby's was a dramaturgy in which puppets figured forth human instincts and faculties. He drew the numinous circle around these human things in order to show, as myth does, how interfused they are with a universe of powers transcending them.

Our journey out of the little circle and into eternity was Robby's mature subject. Among his possessions was a homemade faith enabling him to look on mortality as a deceit of the senses. He would have understood at once the famous words Blake wrote to Henry Crabb Robinson in April of 1824: "I have been very near the Gates of Death, and come back very weak, but not in Spirit & Life, not in The Real Man The Imagination which Liveth for Ever." The fallen world was temporary. The true, ever-living world, all around us but unseen, a holy secret, revealed itself through mystical experience. Although a marvelous draftsman, Robby had (again in common with Blake) no real interest in landscape or in depicting the human form from nature. I see this now as of a piece with his transcendental preoccupations.

Such, briefly told, was how the deliciously silly companion of my childhood became the fearsome magician known as Robert Anton. Everything the romantics taught about the momentousness of childhood, about original untutored prowess as the enabling source of art, was borne out in

Robert Anton's sculptured puppet heads. From a Bette Stoler Gallery promotional card.

him. What happened is what always happens in such cases: maturity intensified by orders of magnitude the early promptings and intuitions. The cabinet of curiosities from F. A. O. Schwarz gave way to a visionary company of Robby's own furious making.

They delighted the eye and filled the mind, these creatures who would, in performance, turn to their maker with love, fear, bafflement, the whole range of feeling. It was something to see. Among them Robby functioned as a deity, of course. He'd made them, nobody had made him. Nobody but himself, that is.

Not at all surprisingly, Robby tended to be reticent about his family. The self-created are leery of where they've come from, of the accidents of genealogy and place, considering it unacceptable to have had these matters decided for them. But genes are genes and native ground is native ground, despite all claims of the greatly gifted to parthenogenesis. (It is said that Blake, who hated the idea of being anybody's issue, tried late in life to read aloud the parable of the Prodigal Son but broke down at the line, "When he was yet a great way off, his father saw him.") A little stranger in the midst of his people, vaccinated by destiny against their ordinariness, Robby must have wondered why he'd cropped up there and then. The parents, for their part, must have wondered what they'd wrought in him. But along with the bewilderment there was love on offer, and adequate wherewithal—and the hothouse flower was suffered to bloom.

He had pictures to look at, movies to go to, books to read, records to listen to. A canon of taste declared itself: the art of Dürer, Blake, Fuseli, Redon, and Grosz; the films of Fellini (especially *Juliet of the Spirits* and *Toby Damit*) and Kubrick (especially *2001*); the writings of Paracelsus, St. John of the Cross, Jakob Boehme, Meher Baba, and C. G. Jung; the songs of Brecht and Weill (especially *Mahagonny*) and of Cole Porter (especially *Kiss Me Kate*). The American musical theater in general was Robby's Great Code. Expectable in someone of our bent. But "Havana Lied" or "Begin the Beguine" or "Another Opening, Another Show" interpreted in the light of Meher Baba? That was new. As in childhood, so in adolescence: I was his slave, doing my best to like *Juliet of the Spirits* or wade through Paracelsus, even immersing myself in the truly odious Dr. Jung.

Several years ago I tried, in a novel called *Tales out of School,* to communicate some sense of what his puppet theater was like. Much the most fantastical thing in the book, it was the only part I didn't make up. I was challenged by the strict impossibility of rendering justice to what had stood venerable and complete without the supplement of words. There are so many superb examples of writers attempting to claim for language what is really only for the eyes: Ruskin on the Alps, Rilke on Rodin, Zbigniew Herbert on Piero della Francesca, James Merrill on Ravenna and so on. This tradition of doing verbal honor to the silently sublime is one I tried to participate in, however feebly, when I described Robby's theater. I'm aware that his puppets will never be as famous as the sculptures of Rodin or the paintings of Piero. Indeed, Robby's puppets lie orphaned in a trunk somewhere and will never be famous at all. But fame and the sublime are only accidentally related. This we must believe, or else surrender to a worldliness honoring only success. Robby's immense gifts were not known to more than a handful of people, and it may be, given his indifference to recognition, that he'd have remained a close-held secret even if allowed by fate to live out a long life. Once in a while, however, I do still meet someone who actually saw a performance of his. It happens less and less, of course, and at some unspecifiable but roughly calculable point in time the next-to-last and last of us who saw the thing will disappear. For now, though, we are a happy few, content in the long-ago to have sat before a tiny stage beholding a human awful wonder of art.

The long-ago: that is to say, the sunlit late seventies. Then a cloud settled down on earth to see how many of us it could devour—the part of the story everybody knows. Robby fell ill in the spring of 1983. Watching my adored friend as the darkness enveloped him, I did not imagine how many more I'd watch as they vanished in their turn.

This subtraction of wit, grace, brains, and beauty from our midst has now become unbearable to contemplate. How is it we haven't, in compassionate horror, pulled the earth up over us? How is it we who are spared have gone on creating, laughing, renewing ourselves with love? Is the appetite for life simply too great, greater than our accumulated griefs? And what, for their part, do the lost travelers under the hill think of us? Do they applaud our flinty resilience? When they come back to us in dreams—at least in mine— it is usually to say that, yes, they do.

August of 1824: George Richmond writes to Samuel Palmer, Blake's disciple: "Just before he died His Countenance became fair. His eyes Brighten'd and he burst out into Singing of the things he saw in Heaven." Thus it should have been with my great friend. Justice would have Robby full of years and singing. But Robert Anton died young and alone and frightened—and by his own hand, having endured enough—in a Los Angeles hotel room.

They say that, coming and going, Palmer would kiss the bell handle of Blake's lodgings. As a boy, Robby had a comparably ardent disciple on the threshold at 3912 Ann Arbor Court. My mother would drop me off on Saturday afternoons. After decently greeting his parents, busy with some football game or golf tournament on television, I would make my way to the heaven of art, Robby's bedroom. Here was where the real man, the imagination made abode. Here was where nothing bad could happen. Here was where the master smote me with blessings. When I dream about him we're there again. I find him huddled up, the prodigal come home, sick but hanging on. I say, *You're dead.* He says, *Not for a minute.* I say, *Lo, these many years.* He says, *Illusion.* I say, *The dead are dead.* He says, *Only out of sight.* He asks for news, wants very much to know how we've all been getting along . . . .

The parents are still at the old address. The football game or golf tournament is still on. I think I will not go in, only give the bell handle a kiss, next time I dream I'm there.

Chris DeBlasio
William Berger

Chris DeBlasio died of AIDS in 1993 at the age of thirty-four. His life had been busy, challenging, and intense. He was an ardent activist, a perfectionist who strove for excellence in everything he did, and a great pain in the neck if he felt that he, or you, were not giving one hundred percent to the task at hand. He may not have been the most difficult person who ever lived, but he was easily in the top five. He was also a great artist—a superb musician, and, above all, an extraordinary composer just on the brink of making a remarkable name for himself in the somewhat rarefied world of contemporary classical music.

Everyone wanted to talk about Chris after he died and play his music and run modest magazine articles about him—for a couple of weeks. Americans have a short attention span for death. I noticed this at the time of the Oklahoma City bombing. Dogs were still sniffing through the rubble when a CNN reporter started speaking of closure. You're supposed to cry when the cameras are on you and then get over it. The AIDS front has long since passed through this Village and is now ravishing other theaters of war. No newspaper prints headlines of last year's battle. That much I can fathom, but each passing year magnifies the tragedy from my point of view. Not because My Lover died. That's the easy part, relatively speaking. Evidence would indicate that I have moved on in that direction. The hard part, of course, is wondering what might have been.

The odd thing about a composer dying young is that it doesn't earn him any extra sympathy points. In fact, it's considered quite *comme il faut* to pop off at a tragically young age. People were sympathetic but only up to a point. Perhaps they were hearing a bit more than they could process about AIDS in the art community right at that point. Or perhaps many of my gay friends were uncomfortable with so much attention and even sympathy being given to other gay men. (Sad to say, but I think there is something in this). For a while, I noticed people repeatedly mentioning (as if I didn't already know it) that Mozart had died at thirty-seven and Bellini at thirty-four (like

Chris) and Pergolesi at twenty-seven. And hovering over Chris's death is always the omnipresent specter of the definitive queer composer Franz Schubert, dead, as everyone seems to know, at age thirty-one, before there was any such thing as AIDS.

Drama queen that I am, I refuse to find consolation in the knowledge of Schubert's premature death. First of all, I didn't sleep with Franz Schubert, but trying for a moment to separate my own personal loss from the overall artistic loss, I still find the comparison annoying. It's not the same world. Schubert and Mozart did not have to survive major institutional training in order to be taken seriously as composers. They did not have to wave around degrees from any modern conservatories whose systems methodically wring the creativity out of people. Nor did Mozart have any choice in his career. It was beaten into him, with spectacular success, by his father. Similarly, Schubert had to choose between starving as a schoolteacher, like his father, or starving as a composer. A middle-class American today must choose between getting rich in business or starving as a composer. Harder choice.

Most of all, it simply takes longer for artists to develop now than it did 200 years ago. They didn't have our demons. They had their own, God knows, but demons worked differently then. In those days, demons forced work out of you at the expense of the rest of your life. There was the demon who supposedly possessed Paganini, preventing him from eating or sleeping but forcing him to exist on fiddling alone, and there was Svengali and there was what's her name from *The Red Shoes* who pirouettes herself into the grave and there was the portrait of Antonia's mother from the *Tales of Hoffmann*, who comes to life urging her consumptive daughter to sing herself to death.

All those possessed people didn't know how good they had it. The Devil has learned much in the last two centuries and his methods have become more sophisticated and insidious. Perhaps from seeing himself depicted on stage and mentioned in the media so many times, he has decided to heed the advice of Goethe and Nancy Reagan and Just Say No. He has invented mortgages and family values and a bureaucratic arts establishment and inelegant addictions and that most powerful demonic weapon of modern times, personal "issues." Nowadays, a Paganini would end up on either crack or Prozac before he had a chance to lose his soul to music. Artists only rarely die wearing the Red Shoes these days. They die in support groups or in traffic on the Long Island Expressway, wondering what might have been.

So it very nearly was with Chris, but he beat the Devil at that game, at least, and almost succeeded in triumphing over his own reductive issues. There's no need to list his psychological inventory now. It's enough to say that he had issues in spades, and he faced them, and he dealt with those he could and accepted the rest. And just when it was time to soar, he died. That is his tragedy, and mine, and art's, a story beside which Franz Schubert's enormous catalogue of music seems more like a cause for celebration rather than regret. Let me tell you about what I saw that allows me to make such a ridiculous statement.

I met Chris on January 11, 1986. It was only my second in January in New York City, and I was trying to look like I was quite accustomed to sub-zero temperatures. This fooled no one, since I was wrapped in a winter coat that made me look one of the Wicked Witch of the West's castle guards. For some reason I still cannot fathom, I kept walking up Broadway past my block, West 101st. Fate, I guess. A remarkably handsome man was heading toward me. He had a lopey yet not unattractive gait, long legs, and wore a black leather jacket. His shoulders were hunched up against the cold. We passed each other but both turned around, facing off like gunfighters in the Old West. There was no subtlety in this cruise. It was far too cold for that.

"Hey," he said, very butch.

"Hey," I replied, attempting the same tone. I looked him over. He had devilish eyes and dark curly hair and looked a little like a young Dirk Bogarde. I was tongue-tied, scarcely believing this babe had stopped for me.

"Well," he said at last, "You want to get a slice of pizza?"

Sexiest line I ever heard, or so it seemed at the moment. We went to the nearest pizzeria and ordered and talked about art and *Star Trek* and George Carlin and history. I was almost disappointed to find this guy had brains—half of me was hoping for a dumb stud for the evening. He asked what I did for a living. "File clerk," I answered. "You?" "Composer," he answered, with as much hauteur as that word can bear. I had a momentary desire to leave New York and this weather and these impossible queens and return home to California where people did not introduce themselves as "composers" or "philosophers" or anything of the sort. He invited me upstairs to his apartment, and I went, pomposity notwithstanding. Years later, he confessed that he only diverted us to the pizzeria that night in order to

Chris DeBlasio on Gay Pride Day, 1993. Courtesy of William Berger.

see me without my winter coat and make sure I was remotely anthropoid-shaped. That's Chris for you. Always methodical.

Although his building was next to mine along Broadway, his was rich and spacious and elegant while mine was a crack den. He lived in a three-bedroom apartment he shared with two roommates (who were conveniently absent). The living room was dimly lit with an abundance of old heavy wood furniture and two pianos given pride of place. He rolled a joint and gave it to me, sitting himself at the larger of the two pianos. I lay back, trying in vain to look simultaneously studly and soigné. I stared out the second-floor window as snow fell on the street sign proclaiming "Broadway." Chris's gorgeous hands fluttered over the keyboard picking out the opening roulades of *Gretchen am Spinnrade.*

"Schubert," I muttered. "My favorite. How did you know?" He leered at me and began singing. No one had ever worked so hard to get into my pants. I think I became a New Yorker in that moment. He finished the song and began another, looking back at me to see if I could identify it. "Korngold," I guessed. Luckiest guess of my life. It occurred to me that I had never worked so hard to let someone get into my pants. But I felt he was worth the effort. We spent the night together (good sex, not great) and two days later I received a manuscript in the mail. It was a new song called "To a Friendly Neighbor." It was practically a dare to fall in love with him, with the adjective "Friendly" simultaneously warning me not to.

I already had. He was too attractive and engaging to resist. Even his flaws were rather appealing in their obviousness. Beyond the grandiosity, he was rigid, opinionated, and insufferably organized. He ironed his underwear and I swear (although he denied it till the day he died) I actually saw him measuring water to boil pasta once. He lived modestly (he thought) off the interest and dividends from inherited investments and fussed over every cent. He ran his life like an electric train set and his view of the world was as compartmentalized as his dresser drawers. In his cosmology, Christians (myself included) were either stupid or masochistic, Southerners were all slow-witted, tops were self-accepting and together, bottoms self-loathing, the French were all snobs (!), and so forth. In music, it was much of the same. Verdi's *Falstaff* (which he knew by heart) was genius but in general Italian opera was too "operatic" (his phrase) and anyone who now wrote lyrical melodies that shunned modernist fashions like serialism or atonality was delusional.

He played me his music over the course of the next few months. Since finishing music school a few years before, he had written quite a few scores for avant-garde shows which one couldn't really call musicals, several performance art songs, and some incidental music for plays. He referred to these pieces only cryptically, and instead played me his more recent compositions, which were instrumental and quite daring. It was all very brainy and I could see how this sort of thing scored him high marks at the conservatory but I didn't believe a note of it. I wasn't opposed to atonality or serialism—as an affected young man about town I was quite conversant in both—but his heart wasn't in this music. There's nothing more transparent than atonal music written by someone who, deep down, would rather be writing catchy show tunes. I began to suspect that dear DeBlasio was a closet sentimentalist. I mean—duh!—he played Schubert to seduce his neighbor! I decided to "out" him as a romantic. At our next tryst, I brought him flowers and a note that included the word "love." He freaked and said we couldn't have sex anymore. And we didn't, for four years. My diagnosis of latent romanticism had been exact, but my prescription almost proved lethal.

Chris wouldn't have been able to have sex that summer anyway. He got sick from some vague liver ailment and didn't do much of anything. His face looked gaunt and ghastly. There wasn't a reliable HIV test yet in 1986 so we just uttered platitudes and didn't mention the obvious. He recovered, but I thought of him as a marked man from then on. The vagueness became real the following year. He tested positive. Typically, he decided to approach the situation proactively and rearrange his life accordingly. Did I forget to mention he had a boyfriend throughout this time? Yes, he was involved with a man whom nobody, least of all Chris, liked very much. The two of them had a great deal of psychodrama but didn't seem to spend much time together. I told Chris they reminded me of one of the great affairs from the previous century, perhaps Boito and Duse, who wrote passionate letters to each other bemoaning the pain of separation while doing everything possible to avoid each other's company. This was all before gay men worried about being paragons of American monogamous virtue. Chris called the boyfriend to tell him about the diagnosis, got a snide answer, stared at the phone a moment, and hung it up. They never spoke again. Chris knew he had no time for excess baggage. The clean-up process had begun.

He had to make sense of his life while there was still time, and his life, as he saw it, was a mess. Most of all, he needed to find out why he ran from love. His relationships had all been abusive in one way or another, becoming progressively more so. I wasn't abusive in any overt way, but I was drinking heavily and living anarchically and was a mess myself so at least he had something to work with and keep him interested. He went into therapy with the same gusto he had once brought to his music studies. In fact, near as I can tell, he went into full-time therapy, as in five days a week. And right about this time, an interesting thing started happening called ACT UP. Chris, the elegant and insufferable snob from the Upper West Side who had never deigned to associate himself with the canaille in the streets, and who in fact had snotty things to say about people like me with a history of political involvement, became an activist. He went to the first demo on Wall Street in 1987, screaming "Smash the Patriarchy!" in his superbly trained baritone voice while knowing full well that his pudgy stock portfolio allowed him the free time to do so. It was another split in his personality, but some ruptures allow for new developments. Chris was growing.

His music was in a sort of limbo at this time. He wrote a song cycle, *Villagers*, for mezzo-soprano set to poems by contemporary poet Ilsa Gilbert. It was performed regularly and well by Sandra Goodman, an excellent interpreter of art songs (for lack of a better word) on the recital circuit. Chris enjoyed this a lot more than he let on to most people. Applause was sweet. Taking bows in recital halls was fun. Who knew? He moved to a very small apartment in the Village and began participating in life. I moved to a large apartment in Harlem and fell further out of life, but we talked every day on the phone and met about once a week. He was devoting himself to ACT UP with revolutionary fervor, but also with brains and discipline. He immersed himself in medical knowledge enough to be regarded as an authority and was interviewed and quoted by mainstream journals. He wrote and edited articles. He discovered that he was, after all, teachable, and allowed himself to listen to music that had not been on the syllabus of his conservatory. He continued fearlessly in therapy, confronting his demons and even his family in ways that eventually transformed their lives. Composing took a short break. It had been temporarily replaced by living.

Meanwhile, we each dated other guys half-heartedly and consigned each other to brotherly, best friend roles. We even played this sick game where we automatically introduced any new men in our lives to each other, ostensibly for approval. Later, we called these guys our "interim boyfriends," but "hostages" might have been a better term. We fooled no one but ourselves. On Christmas 1989, I invited people up to my apartment for dinner. There were three couples, and Chris, and me. The others were all straight (or "gender-discordant couples," as we now say), and this only made the spotlight shine more glaringly on us. I had decorated like a mad queen on a coke binge, with a red velvet tablecloth and gold-painted leaves between the place settings—all this, mind you, in a drug-infested tenement in Harlem. Reality and fantasy were at great odds for me just then. I served martinis with the hors d'oeuvres and champagne with the first course, scallops in Pernod. The guests were giddy, and Bonita, my dear chic blond friend who always speaks her mind when intoxicated, brandished her champagne flute with one unsteady hand while wagging an accusing finger at me and Chris with the other.

"When are you two going to cut the shit and get married?" she said bluntly. The blood rushed to Chris's cheeks and his jaw clenched. I got drunk and burnt the turkey and don't know what happened the rest of the evening. But a seed had been planted. The Unspeakable had been uttered.

Somewhere in this time, I moved to a dump in the East Village and saw Chris more frequently. He left town in summer of 1990 to live at an artists' colony in Taos. We wrote each other letters which were emotionally guarded in terms of our relationship but which showed a distinct increase in emotional pragmatism on his part. He called to tell me when he was coming back and asked me to come to his apartment that very day since he had something important to show me. Whenever he used the word "important," I knew music was involved.

It was a perfect afternoon in September, the light streaming through the venetian blinds of his apartment on Thompson Street. He was boyishly excited as he rolled me a joint and planted me, once again, on the sofa facing his piano. With his back turned to me, so that he was playing as if privately and I were eavesdropping, he played and sang the piece he had written that summer. *All the Way through Evening* is a cycle of five songs with poems by Perry Brass, dealing with the tragedy of AIDS. There was no way Chris could be arch or detached from this subject matter. This would not be about music theory or innovations in composition technique. It was written for baritone voice (Chris's own, in fact). I have attended many performances of every type of music all over the world. I have been at events that have become part of the canon of musical mythology. But I have never heard anything like what I heard that afternoon. It was just me, stoned, on the sofa and him at the piano, a handsome, thirty-one year old, overeducated gay man crying from the heart that life is, after all, precious and beautiful and painful to leave. The beautiful vocal line died away, leaving the soft but relentless repetition of the final ostinato chords, like the ripples on the river of death they describe. Before the piece ends, there is a delicate run of rapid high notes over the lower

chords, then another, perhaps depicting a shimmer of light but also implying a soul leaving the body. Musically speaking, it is also an obvious reference
to the orchestral denouement of Richard Strauss's *Four Last Songs*, which is
perhaps romanticism's final and supreme encapsulation of the moment of
death. I had to laugh aloud—with joy, actually, but he wondered why I
laughed.

"Been listening to our Strauss lately, haven't we?" I said.

His face took on a look of genuine concern. "Do you think that's OK?"
he asked.

"I think it's more than OK," I said, standing behind him and kissing
the back of his neck. "In fact, I think you have just become an artist."

It was true. A huge membrane had snapped somewhere inside Chris.
Love and life would be allowed to flow in while music would gush forth for
a brief but excellent moment. Now, if this were a screenplay, Chris and I
would have fallen into each others' arms at this point, making mad passionate love to a swelling C-major soundtrack climax, and it would cut to our
imaginary splendid gay wedding at Cooper Union with all of ACT UP in at-
tendance and the choir of Trinity Church singing a new anthem of love written for the occasion by DeBlasio himself. Roll credits. There may be some
metaphorical truth in that version of events, but it wasn't actually quite how
it happened. We continued to parade men in front of each other for a bit. (I
have since apologized to the guys in question—those who lived long
enough, at any rate.) One night after he returned from Taos, we were to meet
each other and our prospective dates at the Eagle, a rather homey leather bar
by the waterfront which has since become a grande dame of the New York
scene but a decade ago was delightfully generic. Neither date showed up.
Chris and I were stuck with each other. I drank bourbon on the rocks and
shot pool. He twirled on a bar stool and stressed. I walked over to him and
smiled as if I were up to something. I was.

"It doesn't matter that we've been stood up, Chris," I said.

"Why not?"

"Because," I said, glaring into his eyes, "in the end it's going to be you
and me anyway."

Thank God I said that. Thank God he heard me. Thank God for bourbon. Chris glared at me, twitched, and left. I stayed and shot pool. In fact, I
think I won the tournament that night, but that might be more cinematic re-

visionism speaking. He called a couple of days later, furious, and ordered me to meet him at a café in the Village. The café, delightfully enough, was called Dante and I headed over for my little slice of purgatory. He broke down, cried, and confessed (or was it professed?) love. I was very together that night and miraculously not drunk and said some really fine things, the gist of which was that there was no reason to be sad. He would always be the most important relationship in my life, however we cared to define it. There was love here, so what did we need to fear? We agreed to meet again the next morning and go blading, which we had intended to do anyway. He came upstairs to my hovel the next morning and without a word made love to me like he never had before, and it wasn't only due to the rollerblades which, in his effort to make up for lost time, he never got around to removing.

We were lovers at last, walking around New York holding hands and kissing and, I'm pretty sure, nauseating everybody. We got into the habit of going out to breakfast together at a health-food restaurant. This was during that moment of folly when we thought oat bran pancakes could cure AIDS. As it turned out, I gained ten pounds and Chris died anyway, but at least we were fighting. Life was more worth fighting for than ever before. Music continued to flow out of Chris. He wrote a group of four motets for chorus and string orchestra called *The Best-Beloved,* to homoerotic/religious Jacobean texts, no less. It is a shamelessly gorgeous piece, lush and sultry and inspired. It showed yet a deeper level of emotional truth. He even invented some new musical directions for the piece. At one point, a cello passage is marked *scavando,* meaning the cellos should *dig out* the notes, kind of like Scarlett O'Hara digging up that carrot or whatever it is. Art was reflecting his acknowledgment of the inherent hunger of life for life. In my vanity I'd like to imagine that *The Best-Beloved* is a love song to me, but it isn't. It's a love song to love. I just happened to be there at the time. I accept this. He probably would have written it even if I hadn't been there. But—and I take great pride in this—he wouldn't have allowed himself to enjoy the applause and the accolades so much if I hadn't been at his side.

One day that spring, we woke up, made love, ate oat bran pancakes, and listened to the broadcast of *The Marriage of Figaro* from the Met. One very short passage caught his imagination. I wasn't quite sure why, out of everything from that magnificent score, he focused on this particular, seemingly incidental passage, but he kept humming it after the broadcast. We walked down Charles Street as evening came, both of us in awe of the trees in their full moment of April bloom. We sat on somebody's stoop and he asked me to keep quiet as he breathed in the scent of the trees, nostrils flaring and brain-wheels obviously turning. That night, he began work on his loveliest piece of music, a prelude for soprano saxophone and string quartet. Although I can't hear this piece of music's relation to the Mozart passage, Chris swore that his piece was the Mozart transformed through his body by the perfect afternoon on Charles Street. It's a very easy piece of music to love, approachable and almost jaunty. Chris felt it was incomplete. He used the prelude as a departure point, and composed a fugue as a companion piece. The fugue is fascinating and lively and also happens to be among the era's most difficult pieces of music to perform. It has tripped up some of our most respected musicians. It is tonally related to the prelude, and although the forms are antithetical, they are clearly two sides of the same coin. In fact they are the two sides of Chris as they existed at that moment—at odds yet entirely interdependent. The *Prelude and Fugue* are the integration of a schizophrenic existence. He could not have written them at any earlier point in his life. He began writing his best cycle of songs, *In Endless Assent,* setting poems of Elizabeth Bishop, while we were on a vacation in northern Maine. At night, the aurora borealis shone and Chris was entirely freaked out by it while unable to quit staring at it. When we returned to New York he looked up all he could find on that phenomenon and became an amateur expert on the subject.

He went back to Taos for a month to work on *In Endless Assent.* While there, he saw *Thelma and Louise* and broke down. He wrote me a long letter telling me he was ready to quit running. Was I? I assured him I was, and when he returned we got an apartment together, the first time either of us had officially lived with a lover. I took measures to get my life together and Chris encouraged me, rolling pin firmly in hand, every step of the way. He didn't have time for my shenanigans. Neither did I, of course, but I couldn't see that while I was living in them. He could. Behold the legendary wisdom of the terminally ill.

His health was holding up well, and for one year we had everything we needed and, moreover, the presence of mind to know that, whatever might happen the next day, we were fine for the time being. He worked diligently at the piano every day, writing a *Serenade for Violin and Organ* that reminds many people of Vaughan Williams's *Lark Ascending*. We were married by a Catholic priest (to humor me, but it shows how Chris's rigidity had mellowed over the years) in January on the anniversary of the night we met. Chris became the consummate homemaker, gleaming over his perfect pie-crusts as I came home, suited and tied, from my corporate job. I had to laugh. When I met him, he was decked out in leather from head to toe. Now I didn't know whether I'd be coming home to find Rambo or Hazel in the kitchen. Nor did it matter. What mattered was the moment. Chris actually talked about writing an opera—even an "operatic" one. I found scores of Puccini and Donizetti on his piano, and he confessed that he was astonished to find that their music and dramatic abilities were really quite good. Doors were opening.

That year was a brief moment. His health began failing the following autumn. The grotesquerie of AIDS treatment, circa 1992, began. There were pills and shots and tubes and shit attacks and major food issues. There was also a little more talk about death around the house. I had told him about a José Carreras recital I went to at Carnegie. It was Carreras's first "return" concert after the grueling treatment for the leukemia that almost killed him. Carreras sang the song "Pietà, Signore" by Stradella, written in 1682 shortly before the composer was murdered at the age of thirty-eight, I believe. It was a harrowing performance. The song is a distinctly premodern wail of a dying man begging God not to punish him eternally for his sins. As remote as this may seem to us, it faces up to the terror of death and the unknown in a way most modernists circumvent. When Carreras sang it at Carnegie, it was followed by an eerie silence. Although the song is familiar to many people, nobody had ever heard it sung with so much feeling before. Carreras had recently been close to death—even dead at one point, according to certain medical definitions. He knew what he was singing. Chris didn't say anything about that story when I told it, but apparently it affected him and he got a copy of the sheet music of "Pietà, Signore." One night, I came home to find him at the piano, ball of Gancyclovir and God knows what else hanging from the IV pole and hooked up to his heart through the Hickman catheter on his chest, singing the Stradella song from the depths of his soul. I defy any horror movie to scare me after that vision. And yet there was something impressive about it too. Chris was forcing himself to look into the void, and was using music as his medium.

There was no more talk of an opera, or any other large project. Chris kept working, but on smaller projects. Commissions were being thrown at him from many quarters, but he refused to accept any money for a project he might not finish. He became angry about it. He was enough of an artist, or maybe just enough of a queen, to resent the loss of his looks and the desecration of his once beautiful body. He said rude things to people, especially to anyone wearing a red ribbon, his favorite pet peeve. Dying people only become saintly in movies. He told me that I needn't worry if he ever went into the hospital, since he would endure that only once and would not come out again. I assumed this was another bit of bile being coughed up, but I should have listened to him. Chris never wasted words. He checked into St. Vincent's (the "Undiscovered Country," we used to call it, since so many we knew never returned from its shore) on the 15th of July and died on the 20th.

That day, July 20, 1993, was hot and oppressive. I went to work as usual, planning for a long siege at the hospital and not believing the situation was yet critical. Or maybe I was just in denial. I got a call and ran downtown, sitting there in my light blue suit and preparing for a long vigil. Hours went by. We said things we had to say, or thought we had to. Finally, there was a change in the breathing, and the death decline set in.

The nurse, automatically adopting that concerned yet measured tone of voice that comes so easily to people who work around death, offered Chris a morphine drip to ease the pain of—well, you know . . . . I rolled up my sleeve, ready to accept the drip myself. You never know. Sometimes the nurses who come around offering juice or soda to the patients will offer one to the visitor as well. Perhaps she might hand out a little morphine to me. I could have used it at that point. She didn't give me any morphine, and, as it turned out, Chris refused it also.

"No, I don't think so," he said quite matter-of-factly, as if he were speaking to a waiter offering after-dinner coffee. "I'm going to need all my wits about me for this experience."

At the time, the remark struck me as unbearably noble and brave. It was like one of the great defiances of death from history and literature, on a par with blind old King John of Bohemia's final charge into the line of English archers at Agincourt (or was it Poitiers? Who cares. Agincourt sounds better). I thought of Pickett at Gettysburg and Leonidas at Thermopylae and Hotspur ordering the alarm even after he knows his father's troops will miss the battle. At that moment, Chris seemed to me like all these heroes, but most of all like Hotspur—noble, defiant, *sexy* Hotspur, declaring, "Sound all the lofty instruments of war, and by that music let us all embrace: For, heaven to earth, some of us never shall a second time do such a courtesy." Chris was uttering last words worthy of Shakespeare. Stage directions: The trumpets sound. They embrace, and exeunt.

I don't see it like that anymore. I wonder why anybody would want their wits, of all things, at the moment of death. What for? To take notes? Did he imagine he might need to be in top mental form for St. Peter's great Entrance Exam at the Pearly Gates? It occurs to me that Chris's comment was the last utterance of an exceedingly controlling personality. It was vintage DeBlasio. He needed his wits about him to comprehend (that is, to encompass, to "top," we might say) the experience of death. He always maintained that no one could possibly know anything about the existence or nature of an afterlife. He called himself a "confirmed agnostic," a term that still leaves me scratching my head. But the term applied well to him. He didn't know one way or the other, and was as open to the possibility of the soul's immortality as to any other eventuality. Perhaps a soul might be able to telegraph, in some way, its sensations to a living person, who could then translate these transmissions into splendid art for the edification of the living. Chris, I believe, was preparing for the possibility of becoming somebody's muse. Whenever he began a project, he got very organized and methodical. And who, after all, would be better qualified for the job of muse than he? Whose soul could be as disciplined, as conscientious, as well grounded in the basics of theory and composition?

In his final months, Chris spoke a lot about the requiems of Verdi and Mozart and about Richard Strauss's tone-poem *Death and Transfiguration*. He praised those composers' encapsulation of the death experience and regretted that he was not up to the task of emulating them. The little flutter at the end of Strauss's *Four Last Songs*, and Chris's evocation of it in *All the Way through Evening,* was but a gesture, and moreover was from the point of view of a person beholding death rather than experiencing it. At the moment of death, then, I am convinced that he decided to do all those composers one better, so to speak. He would actually die, and while doing so lay all the preliminary groundwork for the supreme piece of death music (since, in his estimation, even Mozart, Verdi, and Strauss had not gotten it quite exactly right). Once safely on the Other Side (assuming there be one) and fitted out with a halo and a well-tuned harp, he would telegraph his notes to some worthy vessel back in New York. In other words, he may have been ready to die, but he was not ready to stop composing.

Can anyone blame him? He was thirty-four fucking years old and had only just found his true creative voice. All the counselors with their *concerned* voices in all the support groups of New York might have felt better if he had told them he was ready to let go and "make the transition" or whatever euphemism our thanatophobic culture has devised. Screw them. He wasn't ready to let go, to allow others to do or to fail without his guidance. And that, I think, is a true mark of an artist. That shows, in an artistic sense, more commitment, more credence, and more *balls* than all the cavalry charges at Agincourt.

If Chris's afterlife plan was successful, I have yet to hear the results. I eventually remembered that Hotspur's actual last words are not defiant at all. He declares "Percy, thou art dust and food for . . ." leaving it to his killer to finish the sentence with ". . . worms."

We held the memorial at Calvary Church a week and a half later. Don't die in New York in the summer if you can at all help it. People don't know what to wear and balancing everybody's beach and weekend house schedules is damned near impossible. Harry Huff, Chris's good friend, organist at Calvary Church, and executor of his musical estate, did wonders with the available resources, but we decided to do more. Instead of waiting for Chris's spirit to inspire some other composer, we decided he had written enough music while among the living. We wanted to hear his music under optimum conditions with the best performers possible. The concert was held at Alice Tully Hall on January 11, 1994, quite coincidentally. It was the only night the hall was available.

The *New York Times* refused to send a critic, telling us it was their policy, out of consideration for the deceased, never to review memorial concerts of any sort. I pointed out that this was no more a memorial concert than Mostly Mozart was a memorial festival, dear Wolfgang, in case they hadn't heard, having been dead as well for some time now. That didn't work. People can justify much apathy under the guise of being considerate. If AIDS teaches us anything, it shows that misguided compassion can sometimes be as lethal as outright hostility.

Other critics came, and the reviews were favorable. They tended to dwell on what excellent potential the DeBlasio corpus of music showed, and spoke on about what might have been. And that's where it remains today, amplified (I insist) rather than dulled by six years of resonance. The trees on Charles Street are still there, and they bloom every April as splendidly as they did when they inspired Chris to write music. I avoid that block, but sometimes I have to walk down there and I see all the photographers and painters who hit the sidewalk on perfect spring days trying to capture the moment. That should give me a sense of the continuity of art and the human longing for beauty, but instead I get a little bitter wondering what new sonata Chris might have written to transform, rather than merely capture, the moment.

Or perhaps he wouldn't have. The supreme irony is that Chris might never have blossomed at all if it hadn't been for AIDS. It was his diagnosis that spurred him into demon confrontation and therapy and activism and opened him to the dangers and thrills of human interaction and love and the joy of being alive. I can't bring myself to say, as others have, that I am grateful for AIDS. I'm not that spiritually evolved. But Chris taught me to look things squarely in the face and call them by their real names and, ultimately, give the Devil his due. I would be betraying Chris if I didn't acknowledge the role AIDS played in his development, in our relationship, and in his art. The most devastating aspect of wondering what might have been is that one possible answer is "nothing at all."

Those doubts are as gnawing as the unfulfilled aspirations are tantalizing. Chris's untimely death leaves us who knew him in perhaps the worst place of all, a place of not knowing. We, though living and going on with our lives, remain where Chris's soul would have been assigned by a Dante or an Aquinas—in some sort of purgatory of agnosticism.

Remembrance of Things Past
Marc Lida's Proust Watercolors
Jonathan Weinberg

"Art is long, life is short," or so we are told. Art bestows immortality on the artist. But what if the artist never becomes famous and death comes before his or her art ever becomes known? Another cliché has it that works of art only become really valuable after their creator dies. Of course, it is the story of van Gogh's troubled life, and the astronomical auction prices of his canvases, that fuel this myth. In truth, it is rare for an artist to achieve posthumous fame after a career in obscurity. Even van Gogh's life does not quite fit the myth, since before he died his work was already well known to the French avant-garde, and his brother was an influential art dealer. Indeed, how could it be otherwise? How can works of art be known if there is no one to care for them and put them before the public? These are tasks that initially fall on the artist. If lack of fame hinders an artist's life, creating poverty and depriving him of the time and space to make art, it can be equally devastating to the works themselves after the artist's death. Since such art has little monetary value it may not be properly preserved or documented. After all, there is rarely a financial incentive for a gallery to represent the estate of an artist who failed to win an audience when he or she was living.

This problem of what becomes of works of art when their maker dies in obscurity began to haunt me when my best friend, Marc Lida, died of AIDS/HIV at the age of thirty-four, in 1992. He was not entirely unsuccessful. His illustrations were published in the *New York Times* and the *Village Voice*, but he never was able to live by selling his art. In part he became a social worker to help people with AIDS/HIV because, as he wrote in his application to graduate school "I have no indication whether I'll ever be able to support myself as an artist" (this and subsequent quotations are from typed manuscripts owned by Marc's brother, David Lida). Part of the problem was that he

Figure 1. *Marc Lida,* The Mindshaft, *watercolor on paper, c. 1982. From the collection of David Lida.*

worked in watercolor and made illustrations—two modes usually considered minor in the art world. But if by illustrating he seemed to forego the high art venues of galleries and museums, the exalted texts he liked to illustrate made his work unmarketable among art directors and publishers. Until the early part of this century novels were customarily illustrated, but today fiction rarely is presented with pictures.

Marc's other great subject, gay night life, had a limited commercial audience as well. Paradoxically, to art editors his illustrations seemed too much like high art, whereas to gallery directors they seemed too much like illustrations. His line was a bit too crude and expressive to sit passively on the page, his color too variegated to be easily reproduced, and his typical figures too mannered to fit the needs of advertisers. He might have done children's books, but somehow he was never able to focus on an appropriate story for children. Also there would have been the problem of his overtly gay work. Is it possible for a successful children's illustrator to exhibit pictures of such homosexual night spots as the Mineshaft (fig. 1) or the Saint?

His heart was in making pictures like *Freud Wrestling with Dora's Demons* (fig. 2). For Marc, Dora's analysis was a kind of fairy tale with a beleaguered heroine, the patient, and a courageous hero, the doctor. The wa-

Figure 2. Marc Lida, Freud Wrestling with Dora's Demons, *watercolor on paper, 1983. Private Collection.*

tercolor transplants Henry Fuseli's *Nightmare,* which was an image Freud liked, to the Viennese psychoanalyst's office. Like Fuseli's tormented female, Dora's head is thrown back, her body splayed across the analyst's couch. In place of Fuseli's incubus, Dora's dreams take the form of the characters of her case study. The humor of the picture is less a matter of its exaggerated gestures than of Lida's irreverence in daring to illustrate such a serious text. Freud, rather than Dora, becomes the target of Lida's absurdity. Dora's nightmares share the same visual space as that of the doctor's office. There is no boundary between real and unreal. Here, the patient-doctor struggle—the so-called talking cure—seems like a dream, or just another fiction. There is no difference between Dora's fantasies and the fantasies of psychoanalysis.

Although Dora's pose is lifted from Fuseli, Marc Lida used as his real model the watercolor illustrations of the early twentieth-century American painter Charles Demuth. One of the things that cemented our friendship when we met in 1972 was our shared love of Demuth's watercolors illustrating the writings of Émile Zola, Walter Pater, Edgar Allan Poe, and Henry James. Intensifying our pleasure in these well-known works was our knowledge that Demuth had also done private pictures of homosexual bathhouses and sailors having sex with each other. I went on to write my dissertation and later book on Demuth's erotic work (*Speaking for Vice: Homosexuality in the Art of Charles Demuth, Marsden Hartley, and the First American Avant-Garde*). Marc went on to learn from and transform his style and take on similar subject matter. Demuth's pictures of avant-garde hangouts, vaudeville theaters, and bathhouses of the teens were a model for Lida's extensive recording of bars, discos, and sex clubs of the eighties.

In 1927 Demuth wrote to Alfred Stieglitz that he had been reading Marcel Proust's novel: "So I have joined the others, not without reservations, however. He's too much like myself for me to be able to get a great thrill out if it all, marvelous, but eight volumes about one personal head-ache is almost unreadable, especially when you have your own head-ache most of the time" (letter in Alfred Stieglitz/Georgia O'Keefe Archive, Yale Collection of American Literature, Beineke Rare Book and Manuscript Library). Despite his ambivalence, or because of it, Demuth planned to illustrate the "marvelous" opus. He insisted that he needed to do the work in Paris, but he succumbed to his own "personal headache," diabetes, in 1935 and never began the work. And so in taking on Proust's work, Marc was taking up the project of his chosen master, even as his paintings augmented the work of his favorite writer. In bringing Proust and Demuth together through his art, Marc was merging two aspects of his own ambition, since throughout his adolescence he imagined himself a writer. When we first met at the age of fifteen at Buck's Rock, an art camp in New Milford, Connecticut, that catered to the creative children of New York intellectuals, he boasted that he had written dozens of plays. I was suitably impressed: only later did I find out that they were very short, with plots borrowed from *I Love Lucy* and old thirties movies. (One of our counselors at Buck's Rock was the New York City artist Arnold Fern, who wore a kimono and insisted on painting our toenails gold. This gave our *camp* experience an entirely different shade of meaning.) It was during our second summer at camp that I remember Marc announcing he was reading Proust. Surely, at sixteen, he was too young to understand the novel's daring formal invention or to appreciate the significance of its theme of time and memory. Instead, he was reading for the plot, such as there is, and enjoying Proust's fascination with gossip, particularly his descriptions of clandestine sexual behavior. And so that summer the melodramas of *All About Eve* and *Gaslight* merged with the sexual exploits of the M. de Charlus; all the time Marc spoke of these fictional characters as if they were living acquaintances.

When Marc was older he reread Proust several times with a greater understanding of the novel's stylistic complexity and a heightened awareness of its depiction of homosexuality, prejudice, and illness. He did several sketches based on the novel in the mid-eighties, but it was not until 1989 that he began to work on his Proust series in earnest. It was around this time that he was diagnosed with HIV/AIDS.

The Proust series was exhibited in Marc's lifetime, but only under fairly modest circumstances. He was a student and friend of the well-known children's illustrator Maurice Sendak, who bought the Proust watercolors and helped to arrange for their exhibition at the School of Art of Yale University in 1991. Unfortunately that show was not noticed by the New York critics. When Marc died the following year he did not receive an obituary in the *New York Times,* one of the bellwethers of mortal fame. Since his death, his work has for the most part been seen only in group shows that focus on art by people with AIDS/HIV. It remains little known outside a small group of friends and colleagues.

At the end of *Time Regained,* the final section of *Remembrance of Things Past,* Proust insists that art has the power to live on after its author's death: "the cruel law of art is that people die and we ourselves die after exhausting every form of suffering, so that over our heads may grow the grass not of oblivion but of eternal life, the vigorous and luxuriant growth of a true work of art, . . ." But a few pages later he remarks, "Eternal duration is promised no more to men's works than to men." In other words, the work of art itself may not endure any longer than its creator. What can I do to assure that Marc and his work do not disappear? If there was ever a noble use for my training as an art historian it is to focus attention on the work of my friend and rescue it from oblivion. This essay provides such an opportunity, but I have another motive for writing about Lida's watercolors that goes beyond that. As illustrations of Proust's text, their very subject is the problem of memory. To confront Lida's and Proust's work is to grapple with the question of how works of art help us or fail to help us remember.

Marc Lida's Proust series provides a way to discuss the problem of public memory and the process of personal loss. How does a life's work survive? How do I remember a friend? My relationships to the work as an art historian and as a friend come together in these works and also diverge.

It turns out that the friendship almost derailed the work of scholarship. In 1997 I volunteered to give a presentation to a seminar devoted to Proust at Yale University, thinking that this would be a perfect opportunity to publicize the pictures. I assumed it would be an easy matter of assembling slides of the pictures so that they followed the novel's course. To my dismay, I found out that neither I nor Marc had put titles on the transparencies when they were made. I contacted Maurice Sendak who told me that the originals also were without titles. What were we thinking when we carefully stored these pictures away? Our very intimacy with Marc and our fear of death got in the way of properly documenting his work. It always seemed as if there would be a little more time to ask questions of the artist about his pictures. Fortunately, when they were first exhibited, Marc had provided passages from Proust that had inspired his images. These quotations had been placed on small panels that originally accompanied the pictures. The panels had been preserved but not with the original watercolors, and they lacked the citations to the novel. My task was therefore to figure out which quotation went with which picture, and then also to find out where the quotation fell in the novel to determine the proper order of the pictures in the series. The job is exacerbated by the fact that Proust's work is some three thousand pages long in the 1981 Random House edition.

Marc died before he had properly prepared his work. I share the blame. In the last months of his life I was uncomfortable discussing anything that might suggest that he was dying. And so I let the chance pass to interview him about the meanings of his pictures. I also failed to do the most rudimentary job of art historical scholarship, that is to properly document the work in terms of its titles and dates. But four years later the process of reassembling the text and images forced me to reconsider the meaning of the watercolors and their relationship to Proust. I discovered certain aspects of

Marc's work that I had not noticed. For example, I had wrongly assumed that the pictures worked like an informal homage to Proust; that is, they did not really illustrate the novel in a systematic way. In fact Marc was far more serious about illustrating the complete text than I had imagined. Although he was clearly drawn to dramatic moments of scandal and humor, such as the scene when the unnamed narrator sees two women kissing, or when the Baron de Charlus reveals his homosexuality, he was careful to distribute the pictures uniformly throughout the book. It is as if he imagined the novel would someday be accompanied by his pictures.

In trying to reconstruct the sequence of the pictures in relationship to the text, I found myself trying to remember my experiences with Marc as well. It was as if I were ritualizing the major theme of Proust and of Marc's series, "The Search for Lost Time," or as it was creatively mistranslated by C. K. Scott Moncrieff, "Remembrance of Things Past." During the process of rereading I came upon this famous passage:

And so it is with our own past. It is a labor in vain to attempt to recapture it: all the efforts of our intellect must prove futile. The past is hidden somewhere outside the realm, beyond the reach of intellect, in some material object (in the sensation which that material object will give us) of which we have no inkling. And it depends on chance whether or not we come upon this object before we ourselves die. (*Swann's Way*)

It is Proust's conceit that certain pedestrian events, such as tasting a madeleine dipped in herbal tea, or stepping on an uneven flagstone, can bring back the past "complete with all the other sensations linked on that day to that particular sensation, all of which had been waiting in their place— from which with imperious suddenness a chance happening had caused them to emerge—in the series of forgotten days." He opposes this complete, almost hallucinogenic memory, to the usual idea of remembrance, which is only a series of conscious recollections: "the truths which the intellect apprehends directly in the world of full and unimpeded light have something less profound, less necessary than those which life communicates to us against our will in an impression which is material because it enters us through the sense but yet has a spiritual meaning which it is possible to extract" (*Time Regained*). Unfortunately we can have no control over when these accidents that spur involuntary memories may occur. They may never happen. But even if these sensations do take place, the very moments they bring back will not last. These moments that were so vividly recalled will be buried again in the past.

The sensations Proust speaks of are so subjective, so highly personal, that in a certain sense they cannot be fully shared. We cannot taste the madeleine and have Proust's epiphany. In the end, Proust is not so much presenting us with lost time as with a description of what it might be like to find it. By suggesting that time can be recovered in such a way, however, he is also insisting that it was never really lost, that it stays with us as part of our very being. It is "embodied, of years past but separated from us" (*Time Regained*). We carry it with us to be restored in brief moments, involuntarily, during key accidental events. Yet in the end it is not chance or random objects that give us a sense of what it is to recapture time, it is Proust's art: "the task was to interpret the given sensations as signs of so many laws and ideas, by trying to think—that is to say, to draw forth from the shadow—what I had merely felt, by trying to convert it into its spiritual equivalent. And this method, which seemed to me the sole method, what was it but the creation of a work of art?" (*Time Regained*).

Proust's descriptions illustrate themselves by creating a picture in our mind. By making Proust's text concrete, illustration runs the risk of providing too much of the materiality and not enough of the elusive "spiritual meaning" that Proust wanted to extract from experience. Yet the very translucency and insubstantiality of Marc's watercolor technique has the effect of describing characters without fixing their corporeal presence. Marc once wrote a description of the work of Sendak that is also an apt description of his own style: "Though the viewer can make out the subject of the drawings, many of the images seem to be juxtaposed on each other, lending an almost collage-like quality to the pictures. Figures strike operatic, gestural poses; the backgrounds become like stage settings, with the action of the pictures played in the foreground." He goes on to comment that these techniques, "which might be used by twentieth-century artists for distancing effects   irony, parody or camp . . . engage the viewer, . . . move the viewer, bring him or her into a state of interest, and hopefully, emotional intensity."

Marc's characteristic mode is comic and grotesque. There is little sense of the narrator's inner struggles. But rather than undercutting Proust's high seriousness, the result is to augment the social and erotic aspects of *Remem-*

Figure 3. Marc Lida, Proust Watercolors: The Lady in Pink, *watercolor on paper, 1989–90. From the collection of Maurice Sendak.*

brance of Things Past. Marc reads for moments of both private scandal and public spectacle. And so he begins the series with the scene in which the narrator meets his uncle's mistress, the lady in pink, a famous actress, and impulsively kisses her hand (fig. 3). Rather than show us the key moment in which the narrator eats a madeleine, thus introducing the major theme of the novel, he instead emphasizes a moment when the narrator learns something about sexual desire. Taking his lead from Proust himself, Marc makes the narrator in his watercolors a self-portrait. But where Proust's hero is in search of lost time, so that his entire project reads like an extended memory, Marc's alter ego seems to be in pursuit of experience itself. It is almost as if the novel has come to life around him. Perhaps this difference is a matter of the different mediums of author and painter. The watercolors suggest the action is occurring directly in front of the viewer in the present, while the text is written as if the author is recalling events. In general painting tends toward immediacy—it is about presence—while writing even when it takes the present tense always seems mediated by time.

Marc is particularly drawn to the voyeuristic element in Proust's novel. In the second illustration he depicts the narrator as a shadowy figure outside

Figure 4. Marc Lida, Proust Watercolors: M. Charlus and Jupien, *watercolor on paper, 1989–90. From the collection of Maurice Sendak.*

a window, spying on Mlle. Vinteuil as she embraces her lesbian lover. Later in the series, he shows the narrator looking through a transom window at Charlus and Jupien (fig. 4). This is the moment in which Charlus's and Jupien's masculinity becomes "inverted." (Here Lida is quoting directly from a Demuth watercolor, *Nana's Awakening,* which illustrates a scene from Zola's *Assommoir* in which Nana as a young child spies from a transom her mother cheating on her father.)

In representing clandestine sexuality, Marc represented his own homosexuality. But perhaps more evocative of Marc's life are the depictions of Swann's terminal illness. He illustrated the key scene in which Swann tells the Duchesse de Guermantes that he is dying (fig. 5):

"Very well, give me in one word the reason why you can't come to Italy," the Duchess put it to Swann as she rose to say goodbye to us.

"But my dear lady, it's because I shall have then been dead for several months. According to the doctors I've consulted, by the end of the year the thing I've got— which may, for that matter, carry me off at any moment—won't in any case leave me more than three or four months to live, and even that is a generous estimate . . . ."

Figure 5. Marc Lida, Proust Watercolors: Swann Tells the Duchess That He Is Dying, *watercolor on paper, 1989–90. From the collection of Maurice Sendak.*

The Duchess stops for a moment, caught "between two duties as incompatible as getting into her carriage to go out to dinner and showing compassion for a man who was about to die." She decides that the "best way of settling the conflict would be to deny that any existed. 'You're joking,' she said to Swann" (*Guermantes Way*).

As if the two shared the same disease, Karposi's sarcoma, Marc painted blotches on Swann's skin. Depicting Swann's conversation with the Duchess and his later appearance at a reception was a way for Marc to represent the difficulty of living with a disease that society would rather not discuss or see. It must have taken courage to give form to this scene, believing that Swann's death sentence was his own fate. The pictures' glowing color, and their extraordinary humor, are in stark contrast to the condition of their making—the onset of a wasting disease that eventually left Marc unable to work.

In 1983, years before he learned he was HIV positive, Marc represented the disease directly in a series titled *Drawings of Sex and Death* (fig. 6). He placed explicit images of orgies and backroom sex next to jolly pictures based on song titles. This attempt at a modern day dance of death was ex-

Figure 6. Marc Lida, Drawing of Sex and Death: AIDS #7, *watercolor on paper, 1983. From the collection of David Lida.*

hibited in the basement of the Pyramid Club, a hot spot in the East Village of the early eighties. Lida's intent was to shock his audience:

I do think that sex is shocking again, homosexuality in particular, because sex is associated with getting sick. Obviously, I am not advocating this kind of sex; there is a certain nostalgia for this kind of sexuality, and it's a different kind of nostalgia than the other paintings, because it's something that I've actually lived through. . . . I think that in the age of AIDS, it is almost distasteful to deal with sex like this, certainly, uncomfortable. I do want to make people uneasy with it because I think sex is fundamentally an uneasy thing and in America people try and prettify it.

Marc claimed to be representing a world he knew well, but the drawings of *Sex and Death,* for all their baroque horror, lack the intensity and humanity of the Proust series. In the Proust watercolors the combination of sex and death is still the main theme, but it is mediated through a complex narrative that finds in art precisely the means to hold mortality at bay through the recovery of the past. However distant Proust's time is to the Age of AIDS, it provided Marc with the means to directly confront his own illness. The attempt to shock people in the earlier series by explicitly representing sexual encoun-

Figure 7. Marc Lida, Proust Watercolors: Mme. Swann in the Allée des Acacias, *watercolor on paper, 1989–90. From the collection of Maurice Sendak.*

ters is replaced by the dignity of Swann as he calmly tells the Duchess he is dying.

In the end, Marc Lida was unable to finish his Proust watercolors. The illustrations stop at the final two volumes of the series, the very two volumes that Proust himself never lived to see published. One of the earliest sketches for the series shows Charlus being whipped. This was one of Marc's favorite scenes in the novel. Yet as he worked on the final series, I think he became increasingly drawn to the novel's scenes of people simply meeting. Perhaps he had come to realize after all that private sexual perversions do not necessarily convey much about one's inner life.

My favorite picture in the series, *Mme. Swann in the Allée des Acacias* (fig. 7), is not a particularly dramatic moment in the novel. It illustrates a scene when the young narrator lifts his hat to Odette: "I was now close to Mme. Swann, and I doffed my hat to her with so lavish, so prolonged a gesture that she could not repress a smile" (*Swann's Way*). The picture is about the way the common world can be miraculously transformed into diaphanous lavenders and greens through a mere exchange of gestures between human beings. The search for lost time that is the novel's theme is above all an attempt to salvage and heighten such moments.

The Proust watercolors are extraordinarily beautiful, but they are no substitute for Marc's presence. With each year I find it harder and harder to conjure up the friend I knew. As Proust suggested, we cannot summon the past. The most powerful memories come through to us at the most unlikely times and through what otherwise might be the most trivial experiences—if we are lucky. Despite all the clichés, art is not the place where the essence of a person is encapsulated or lives on. My task as an art historian is to make sure that Marc's work continues to be seen, not because it is a way to keep his memory alive, but because it is splendid painting. Although he worked in what some might deem a minor form, in a minor medium—watercolor illustration—his ambitions were high. He courageously and outrageously took on one of the most admired works of literature of the twentieth century. He demonstrated that painting can still take on the great themes, that it can confront questions of death and memory, in a manner that is immediate and pleasurable. Perhaps one day, Proust-like, I will trip on the pavement and find myself carried back to Buck's Rock to hear stories about Lucille Ball or Charlus. Until then I will console myself with the joy of looking at Marc Lida's very present paintings.

I would like to thank Nicholas Boshnack, Bruce Kellner, David Lida, and Maurice Sendak for their help preparing this essay.

Artists with AIDS/HIV and their friends and families interested in getting information on how to prepare their estates should contact the Archives Project, c/o Visual AIDS, 526 West 26th St. No. 510, New York, NY 10001.

Trying to Find Words for Things Unspeakable

Philip Yenawine

David Wojnarowicz lived a bizarrely harsh life—most of it mean beyond easy comparison—and events of his past were both his motivation to create and his subject. He described what he lived and dreamed, recounting events of his external and internal life. He especially addressed sex and sexuality, finding it "necessary to define [his] sexuality in images, in photographs and drawings and movies in order to not disappear" (*Close to the Knives: A Memoir of Disintegration*). What he described was uncommon experience but what he illuminated was shared. Somehow, his story fit my relatively benign circumstances, roughly, like waves take a body. More than anyone else, for me David excavated the sadness and difficulty involved in being gay in America, and the pain of living with AIDS. He did this for himself—it saved him from being destroyed by bad news—but he did it for me, too, and he knew that I knew.

We met through others we both cared about, but our relationship was between us and it was unexamined, not discussed, and based on a recognition that we immediately had: we understood and needed one another. To him, I think I represented an art world insider whom he could trust, at least as much as he could trust anyone. And I was trustworthy, because I respected him and loved him even before I knew him, pulled irresistibly toward him because of his art. It stunned and fascinated me from the early 1980s—altered posters, street stencils, and harsh stories of life on the street, a life I did not know but which left me feeling intensely. He was still "emerging" when we finally met, meaning that he was being watched by those who were powerfully connected, those who opened the doors to new artists, and gave them recognition. I think he was afraid of their increasing interest in him and the attention to his work by people he did not know, and he needed me, or someone like me, to help him sort out who was who and what meant what. I, on the other hand, needed his acceptance of sex to address my internal phobias

182

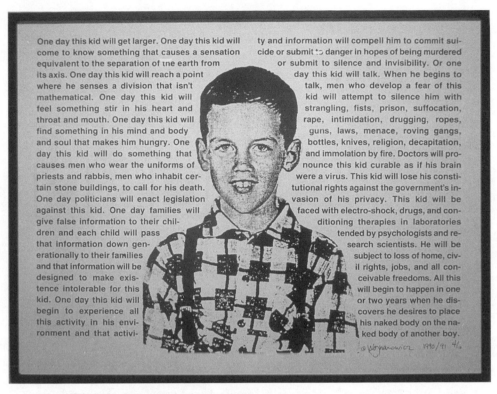

One day this kid will get larger. One day this kid will come to know something that causes a sensation equivalent to the separation of the earth from its axis. One day this kid will reach a point where he senses a division that isn't mathematical. One day this kid will feel something stir in his heart and throat and mouth. One day this kid will find something in his mind and body and soul that makes him hungry. One day this kid will do something that causes men who wear the uniforms of priests and rabbis, men who inhabit certain stone buildings, to call for his death. One day politicians will enact legislation against this kid. One day families will give false information to their children and each child will pass that information down generationally to their families and that information will be designed to make existence intolerable for this kid. One day this kid will begin to experience all this activity in his environment and that activity and information will compel him to commit suicide or submit to danger in hopes of being murdered or submit to silence and invisibility. Or one day this kid will talk. When he begins to talk, men who develop a fear of this kid will attempt to silence him with strangling, fists, prison, suffocation, rape, intimidation, drugging, ropes, guns, laws, menace, roving gangs, bottles, knives, religion, decapitation, and immolation by fire. Doctors will pronounce this kid curable as if his brain were a virus. This kid will lose his constitutional rights against the government's invasion of his privacy. This kid will be faced with electro-shock, drugs, and conditioning therapies in laboratories tended by psychologists and research scientists. He will be subject to loss of home, civil rights, jobs, and all conceivable freedoms. All this will begin to happen in one or two years when he discovers he desires to place his naked body on the naked body of another boy.

David Wojnarowicz, untitled photograph. Courtesy of P.P.O.W. Gallery, New York.

(I was way out publicly but still full of conflict internally) and his rage to help delineate my mostly unvoiced horror at what was happening to so many men I loved. He needed my insights into the art world. I needed his into life as a sexual being in a hostile environment.

David's art pulsates with his anger at America and its intolerant and unempathetic social culture, one that only pretends to celebrate difference, to care about the young or to care for the ill and the weak. This anger propelled his creativity, but his creative output seemed to free him from it. The David I knew was gentle, quiet, reserved, kind, open. He drove his stories forward with rage, but then, out of nowhere, rounded corners, leaving bitterness and arriving at soulful, mournful songs. Ones that I sing to myself in dark moments, and for which I am grateful.

David described his American nightmare using both words and images, sparing nothing and no one, trying to reach "the necessary things in my history that would ease up the pressure on my mind" (letter to Marion Scemama). He limned his childhood abuse, his life on the streets and on the road. He also mined his dreams and fantasies for the meanings that underlie experience. He told of how being in nature—he so totally urban—fed him. Here's a mini-autobiography, cutting to his teen years on the street:

I had been drugged, tossed out a second story window, strangled, smacked in the head with a slab of marble, and almost stabbed four times, punched in the face at least seventeen times, beat about my body too many times to recount, almost completely suffocated, and woken up once tied to a hotel bed with my head over the side all the blood rushed down into it making it feel like it was going to explode, all this before I turned fifteen. I chalked it up to adventure or the risks of being a kid prostitute in new york city. (*Memories That Smell Like Gasoline*)

This litany of abuses is prelude to the first time he got fucked, which was by rape. He was hitchhiking back from one of his periodic escapes to nature. He had taken a bus out of the city and found a pond in New Jersey where he had floated, still wearing his street-filthy clothes and shoes, "pushing my face under water looking for signs of life. It was rapidly turning to dusk and I was wet and feeling cold. The town was too small to offer much evening traffic so it was hard to get a ride. I didn't really know where I was. I was gray inside my head and wishing that killing myself was an effortless act." He caught a ride from a man who said he worked in a bank and who detoured onto a deserted road. There the man threw David into the back of his truck, pummeled him, and forced himself inside this rangy fifteen-year-old. Even years later, when he saw the man again in a movie theater, the memory smelled like gasoline, "lingered like the stink after a bad fire."

    Like most of his narratives, David's description of this abuse was rendered with the fractured brilliance of strobe light. Splintered among the flashes of brutishness were recollections of another sort. He remembers that the man, mounting from the rear, pulled his head back and kissed his eyes. And while he raped, he also mumbled, "Oh, what a gift you are giving me." David pieced these details into the tumble of his account, complicating the picture of this man and this act. The man is not redeemed but neither is he left utterly devoid of consciousness, of humanity.

    The intensity of the man's sexual desire, and the end to which it drove him, are inexcusable, but lust is ordinarily imbalanced—and this David acknowledged. He often described the way it feels to be caught up in longing, feelings powerful and irrational, "a humming gathering from my stomach and rising up past my ears" (*Close to the Knives*). He went on, "I feel the fist of tensions rising through my solar plexus beneath my t-shirt and the sensation grows upward, spreading like some strange fever in my chest, catching only at the throat where small pockets of sound are contained." No matter his early history, he believed in sex as an act of communication. He saw it as essential and good, even as desire pushes reason and safety aside.

Halfway through my meal the door swung open and this deaf mute walks in and leans against the counter a couple of seats from me. He uttered a series of squeaks and grunts and flashed me a smile. Something clicked in my head, I mean, he was intense and oddly sexy with a muscular body covered in scrapes and a few bruises. He looked like he just walked out of some waterfront in an old queer french novel. He managed to order a burger to go and as the counterman went in the back to place the order he leaned over the counter and lifted the plastic lid of the danish case and slipped one inside his filthy shirt. He winked at me as he speared a second danish and dropped it down his neckline, then he walked over and extended his hand and I shook it. Something was clicking somewhere. When I shook his hand he made a odd little gesture with his middle finger against my palm and winked again. There was an air of desperation and possible violence around him like a rank perfume. And that was what suddenly became sexy to me. I tried to understand this sensation, why the remote edge of violence attracts me to a guy. (*Memories*)

David dissected the attraction, finding a useful metaphor: that the life of a gay man is, essentially, that of an outlaw. Since social mores disapprove of, and in some states criminalize, sexual acts of intimacy and love, and since more casual or public encounters are commonly policed, we are inherently lawless whenever we express our sexuality. The queer is a short step away from the one who has completely given up society's rules. David, at least, saw common ground between his sexual nature and that of one who stepped further out of line, whose behavior was even unpredictable and possibly violent. So he let this guy follow him into the subway and to a deserted spot where they began an encounter that was a mess of conflicting impulses. Wanting sex, but not wanting his pocket picked, David eventually kneed the guy in the chest, and barely managed to outrun him onto a departing train. "He never got in and I turned and slumped into a seat and realized the car was filled with sleeping winos. Christmas eve and I'm on a train full of drunks heading toward another future." It is not a pretty picture, but it still implies hope, "another future."

Reading the likes of this was incredibly revealing for me. I judged my own desire harshly. I did not easily forgive myself for getting into situations that went in directions I did not want. And David made me see the foolishness in this. What indeed is wrong with desire, with sexual desire, with desire for being with men, with desire for the wrong men? How had I become convinced that desire was bad, therefore I was bad? Or a less easily answered question, why did this feeling stick so long with me, given that it seldom stopped me, was only effective at producing guilt?

In another story from his teenage days as a Times Square hustler, he tells of a man who

would have me put on these pure rubber sneakers and the sergeant's outfit and then a rubber trenchcoat and then he'd grease up his dick and he would start fucking another rubber sneaker while on his belly and I'd have to shove my sneaker's sole against his face and tell him to lick the dirt off the bottom of it and all the while cursing at him telling him how stupid he was. (*Close to the Knives*)

Someone else might have left us with a sense of pity or revulsion for a man who picked up kids and made them partners to his weirdness. But David saw beyond the sex. He concluded this tawdry little tale by adding that the guy "says he loves the way my skeleton moves underneath my skin when I bend over to retrieve one of my socks." The man becomes sympathetic not simply pathetic, weird but human. There is no sexual perversity. All sex is legitimate.

One way David conveyed this accepting stance was to remain a partner to the sex he described, even when it was taking bizarre turns. He could watch, but was never a bystander. His own sexual nature and his intense desire were givens and accepted, no matter how much religion and family had tried to teach him to think otherwise. There was no guilt which meant also no innocence. And for him, sex happened all the time, all over the place. He described a tableau at a sex club:

There is a clump of three guys entwined on the long ledge. One of them is lying down leaning on one elbow with his head cradled in another guy's hand. The second guy is feeding the first guy his dick while a third guy is crouching down behind him pulling open the cheeks of his ass and licking his finger and poking at its bull's-eye. . . . One of the guys, the one who looks like he's praying at an altar, turns and opens his mouth wide and gestures towards it. He nods at me but I turn away. (*Memories*)

He turned away because at that point he carried the virus, and it complicated participation. But he still relished what he saw. For him, sex was matter-of-fact, the same subject addressed by pornography. As he experienced it and as he described it, however, he added subtext. A leer from someone who was "praying at an altar," his head "cradled": this language transforms a sexual encounter from tired and tawdry to weirdly holy. David talked about sex with grit, no dressing up, no glossing over, and he seldom associated sex with romance. Still, he saw sex as having a kind of sanctity, and he certainly saw it as an aspect of love. In describing what is usually referred to as casual sex with a stranger in an abandoned building on a Hudson River pier, David wrote,

In loving him, I saw men encouraging each other to lay down their arms. In loving him, I saw small-town laborers creating excavations that other men spend their lives trying to fill. In loving him, I saw moving films of stone buildings; I saw a hand in prison dragging snow in from the sill. In loving him, I saw great houses being erected that would soon slide into the waiting and stirring seas. I saw him freeing me from the silences of the interior life. (*Close to the Knives*)

He continued to write this way despite AIDS. AIDS was a virtual gift to homophobes, and to those who disapproved of sex separated from procreation. It offered the perfect opportunity to demonize the sexual urge and promiscuity. People brought up like me, and David, too, were vulnerable to this message. Already complex for most of us because of ingrained sexual phobia and internalized homophobia, AIDS did something horrible to our chances at intimacy, already challenged, as we gay men now faced the distinct possibility of killing each other as we made love. David knew that he'd contracted the virus through sex, and he watched with horror as AIDS killed way too many of his friends and as it exacted its toll on him. But his stream of sex stories and his images about gay sexual experience continued defiantly. He implied that sex would redeem us because it brought us together; we should not abstain. I believe him to this day.

    In 1989, David contributed an essay to the catalog of an exhibition called *Witnesses: Against Our Vanishing*, organized by his friend, the photographer Nan Goldin. The show was at Artists Space, a nonprofit gallery in Lower Manhattan. Funding for the show had come in part from the National Endowment for the Arts (NEA). The NEA was already under scrutiny by the religious right and conservative members of Congress for its support of a fellowship to Andres Serrano, the maker of Piss Christ—in truth, a profoundly spiritual meditation on Jesus—and a show of Robert Mapplethorpe photographs that included several staged, highly aestheticized images of some gay sex practices. David's essay was a brilliant polemic entitled "Postcards from America: X-rays from Hell," and it hissed with anger. It was vaguely diaristic, probing conversations and recalling events in order to describe what it is like to deal with illness, dying, and death, although it was very much a tale of how AIDS was a very particular way to die:

The rest of my life is being unwound and seen through a frame of death. And my anger is more about this culture's refusal to deal with mortality. My rage is really about the fact that WHEN I WAS TOLD THAT I'D CONTRACTED THIS VIRUS IT DIDN'T TAKE ME LONG TO REALIZE THAT I'D CONTRACTED A DISEASED SOCIETY AS WELL.

The essay included powerful condemnations of Roman Catholic efforts to keep safe sex a nontopic, of the politicians who were swayed by them, and of the bureaucrats who did too little too late to help with treatments and education. He even vented on gay critics who wrote rebukes of others who continued to write of unfettered sexual experience:

we have people from the thought police spilling out from the ranks with admonitions that we shouldn't even think about anything other than monogamous or safer sex. I'm beginning to believe that one of the last frontiers left for radical gesture is the imagination. At least in my ungoverned imagination I can fuck somebody without a rubber, or I can, in the privacy of my own skull, douse [Senator] Helms with a bucket of gasoline and set his putrid ass on fire or throw congressman William Dannemeyer off the empire state building. These fantasies give me distance from my outrage for a few seconds. They give me momentary comfort. Sexuality defined in images gives me comfort in a hostile world.

Throughout his youth, and again as a person with AIDS, all social welfare systems failed him miserably, including schools and the neighbors who took no notice of his father's repeated and public beating of his children. Think of what he might have become. But, instead, he used art as his way out, even of bitterness.

He channeled his anger into creativity, and it was preposterous to watch how this frightened our leaders in Washington, and even conservatives in the art world.

Given the hell-bent determination of the right to still voices such as his—triply troublesome because he was queer, angry, and aesthetically challenging—David's hyperbole forced the NEA to threaten to rescind its grant for the show, creating a major early skirmish in the culture wars that had begun in earnest in the late 1980s. In response, the art and civil liberties worlds accused the NEA of attempting censorship. Summit meetings were called between free expression advocates and bewildered bureaucrats who were being lobbied in less public forums by those who wanted to obliterate the agency for a whole slew of reasons, using artistic effrontery as their ammunition. A compromise was eventually achieved: the NEA slapped the hands of Artists Space, but it was allowed to keep its grant for the show as long as no government money went to pay for the offending catalog.

As the public controversy raged, there was another side to the story that seldom gets told. At a meeting of some art world activists addressing the situation, I watched a conversation between David and the director of Artists Space, a good person by all standard measures. I knew it was their first encounter since the fracas had begun many days before, and that David was dismayed not just by the NEA challenge but also by the way it was being handled. I could not hear them talk, but I could certainly see the tension, quiet as it was, and knew that it ended badly. David was already aware that the director, fighting the NEA as she was, and truly beleaguered by countless people applying different sorts of pressure, had a very practical basic issue: keeping her grants coming. There was of course a brave side to her stance, namely that she—and soon enough, scores of other managers of art presenting agencies—was defending Artists Space's right to determine what it showed based on aesthetics, not politics. She and others fought for funding without strings attached. And this basically meant arguing for artists' rights to free expression, a worthy cause. It is not unimportant here, however, that the legal experts carried the ball throughout the fight, not the arts community. The art world enjoined the lawyers to defend its right to free speech—but its contribution was usually to claim authority to establish what was and wasn't art, virtually never to justify art's sometimes contentious nature.

David knew that he was invisible in the fight. Like most other artists who experienced this discrimination, he was never asked to speak for himself. And no one with authority—i.e., credibility that extended beyond the confines of the contemporary art world—stepped forward to argue that, in its challenges, his work was art of a most potent sort, voicing the sentiments of many, making pointed (but defensible) social criticisms, and extending aesthetic terrain. The art world has historically been ambivalent toward artists who make social issues a primary focus, and when such content is combined with cutting edge expression—familiar behavior since the Renaissance—even those "in the know" are often at a loss for words of explanation and apologia. But art world institutions—major museums and their curators as well as respected critics, for example—either kept their distance or, when forced to speak out, hid behind the privilege of expertise without taking on the admittedly difficult task of justification.

While David as the maker of troublesome work was vilified, misrepresented, and misunderstood in the press and elsewhere, he as a person was all but eclipsed. He had created his work in the till-then protected arena of the art world. When the external world invaded, the paper-thin line of defense around those who trekked furthest out became obvious. As one willing to baldly expose his heart and gut, he was de facto abandoned by all but friends. The invisibility of the queer in the larger society existed even here. It hurt him deeply to be betrayed by the world that had given him life.

More difficulty was to come, however: an exhibition of his work by the bravely supportive gallery at Illinois State University also received NEA funding. The show was accompanied by a well-illustrated catalog which contained reproductions of large works, embedded in which were drawings based on pornography, some altered photographs that also originated as porn, and one print that showed Christ with a hypodermic in his arm—truly the man of sorrows, one of the downtrodden. The fundamentalist American Family Foundation unlawfully excerpted the images from their surroundings and mailed them to its constituency as a fund-raiser (purportedly one of its most successful) to support its efforts to bring down the NEA. David sued, both for copyright infringement and for malicious intention to defame his character. He won the case, at least from the standpoint of the illegal use and misrepresentation of his work. But the arguments that his career was damaged were apparently unconvincing. As his one expert witness, I have had a hard time forgiving myself for this. David was awarded one dollar in damages. The judge apparently believed that notoriety was an aid to any career.

There was, however, no evidence then that this was true for him, and there is none now.

What the judge did not, perhaps could not, understand was the nature of creativity, what a delicate matter it really is. Nor the heavy toll it takes to go public as a queer. Nor what it is to live with a life-threatening illness, particularly one that comes with social stigma—the draining strain of it. Although not writing about the judge, David described an encounter with someone else who approached him as if he were "normal": "too bad he can't see the virus in me, maybe it would rearrange something in him. It certainly did in me" (*Memories*).

It appeared to be too much to hope that the religious right could act with any generosity toward any person of different views or behaviors, but I, optimistic to the point of naïveté, wanted to believe that the judge could hear what David was saying—an argument for civil rights, not to mention common sense and basic humanity. How could he miss the pathos in David's description of living with AIDS? In this excerpt from the Artists Space essay, David recalled a conversation with a friend in which he opens a window into how he dealt with the omnipresence of his own deterioration and with the dying and death of others:

My friend across the table says, "There are no more people in their thirties. We're all dying out. One of my four best friends just went into the hospital yesterday and he under went a blood transfusion and is now suddenly blind in one eye. The doctors don't know what it is. . . ." My eyes are still scanning the table; I know a hug or a pat on the shoulder won't answer the question mark in his voice. The AZT is kicking in with one of its little side effects: increased mental activity which in translation means I wake up these mornings with an intense claustrophobic feeling of fucking doom. It also means that one word too many can send me to the window kicking out panes of glass, or at least that's my impulse (the fact that winter is coming holds me in check). My eyes scan the surfaces of walls and tables to provide balance to the weight of words. . . . My eyes settle on a six-inch-tall rubber model of Frankenstein from the Universal Pictures Tour gift shop, TM 1931: his hands are enormous and my head fills up with replaceable body parts; with seeing the guy in the hospital; seeing myself and my friend across the table in line for replaceable body parts; my wandering eyes aren't staving off the anxiety of his words; behind his words, so I say, "You know . . . he can still rally back . . . maybe . . . I mean people do come back from the edge of death. . . ." (*Close to the Knives*)

Why didn't the judge get it? Why could he not see the effort required to make sense of a life so often under fire? David spoke out in order to understand himself but also to make others, including me, grasp what we witnessed and found so hard to process.

I am a bundle of contradictions that shift constantly. This is a comfort to me because to contradict myself dismantles the mental/physical chains of the verbal code. I abstract the disease I have in the same way you abstract death. Sometimes I don't think about this disease for hours. This process lets me get work done, and work gives me life, or least makes sense of living for short periods of time. Because I abstract this disease, it periodically knocks me on my ass with its relentlessness.

Words can strip the power from a memory or an event. Words can cut the ropes of an experience. . . . Describing the once indescribable can dismantle the power of taboo. To speak about the once unspeakable can make the INVISIBLE familiar if repeated often enough in clear and loud tones. . . . IF PEOPLE DON'T SAY WHAT THEY BELIEVE, THOSE IDEAS AND FEELINGS GET LOST. IF THEY ARE LOST OFTEN ENOUGH, THOSE IDEAS AND FEELINGS NEVER RETURN. This was what my father hoped would happen with his actions toward any display of individuality. And this is the hope of certain government officials and religious leaders as well. When I make statements like this I do not make them lightly. I make them from a position of experience—of what it is like to be homosexual in this country. (*Close to the Knives*)

Why could the judge not understand that when the bigots attacked David's art, they attacked him, severely affecting his ability to work? As I see it, the judge's decision was as debilitating to David as the virus, and it crippled his capacity to create. It in no way accommodated the fact that David's time was running out. Thirteen months after the decision was handed down, David wrote to a friend, "I haven't worked in almost a year" (letter dated August 1991 from his journal, Fales Library, New York University). A bit earlier he had written, "I can't form words these past few days, sometimes thinking I've been drained of emotional content from weeping or fear. I keep doing these impulsive things like trying to make a film that records the rituals in an attempt to give grief form" (*Close to the Knives*). Images and words that had sprung from his life, dreams, and fantasy and which were his weapons against society as well as his own physical deterioration began to fail him. "I am a prisoner of language that doesn't have a letter or a sign or gesture that

approximates what I'm sensing" (*Close to the Knives*). In New Mexico, standing in a landscape from which he sought comfort, nature having given solace
to him since his early childhood escapes from his father, he wrote, "I didn't
trust that fucking mountain's serenity. I mean it was just bullshit. I couldn't
buy the con of nature's beauty; all I could see was death" (*Close to the Knives*).

By the time he died, on an otherwise gentle July night in 1992, something in me was dead. As David so often lamented about most of us, I had inherited the American inability to deal with death and dying. I had found out,
too late, how the denial of these things—the only inevitabilities—leaves us
emotionally inept at dealing with them. When most of my waking time was
spent dealing with bad news, I had no clue about how to act or react. I could
talk, sort of—more like stuttering—but I could only approximate feeling. I
ignored and glossed over. I overworked. I misdirected anger. I pretended. I
joked. But I had no clue how to grieve the passing of days that lacked both
joy and hope. David: "My life is no longer filled with poetry and dreams. I
can't even smell rust in the air" (journal entry, 1991). I could not process the
losing of so many—oh so many—people I had thought I would grow old
with. David articulated the words I could not find in myself to fathom and
describe a very long nightmare. He wrote: "Sometimes it gets dark in here behind these eyes I feel like the physical equivalent of a scream" (*Memories*).

By the 1980s I had long lost any religious faith, yet I wanted the solace that it promised. My brushes with it at memorial services only seemed to
make it worse. Though he too saw spirituality as a need and a possibility in
all of us, David wrote of how religion fucked it up. Listen to this, written after asking a nun to leave the hospital room in which Peter Hujar—David's
best friend, mentor, and briefly his lover—had just died. The sister had been
going on about how Peter had accepted the church, in her mind thus insur-
ing his salvation. As he wrote about that moment later, David's terse, quirky
prose cut through the tired promises of Christianity:

He's more there than these images of spirituality—I mean just the essence of death;
the whole taboo structure in this culture the mystery of it the fears and joys of it the
flight it contains this body of my friend on the bed this body of my brother my father
my emotional link to the world this body I don't know this pure and cutting air just
all the thoughts and sensations this death this event produces in bystanders contains
more spirituality than any words we can manufacture.

So I asked [the nun] to leave and after closing the door again I tried to say something to him staring into that enormous eye. If in death the body's energy disperses and merges with everything around us, can it immediately know my thoughts? But I try and speak anyway and try and say something in case he's afraid or confused by his own death and maybe needs some reassurance or tool to pick up, but nothing comes from my mouth. This is the most important event of my life and my mouth can't form words and maybe I'm the one who needs words, maybe I'm the one who needs reassurance and all I can do is raise my hands from my sides in helplessness and say "All I want is some sort of grace." And then the water comes from my eyes. (*Close to the Knives*)

With spirituality that existed without boundaries, he bore the virus's ravages, coping for more than two years after writing this. He was not quite thirty-nine when he died. ("My eyes have always been advertisements for an early death" [1991 journal entry].) I live on, of course, like others, weighed down with loss, feeling abandoned and dried up. Trying to conjure hope. Facing unrelenting depression as I try to get on with work which doesn't seem satisfying, certainly no reason in itself for living. Wondering if I should risk making new friends or searching for lovers in a reduced pool of people who might also get/be sick. Dealing with disclosures of status, and the possibility of rejection or repulsion on the grounds of it, of dicks that won't get hard because of medicine or fear. I wonder how David would have written about this? What more would I have learned from him?

Bruce Kelly,
Landscape Architect
John Berendt

Not long after John Lennon died in December 1980, the New York City Council voted to create a memorial to him in Central Park and to name it "Strawberry Fields." They chose a three-acre site just inside the West 72nd Street entrance, directly across the street from the Dakota apartment house where Lennon and Yoko Ono lived.

In response to the city's gesture, Yoko Ono announced she would contribute a million dollars toward landscaping and maintaining the site. Taking the concept one step further, she ran a full-page notice in the *New York Times,* asking countries all over the world to send rocks, trees, and plants in order to make Strawberry Fields an "international garden of peace."

Gifts came pouring in. The Aleutian Indians sent a totem pole. Morocco offered a mosaic-tile bench, the United Kingdom proposed monumental gates, France would contribute a fountain, Greece would send an enormous slab of marble. There was even talk of erecting a statue of Lennon. Most of the gifts were plants and trees, but many, like Uruguay's kapok tree and Cuba's royal palms, were not suited to the New York climate and would never have survived in Central Park.

Clearly, the proposed memorial was lurching out of control. Henry Stern, the city's Parks Commissioner, remarked that he feared the site would become a "botanical freak show." The Central Park Administrator, Elizabeth Barlow Rogers, became alarmed. For years, she had devoted her energies to restoring and preserving the park's romantic landscape as it had been designed by Frederick Law Olmsted in 1857. Olmsted had laid out the park as a seemingly natural expanse of meadows, clumps of trees, rolling topography, and water bodies that had graceful, undulating edges. He had warned against inserting any grandiose effects for fear they would detract from the overall harmony of the park. Rogers knew that Strawberry Fields, as it was

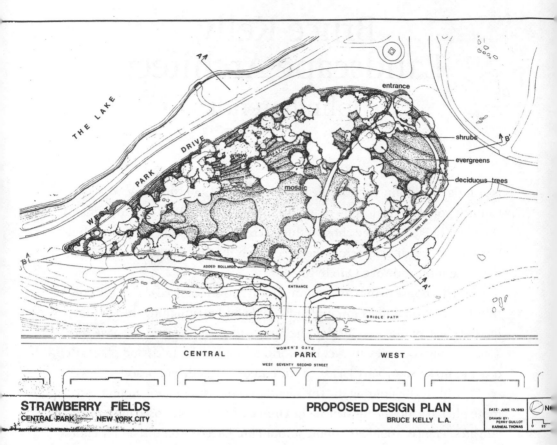

Bruce Kelley, architectural drawing of Strawberry Fields. Courtesy of New York City Department of Parks and Recreation.

shaping up, would never win the approval of the Landmarks Preservation Commission, the Arts Commission, or any of the various community boards that had jurisdiction over it. The park had long ago been declared a historic landmark, and any but the most subtle memorial would be seen as an intrusion.

At this point Rogers turned to Bruce Kelly, a young landscape architect who had acted as a consultant to her and to the Landmarks Commission since 1975. Kelly was an Olmsted specialist. He had coauthored the book *Art of the Olmsted Landscape,* written the title essay, and curated an exhibition based on the book at the Metropolitan Museum. He was one of four landscape architects chosen to draw up the Central Park Master Plan for the fifteen-year, $150-million restoration of the entire 834-acre park. Rogers asked Kelly to take over the design of Strawberry Fields.

A soft-spoken Georgian, Kelly knew this assignment would be a ticklish one. It would require patience and diplomacy if it was to satisfy Yoko Ono, the civic review boards, and over 150 donor countries. Before doing anything else, Kelly researched the site to find out what Olmsted had originally intended for it. The plans, it turned out, called for broad, open scenery with meadows along a rock ledge that served as a north-south spine. In Olmsted's day, the West Side of Manhattan had not yet been built up, and the entrance at 72nd Street Central Park West was little used, so Olmsted planned no pedestrian paths through Strawberry Fields, nor any ornamentation such as gazebos, pergolas, or benches. The most distinguishing feature of the original site was that it served as the southern tip of what Olmsted called the Winter Drive—a continuous swath of evergreen and "winter-interest" plants and trees that stretched from 102nd Street to 71st Street along the western edge of the park.

By 1981, Strawberry Fields had become one of the most desolate patches of Central Park. The soil was eroded and compacted. The wooded areas were choked with weed trees. Fifty of the larger trees were actually dead though still standing, more were dying, and not a single evergreen was left. Meanwhile, the 72nd Street gate had become the most heavily used park entrance, so in 1946 a crude asphalt path had been rolled out across the lawn, without any regard to grading or landscaping. A row of benches had been placed at the 72nd Street entrance, where senior citizens sat facing outward toward the street, inhaling fumes from the traffic passing right in front of their faces.

Strawberry Fields did have its virtues: dramatic topography with steep rock ledges and a gently undulating tableland; lovely views of the Central Park Lake and the East Side skyline; several fine old trees including mature ginkgoes, a huge magnolia, turkey oaks, and one of Central Park's biggest English elms.

Kelly paid a call on Yoko Ono in the Dakota to discuss the project. The windows of her apartment looked out across the park and, directly below, onto the teardrop-shaped Strawberry Fields. She was distant, he thought, and possibly suspicious of him. Two or three times during their conversation, she withdrew to the next room where, as Kelly could see through the open door, she consulted tarot cards. Kelly sensed that it might be worthwhile trying to relate to her on some sort of mystical level, so he revealed that his birthday was December 8—the day John Lennon had been shot. Yoko looked at him strangely, then she laughed. They got along well after that.

Kelly described his vision for Strawberry Fields: a leafy, cloistered bower, carefully planned to appear as if it had occurred naturally. The upper and lower meadows would be rolling lawns, suitable for sunning, reading, picnicking, or napping, but not level enough to encourage ball-playing or other active sports. He would create small grass-carpeted "rooms" elsewhere by the placement of trees and shrubbery. He would move the row of benches that had once stood at the curb several feet into the park, turn them around to face in toward the greenery rather than out at traffic, and screen from the road by a tall, dense buffer of Japanese dogwoods, ginkgoes, katsuras, and an understory of shrubs and plants.

Yoko readily understood that a restoration of Strawberry Fields based on Olmsted's plan would be a more appropriate memorial to John Lennon than a hodge-podge of objects that had no relation to the park. She agreed to accept just one of the elaborate gifts that had been offered and to ask the other countries to select their contributions from a list of plants and trees that Kelly would draw up. Italy's proposal was the one she chose to keep: a round black-and-white mosaic that would have the word "Imagine" spelled out in the middle of a starburst pattern. It would be forty feet in diameter. After the Arts Commission objected to its size, Yoko agreed to reduce its diameter from forty feet to ten. As for the statue of John Lennon, that was never an issue. Lennon had once told his wife that he never wanted a statue of himself, because pigeons would sit on his head.

Today, Strawberry Fields is a magical green glade, "an Arcadian delight" as the *New York Times* has described it. Kelly re-created the Winter Drive aspect by planting five white pines, each fifty feet tall and full to the ground, along with other evergreens and shrubs that had colorful stalks or berries in the winter. He improved the path across the lawn by giving it a gentle curve, grading it into the landscape, and flanking it with an honor guard of shapely cedars and junipers as it made a regal descent to the lake. He set the mosaic into the path so people would pass right by it instead of trampling over the grass to get a look at it.

Strawberry Fields was one of the first sections of the Central Park restoration plan to be completed. It set the standard and, because of its instant popularity, sparked widespread enthusiasm for the larger project, which would eventually transform the entire park. For this alone, Strawberry Fields is a fitting memorial to John Lennon. It is also, sadly, a memorial to Bruce Kelly, who died of AIDS in January 1993 at the age of forty-four.

If Kelly had designed nothing else, Strawberry Fields would be reason enough to celebrate his work. He was prolific, however, and many of his landscapes are public spaces that can easily be seen and enjoyed. Several are in Central Park (the Dene, the Shakespeare Garden, the Point in the Lake, the Obelisk landscape, among others.) His real contribution, however, extends well beyond his landscapes. He was an artist whose work not only influenced other landscape architects but awakened public interest in historic landscapes. Through his writings, his lectures, and his own designs, he promoted the idea that historic landscapes, like historic buildings, were works of art and therefore deserving of preservation.

Surprising as it may seem now, this was an entirely new concept in the late 1970s and 1980s when he was espousing it. Until that time, the accepted manner of dealing with aging public parks was to renovate them, which meant tidying them up, usually with modernizing touches. In the 1940s and 1950s, for instance, New York City's Parks Commissioner Robert Moses carried out dozens of well-intentioned but inappropriate renewal projects in Central Park, such as laying the asphalt path through Strawberry Fields and clamping a concrete embankment around the pond at the northern end of the park (the Meer), thus obliterating its naturalistic shoreline.

In *Art of the Olmsted Landscape,* Kelly identified fifteen elements that typify an Olmsted landscape. He demonstrated in rich detail how they are all in balance and form a single work of art based on what Olmsted called "a single, noble motive." In the case of Central Park (and virtually all other American parks, since Central Park serves as their model), the noble motive was to provide hard-pressed city dwellers with a touch of nature as an escape from the increasingly noisy, dirty, and stressful city.

"That book was a watershed event," says Susan Rademacher, former editor-in-chief of *Landscape Architecture* magazine. "Bruce established the significance of Olmsted's work to the basic concept of an American landscape.

No one had ever written about Olmsted in such breadth and scope. The landscape as a work of art is still difficult for most people to grasp, because it's always changing, but Bruce conveyed the idea brilliantly. He wrote about experiencing a landscape, being 'immersed' in it, how a landscape architect can evoke a variety of moods and stir emotions with a landscape just as a painter does with a canvas. He explained that Olmsted actually designed how we enter and move through a landscape, drawn in by a sequence of vistas that lead us farther into the park. That book had a tremendous impact on the conservation movement. I find myself going back to it again and again, particularly Bruce's essay."

Charles Birnbaum, coordinator of the National Park Service's Historic Landscape Initiative acknowledges Kelly's far-reaching influence. "Bruce opened people's eyes to things they had never thought about. He looked at the landscape comprehensively—as a coherent balance of vegetation, topography, water, buildings, and traffic circulation systems. In the late seventies and eighties—which, for historic landscapes, was a period of enlightenment—Bruce took a stand in favor of viewing landscapes as cultural artifacts; he made the point that the design history and the usage history of a landscape were every bit as important as aesthetics. Landscapes had never been dealt with that way before. Beautification had always been the sole consideration. Government money became available for the first time, and now there are federal guidelines for preserving historic landscapes. Bruce played a major role in it. He was one of the vision people."

With public interest in historic landscapes increasing, concerned citizens in other cities sought Kelly out for help in rehabilitating their own parks.

Buffalo, which has a string of connected Olmsted parks, was one of several cities that called on him. Gretchen and Tom Toles were among the leaders of the Buffalo Olmsted Parks Conservancy.

"Bruce taught us how to see Olmsted's work," says Gretchen Toles. "He was able to translate what a landscape was in terms that we could understand as laymen. I've never encountered anyone as eloquent. He made us see that all the specific elements of an Olmsted landscape related to each other and made it a coherent, finished work of art: the canopy, the understory, the topography, the water, the vistas. He made everyone passionate about it, especially donors. And he was always available for advice and comment. We'd just pick up the phone and call him."

"When Bruce came in," Tom Toles recalls, "it was like a very clear, bright light. He mapped it out for us. What do we have here? How should we think about what to do with it? He wrote a master plan for the restoration of South Park based on Olmsted's plans and offered three alternative courses of action. Twenty years later, that document is still the basis for discussions of how to deal with the park."

Caroline Loughlin met Kelly when he went to St. Louis to consult on Forest Park. She recalls that he was adroit at problem solving. "Bruce validated the history of the park as being important at a time when people were ready for that. But then we were faced with a frustrating dilemma. The park was choked with roads; some people were in favor of removing some of them, but others argued that the roads were historic and belonged there. We asked Bruce what we should do, and he said, yes, they are historic and they do belong there, but they don't have to be twenty feet wide and paved with asphalt. Some of them could be narrow footpaths. It was a revelation! He was right, of course, and it gave us a way of keeping the historic footprint of the park without letting the roads dominate."

Joan Bozer, of Buffalo, recalls falling under the spell of Kelly's persuasive powers. "He could convey, like no one else, the grandeur of the park, the potential of the park, the meaning of the park, and the need to protect and preserve our park system. If you called him in a crisis and said you needed him to resolve issues, he always came. I remember when the city wanted to take part of an Olmsted park for office buildings or schools. Bruce came and explained convincingly, and without ruffling anybody's feathers, that this was not a good idea, because the park was not just an assemblage of parcels but a unified, coherent whole. His death is a great loss to the country. So many parks and historic landscapes would have benefited from his vision. He was eloquent, he inspired us and motivated us. He spoke beautifully, wrote beautifully, and designed beautifully. Everybody liked him. Those qualities are hard to find in one person."

Bruce Kelly's genius showed itself at an early age. He grew up on a farm in Wrens, Georgia. Both grandfathers had been farmers, and his mother's greatest passion was gardening. His childhood friend Paul Powell remembers that at the age of ten or eleven Kelly took to digging things up out of the ground and moving them around, usually without his parents' permission. "He was fascinated by the shapes of plants," says Powell. "One day he dug up his mother's day lilies and put them in a more prominent spot to give them more sun. Another time, he moved some junipers his father had planted on an embankment along the highway for erosion control; he rearranged them to look better. Then there was the hedge on the property line that screened out the view from the neighbors' big picture window. Bruce rearranged those too, to thin them out. His parents were furious, but they had to agree that Bruce did have a good eye."

His "eye" continued to impress people for years after. Geri Weinstein, the director of horticulture in Central Park, tells of accompanying Kelly while he was directing a crew that was planting trees and shrubs on the Point in the Ramble. "Bruce went out in a boat on the lake to get some perspective," she said. "He had the men moving things around. They were positioning a tree when Bruce called out, 'We need a horizontal. Could you lay it down almost flat and set it into the ground at a horizontal angle?' The crew thought he'd gone crazy, but he was right. He had an eye for how plant material distributes itself naturally in the landscape, and he never made a false move. I've seen him place nine or ten pine trees, and they looked as though they'd always been there."

In matters of landscape, his instinct proved correct again and again. "I had annuals in my flower garden," his mother says, "and suddenly a wild oak sprouted up in the middle of it. I was going to cut it down, but Bruce begged me not to. So I let it be, and it grew into the nicest tree. We love the shade of it."

Betsy Barlow Rogers, founder of the Central Park Conservancy and author of the two-volume work *History of Landscape Design: Cities, Parks, and Gardens as Expressions of Cultural Values* (Abrams, 2000), frequently depended on Bruce's eye. "In the summer of 1975," she recalls, "Bruce and I would walk through the Ramble or through the area known as the Loch in the wild and beautiful north end of Central Park. With Bruce's eyes informing mine I would see these abused and weed-choked woodlands as Olmsted and Vaux had planted them. We would look at the barren plain that was once the Sheep Meadow or the dusty plateau of the so-called East Green, and Bruce would conjure in my mind's eye the pastoral beauties of fresh grass and fringing canopies of trees. Then and later when he served as one of the principal members of the Conservancy's master planning team, Bruce helped me to see the Park not as a collection of objects set in a space, but as space itself, space beautifully articulated to induce a variety of moods."

Kelly's feeling for historic preservation also emerged, remarkably, when he was a child. He voiced concern that sharecroppers' houses would one day disappear. They were modest dwellings of the sort that were typical all over the South—a single main room with a sleep shed, a kitchen shed, and a tiny front door and porch. He asked his parents to buy one and put it in the backyard. According to his sister Phyllis Kennedy, the family did not take him seriously. "But he turned out to be right," she says. "Sharecroppers' houses are now lost to the landscape."

Kelly's concern about sharecroppers' houses had as much to do with his social conscience as it did his appreciation for architectural history. He was a liberal democrat and had an outlook very much like Olmsted's. Olmsted was one of America's great democratic theoreticians. As the country approached civil war, he evolved from a liberal to a thoroughgoing radical on the issue of slavery. Central Park was, among other things, an experiment in democratic city planning. It was the first American park to be open to all people free of charge.

Although several of the world's elite were among Kelly's private clients—CBS founder William Paley, Senator John Heinz of Pennsylvania, buy-out specialist Henry Kravis, U.S. Chief of Protocol Angier Biddle Duke, and Baron Alessandro Albrizzi of Venice—he took delight in twitting the high and mighty. For example, when the members of the exclusive Atlanta Botanical Gardens asked him to draw up a plan for Atlanta's Piedmont Park, he proposed that the botanical garden, which itself was located in the park, remove its chain-link fence so that the public could have free access to its grounds.

"He was a social progressive through and through," says Professor James Marston Fitch, who taught Kelly when he studied for his degree in historic preservation at Columbia. "He was very adept at the social graces and made friends easily. But he had a healthy distrust of many of the people he moved with. Politically and philosophically. His opinions were consistent. He had a kind of purity that amazed me."

As one of Bruce's closest friends, I can attest to the truth of Fitch's recollections. Bruce listened well, observed closely, and argued his convictions on all matters strenuously, eloquently, and stubbornly. It was my pleasure, many times, to have that remarkable experience of walking through a landscape with Bruce as a seeing-eye guide. We all think we can look at trees and lawns and hillsides and know exactly what we are seeing. But Bruce's running commentary provided one revelation after another. In Strawberry Fields, he would point out how he created outdoor rooms by positioning trees and shrubs a certain way and how he had selected the plants so that in the fall and winter the proportions of the room would change as the colors became brighter or darker. He would point out Olmsted's main sequence of Central Park vistas that led you from the Plaza entrance at Fifth Avenue up to the Mall, along the Mall to the Bethesda Terrace and the Park's starring vista: the Bethesda Fountain in the foreground, the Lake behind it, the wooded Ramble beyond the Lake and in the distance, poking up above the trees, the Belvedere Castle at the heart of the park.

As a preservationist, Bruce sparred with competing forces working at cross purposes, particularly in Central Park. Visitors who took shortcuts created dirt paths, or "desire lines," across the grass. Fences, he said, would only present a challenge to them, and they would jump over. A row of benches would be subtler and more effective than a fence, as would a banked path or shrubs with thorns. In thinning trees to preserve Olmsted's vistas, Bruce ran up against vocal birdwatchers, who objected to *any* trees being cut down, especially dead trees because they house insects that attract birds. He created a firestorm of protest when he removed five trees to open up the famous view of Belvedere Castle from the Bethesda Terrace. And when he cut down 150 seedling cherry trees in Strawberry Fields to allow the more mature trees to flourish, vociferous opponents set up a table in the park and handed out petitions. "The grabbing phase of Strawberry Fields memorial has developed, as predicted, into a destructive operation," the petitions read, "smashing and cutting down trees and turning this romantic and picturesque part of Central Park into a war zone of politics. This is the beginning of the end of Central Park!" These particular critics have not been heard from since Strawberry Fields was completed.

Bruce was an optimist. No landscape was beyond reclamation. He never gave up hope. He was extremely confident, very sure of his own strengths, and one of his many graces was his firm belief that his friends possessed great talents too. He encouraged them, and he brought out the best in them whether they happened to be lawyers, teachers, artists, or writers.

I had spent my entire adult life writing and editing for magazines. One day in 1985, Bruce said to me, "It's time for you to write a book!" And I knew he was right. When I started casting about for a subject, he said, "You loved Savannah. Why don't you write a book about Savannah?" So I wrote *Midnight in the Garden of Good and Evil.* Bruce took an enormous interest in its progress throughout the seven years it took me to write. He read every chapter as I wrote it.

All of us who knew him feel the loss his death has created and know that the loss is far greater than the landscapes he never had a chance to create. I often walk through Strawberry Fields and admire the katsura trees, which were one of his two favorite kinds of trees (along with the live oak) and stroll through the oak forest that he made visible at the bottom of the hill by clearing away the seedling weed trees that had obscured it. And I always direct a mental salute toward the bench with the small metal plaque affixed to the back of it with the inscription that borrows from the memorial to Christopher Wren in St. Paul's Cathedral. It reads, "Bruce Kelly, Landscape Architect, 1948–1993, 'If you seek his work, look around you.'"

Fucked
Craig Lucas

"What do you mean?"

"You know, cornholing. The guy puts his thing in the other guy's butt."

"Really?"

As shocking as death, this. As absurd as that first rumor of procreative sex. Not right.

Always knew I wanted to be with men, held and holding, caressing and lapping, nursing on their cocks. But this? Going the wrong way where all that shit has been?

The first person who ever fucked me, or tried to, was my classmate at Boston University's School of Fine and Applied Arts. If ever there was a fine and applied art, it's fucking. (And aren't artists supposed to be the best lovers?) His name: Irving Lee, and he was a tall, very dark-skinned actor with a preposterous yet fluid overgrown dancer's body, a beautiful booming voice and dazzling smiles for everyone, his presence to me daunting and electric; I wasn't in love with him, but I knew I wanted to make love to a man, and Irving was so out, there were no secrets in the theater department anyway, and I got really drunk at a party of upperclass students and hung around until Irving had no choice but to deal with me which he did more out of pity, I'm sure, and very soon it became clear even to drunk me that he wanted to put himself inside me, and no one had done that to me, ever, nor was it any conscious part of my sexual imagining. (It would be decades before books appeared with chapter titles like "Privileging the Anus.")

But this is a story about getting fucked. So we tried, and I yelped, and he said, Relax, and I said, I'm trying, and he tried, and I seethed with overeager misery, and he drove me home, even though I tried and tried and tried to excite him with my mouth and my kisses, he wasn't buying.

When I moved to New York, Irving was appearing in the cast of *Pippin*, and I would see him as I walked to my own show, *Shenandoah*, or at auditions. We were never really friendly. There was always that sad, failed fuck between us. And smiles.

It was at that same time I met Henry Post, one of the Merriweather Posts: blond, louche, wry; Hank lived in a loft on Washington Street, and we met in the back room at the International Stud, a bar in the far West Village where they showed dirty videos and men groped and made love, the smell of poppers in your clothes afterwards with the smoke and the seafoam sperm smell. Henry's cock wasn't big, but he really knew how to make love, and goddamit if he didn't want to fuck me, too, and I went home with him and fell in love with him somehow, and he introduced me to people with names like Alpha-Betty Olsen; he talked about Bette Midler as though they'd been married, and he wrote journalistic pieces and treatments for movies with titles like *In Blue Blood* (about some gay poseur), and he found some way to get inside my tight, unfriendly asshole, and it was . . . well, it was amazing. It made me cry. I'd never felt anything like it, the stimulation, the emotional cords which were pulled, and being under him, with my legs up, or on top of him, I could feel how much he wanted me, and I let him fuck me, even when I bled a little bit, I still wanted him to fuck me. As another friend said to me, "You feel like a baby being born." Yes. So I put that in a play. Because the play is the way that you make love to the audience, as a book is the way you make love to a reader, or the reader makes love to the author. Which is why anonymous sex is ultimately so forgettable: little or no dialogue, no ideas, no context. Some people like it, I guess, and I tried it out a couple of hundred times, but . . . I don't know.

The reason Henry and I broke up wasn't the fucking, it was the contempt he expressed for the artists I liked—Britten ("moderne" as opposed to modern, Hank preferred Alban Berg) and Virginia Woolf (indulgent, fey). This rankled.

Hank gave me a copy of Isak Dinesen with this haiku by Teishitsu in the flyleaf: "Icicles and water / Old Differences / Dissolved / Drip down together."

One night after a performance of *Shenandoah*, riding downtown on the subway, I spotted Peter Evans, the Yale-trained actor whom I'd seen in *Streamers* and lusted after. I had a copy of the script for a new musical (*Merlin*) in a blue leather binding which I made a big show of perusing, studying ("What is Merlin's action in this scene?") so he'd know I was in the theater too. Brazenly,

I rode on past my stop, got off at Christopher Street directly behind him, and followed him all the way to his apartment on Hudson Street where he couldn't avoid noticing that I was hovering, and he reluctantly, fearfully, invited me up. And we fucked. Pete had a small, blunt, perfect dick, and it fit inside me without causing me any pain at all. He had a swoopy, pointed nose, sunken English cheeks, hair as soft and fluffy as dandelion silk; he didn't take extra special care bathing or getting dressed or shaving, so there was always a skid mark in his undies, a missed patch of beard, an untucked shirt missing buttons. I adored him, head over heels adored him, and loved to fuck him and be fucked—this was the sexual/romantic relationship I'd always wanted.

And Pete didn't want me. I was a chorus boy, hadn't gone to a "good enough school." But he really did love me, he just didn't realize it. We'd hook up for sex, he took me to the opera (*Parsifal*, I slept, *Peter Grimes*—electrifying). We discovered to our horror that we had the same goal in life: to be geniuses, to win the Nobel Prize. Coming from a Broadway chorus boy with no greater achievements to his credit, this must have seemed particularly ridiculous to Pete. But I could always make him laugh. Hard. And I could make him hard. He left me for a young stage director who is now known for reviving old plays and bringing his Yorkshire terrier to rehearsals, sometimes attributing artistic judgments to the dog.

I tried to kill myself with an overdose of barbiturates and alcohol, and Peter found me, in a coma, and we both survived. Over the years we would continue to meet, to fuck, to talk books. I loved his little dick, his guilt, his Anglophilia. He played a wide array of showy parts—the obese Benno Blimpy, balding Verlaine in *Total Eclipse*, the romantic lead in a musical of *Once in a Lifetime*, Coward and Chekhov at Williamstown's summer theater— taking his work as seriously as his tortured love affairs. The scripts were treated like roadmaps with hidden, underground connections between the major sites; he scribbled and erased and studied them, and repeated his lines endlessly after fucking, before permitting himself to relax over a meal, then fucking. Or he passed up the fucking for more scriptwork. No decision was easy for Peter, every move entailed an agony of protracted, painful reconsideration; but onstage, as in the act of love, he seemed fully spontaneous— alive. An amateur watercolorist, lover of Henry James, he moved on to more exotic lovers, masseurs who would fuck him at the end of the session, dark-visioned painters, costars, Italian strangers, California hitchhikers. Still, Pete and I would travel out to New Jersey to visit his boozy, chain-smoking mother and doddering, Alzheimer's-suffering father, and he'd suck me off in the car on our way to the country club, or we'd fuck in his childhood bed. For old time's sake. Like the ex-husband and wife at the end of *Scenes from a Marriage*. A cabin in the middle of nowhere. Fucking. Talking. Relieved.

Pete introduced me to Rick Sandford, one of the hitchhikers. Rick had introduced Pete, preposterously enough, to a famous English novelist and his much-celebrated younger painter boyfriend who lived together in the hills above Santa Monica. It seemed that all of these people were fucking! At the time I was appearing in the chorus of the original production of *Sweeney Todd*, and Rick attended with the famous novelist and the painter, and when I looked out to see them in the third or fourth row, they appeared to be passing a bottle of poppers back and forth, sniffing them and grinning idiotically. I think the novelist may have abstained.

Looking back, thinking about fucking, and these artists, their faces and careers and all the art everyone was trying to make along with the men, I can mythologize the figures and the acts into a coherent narrative, of sorts. But in the midst of it, then, what did I want but to fall in love and feel the fucking. And the future was, as ever, unwritten. And the fates of the actors in the farce, the drama, are not fully formed. They are plastic and fluid, full of possibility. Or are they there, hidden, all along, like the dark and wet, impossible pleasure of an asshole? On the make is what we were.

Rick pursued me. I was dating someone, so we hooked up for a threesome. And Rick sat on my cock, his boyish, guilt-free face hovering above, and my boyfriend entered Rick from behind, and we both fucked him, together, our two cocks pressed tighter in love. Rick united our two dicks and made us both come inside him.

Later I saw him achieve this same feat in a porno flick. Rick's writing career remained largely private. He came to New York with a strip show. To "Another Hundred People" from *Company*, he arrived onstage with a suitcase, and met invisible New Yorkers, stripping for them, looking for love. Afterwards, we had to wait while older men went into his dressing room to make appointments. Or something. Rick asked what I thought of the performance. Idiotically, to my continuing shame, I gave him notes. "Wouldn't the piece want to be more shaped, cohesive? Didn't it lack an intentionality?" Rick said, "If you don't respect my work, then you don't respect me."

For years we didn't speak. When we hooked up again, the English novelist had died. Rick's nude portraits had appeared everywhere, drawings of him in every conceivable naked pose, executed by the younger boyfriend of the novelist. Rick's film career, under the pseudonym Ben Barker (the real name of Sweeney Todd), had come and gone. Rick lived alone in Los Angeles, across from an Orthodox yeshiva school. He had taken to dating his letters in Christian era time and Judaic time. He sometimes wore a yarmulke and zizith, and continued to keep copious lists of "bests"—movies, books. Rick read everything, had opinions about everything, irritated and delighted me in equal parts. He adored the yeshiva boys. One of them had come to him, drunk, and had sex with him, allowed Rick to suck him off. Rick's fantasy was to light himself on fire in front of the boys and to have them piss on him, too late to save his life. Rick read my play *Prelude to a Kiss* and informed me, on no uncertain terms, that he fully understood why the Tony that year had gone to *The Grapes of Wrath*. Touché. His writing, obsessive and entirely true to Rick, had either improved dramatically, or my perceptions had shifted. I couldn't put them down. Still can't.

"If you don't respect my work, you don't respect me."

Let me just say that no one was ever going to put two cocks in me. I can't get two fingers in me without a pint of vodka and a bottle of poppers. LSD, ecstasy, cocaine—these substances exist to enable me to open up. And when I do, if I do, if I can, then there is the intense wonder of union: How is that possible?

A man I love once said to me, "It's just so sweet, isn't it, being inside another man?"

You see people, marvelous erudite gay men of any age, and you think, "They fuck?" Harry Kondoleon, master of words and wearer of expensive, brightly colored shoes—snakeskin and leather the thickness of smoke—did he fuck, get fucked? Could a man who rode a cock like a broncobuster write a line like this (from *Christmas on Mars*): "I put quarters in the wrong machine at the laundromat and sit and watch other people's clothing spin and spin while mine sits in a wet unattended lump"? I suppose. His plays hide their essence behind elegance and surprise; their skewed wit conceals the theme of spiritual redemption as linen pants conceal genitals—hinted at, outlined, there.

Maurice Grosser, the painter and the ex-lover of the famous and famously cantankerous American composer and nonagenarian who, when I met him and Maurice, was still living in the upper regions of the Chelsea Hotel in a vast, vast apartment filled with memorabilia and glorious woodwork—Did Maurice fuck? Get fucked? Maurice had been to Harvard, lived in Paris with the cranky composer, and collaborated on two operas with texts by Gertrude Stein. Maurice made his own pasta and hung it on towel racks in the kitchen to dry. For all his years in Paris, he still managed to speak French in a flat American accent, a parody of tone-deaf Americans. His paintings, academic in the best sense, were large canvases of bowls filled with eggs, or fruit, or small paintings of the faces of friends. Elegant, unexperimental, sensual, yet respectful of tradition. Maurice stuttered slightly, read voraciously, loved Mozart, hated Strauss, and in his eighties still carried his own groceries up the grimy stairs of his apartment on Fourteenth Street. His boyfriend, much younger, continued to fuck him AND the famous ex-boyfriend. On a regular basis. This dapper old man who could quote whole passages of *Tender Buttons* . . . he lifted his legs in the air to take that shared cock inside him?

One night we were at a highfalutin' Spanish restaurant and Maurice was telling a story about a Moroccan he'd seduced on a beach in Tangier, and his boyfriend couldn't hear the last line of the story and kept asking Maurice to say it louder, and finally Maurice shouted it to all the startled diners assembled in the plush, large room: "SO I SUCKED HIM OFF!"

Who else fucks? I still do, very occasionally, if I'm in love, and in trust. And it is like being born, as Norman said.

My colleague Norman René—director of my plays and movies, with his perfectly correct posture and his delicate fingers and tiny feet ("The Prince" we called him)—he preferred kissing. But he fucked, too. We never did, the two of us, though everyone always assumed we did. Norman hated to discuss the asshole. Even if his doctor asked him something about his asshole, Norman would cringe. He was interested in human behavior, manners, the tiny gesture which revealed a world. A connoisseur of jokes, good food, foreign films, Italian furniture: he would go to the Mineshaft and drink too much and fuck.

Norman teaches me to look for the hidden. He reads every scene of a play over and over, imagining every possible interpretation of every word, line, look, pause, to seek out the deepest meaning behind the obvious. What is behind the obvious? Even the asshole itself is invisible when you look at, well, someone's behind. Standing before you. Lying there. They have to stretch and bend to reveal it. And all it shows then is the entrance.

Who else? Those fucked, those fucking. . . . I'm wearying from trying to remember, because they're all dead, as you knew they would be: Peter, Rick, Maurice, Norman, Hank. Harry. Irving. There are more. Geoff Edholm. I taught him how to fuck: beautiful, a tattoo of a bird on his upper arm, smooth, appears in the movie *Buddies.* My very first lover, Jess Richards, who didn't like to fuck, but taught me to treat the asshole reverently, that if it was clean it was beautiful, and why shouldn't it be? Jess played Ariel to Morris Carnovsky's Prospero at Stratford. Wrapped his arms around me in the bathroom on a break during rehearsals for *Kiss Me, Kate* at the Cincinnati Playhouse in the Park. And Ray Gill who was in the chorus of *On the Twentieth Century,* and created the role of Booly in *Driving Miss Daisy.* Ray could suck himself off. There, I remember that. Who else? Gene Masoner, who was in the chorus of *Shenandoah* and didn't really like to suck cock, had to sniff poppers to bring himself to taste it, preferred to fuck. Stuart White, the stage director, handsome with dark circles under his eyes, who fucked me; I sat on him and threw up all over him while we were fucking. Dead. Who else? Larry Peck, the ballet dancer; my lover and I picked him up waiting for the train in Sayville. Mart Aldré, my first accountant, former child star. Brad O'Hare, my friend, created the role of Griever in my play *Blue Window,* is in *Longtime Companion,* the waiter who goes into the park at night. To get fucked. Tim Wengerd, the ballet dancer I fucked at the baths. Shall I give you all the names? Let's just say everybody. Through with possibility. Spent.

Just writing this makes me wish for it. Say it with me:

Fucked.

Two Deaths, Two Lives
J. D. McClatchy

With a flamboyance that still makes me wince, Paul Monette decided to die in public. I watched it unfold in a small Manhattan movie theater. A new documentary had opened, by filmmaker Monte Bramer. It was called *Paul Monette: The Brink of Summer's End*. For several years before Paul's death, Bramer and his crew had followed Paul through his daily routine and public appearances, lecture circuit, and travel abroad, interviewing him and filming him being interviewed by others, hovering over the writer at his desk. In the film's final segment, the last six months of his dying, the camera with its cruel dispassion records his decline. The skin goes slack and waxy. His hair falls out. His tongue and nails are covered with hideous fungus. Karposi's sarcoma takes over his left leg. By the end, when he has decided to stop the medicines and his mind clears and calms, he has only enough strength to speak to the camera. He reads from an animal fable called *Sanctuary* that he's been bravely working on through his pain and the constant indignities of IVs, syringes, and pills, nausea and overwhelming fatigue. His voice is slurred, thinner. The fable itself—like the stories read to him as a child—has put to one side all the sexual and political battles Paul had been waging for a decade and returns to the themes of his early poetry: love, not rage, the difficulties of freedom rather than the exigencies of death. And then the final day. The film mercifully switches from video to photographs: his body shifted from one side of its pain to the other, the blank staring eyes of the Jew behind barbed wire. One last photo, black-and-white, of his dead body in his lover's arms.

Most deathbed photographs that come to the mind's eye—of Proust, say, or Hugo—have the calm of Veronica's veil. On Paul's lifeless face is still the mask of agony. Though the film quickly skips to conclude with an earnest voice-over and older, sentimental footage of Paul with his boyfriend and dog romping on a beach at sunset, that is not the image that has stayed with me. It is the dead face. It seems heartless to have so recorded what is, after all, the most intimate moment of a man's life. And yet those about to be left behind study the process with a merciless and self-defensive love. Monet, remembering himself at the deathbed of his wife Camille, wrote: "I found myself, without being able to help it, in a study of my beloved wife's face, systematically noting the colors." Or one thinks of Don Bachardy's drawings of Christopher Isherwood as he slowly caved in to cancer, ghoulish in their precision, loving in their ruthlessness. Or Simone de Beauvoir's scathing account of Sartre's physical and moral decay. Very occasionally the dying make their own record. Some novelists and poets have written up their last days. A few— Hervé Guibert, for instance—have made their dying into a performance to be filmed. Ever since I first met him, I was aware that Paul Monette loved having his picture taken. He was what you'd call a shameless mugger. I doubt he realized what he looked like at the end, and if he had, he would still have wanted himself shown—*put on display,* as it were. He wanted himself seen as a martyr, all the arrows of disease and injustice visibly in him. He wanted himself filmed as an example. It was a natural extension of the kind of witness he'd been bearing for a decade. And when he could no longer hold a pen, he wanted his audience to *see* what he'd been writing about.

One brief scene toward the end of the documentary especially haunts me. He's sitting at a table, obviously surrounded by medical technicians and the film crew. The phone rings, and when he hears who's leaving a message, he picks up the phone at once. "Hi, Sandy," he says. "I'm kinda busy right now." Good Lord, that's me on the other end of the phone! I even remember making the call. I was standing in my kitchen in Connecticut. I'd been telephoning every few days, aware at a distance of what was going on. I knew Paul could no longer read, and I'd been sending him coffee-table books filled with photographs of places he'd visited. We must have been trying to find a better time to talk because Paul says "Tomorrow's a bad day?" A further suggestion. "Oh, OK," he says, "Thursday is OK. I'm planning to be here Thursday." And soon enough, one Thursday he wasn't there. What's odd about this scene is that, instead of seeing the situation from my own point of view, I could see myself as Paul saw me. I could see myself as a kind of intrusion, another part of the paraphernalia surrounding him, sweetly or sourly bothering him. How cumbersome and lonely it is to die.

The inscription in my copy of his first book reads, "To my darling Sandy, my other self, my Southern comfort, my Henry Morton Stanley, my dear. Love

Paul Monette in New Mexico, 1986. Photograph copyright by Star Black.

always, Paul. July 1975." We had met a couple of years earlier, by chance invited to the same dinner party by a mutual friend who was teaching that summer at Andover. While our hosts washed the dishes, Paul and I bolted outside and roosted half-drunk on the vast school lawn, smoking cigarettes, and in the dark talking mostly to one another and occasionally to the stars. Right from the start, we adored each other, but for very different reasons. In me, then a graduate student at Yale, he saw an alternative to his gypsy ways; he saw someone in love with learning, with poetry, with Yale—where as an undergraduate he had himself been lumpishly unhappy. During our visits back and forth, either to my little house in New Haven, or to his succession of apartments in Milton, Cambridge, and Boston, we would talk rapturously over pot or pasta about Anne Sexton and Randall Jarrell, Virginia Woolf's newly released diary and the latest poetry gossip from New York. He thought my tastes, my take on things, both severe and serene. I, on the other hand, wanted only to sleep with him. He was everything I couldn't be: impetuous, melodramatic, *free*. Waving a new draft, he played the New England Rimbaud to the audience of my own blocked ambitions. He boasted of sexual conquests in a way that made me jealous—of the conquests, if they had actually occurred, or just of the boasting, if they hadn't. Here was someone—

a handsome, intelligent, self-indulgent, swaggering musketeer—I longed, if
not to *be* exactly, then to *have*. And I couldn't get to first base. Of course I pretended not to care that I might, though Lord knows I tried. The most sustained assault on his love was to be a trip—just the two of us, alone, on the
road!—to my parents' house at a southern seaside resort. As usual, I had
overplanned, fussing with my wardrobe, restaurant reservations, the best
combination of LPs on the spindle to share over nightcaps and unbuttoning.
Years later, in his memoir *Becoming a Man*, Paul himself wrote up the episode.
First he brooded on our teasing relationship: "So I played the same shell
game with Sandy that I'd been playing with César—bonded like brothers,
everything-else-but-sex. And because he was so decent, Sandy never pushed
for more, though now nearly twenty years later I wish he had." (*Now* he tells
me!) And then he describes the trip:

All the way down in the car, I told myself to go with it, not be afraid. I was beginning
to worry that I didn't know how to have sex with someone I *liked*. That I was falling
into the cycle of so many men I'd met at Sporter's, for whom the only hot sex was with
strangers, and it never got better the second time. Maybe I hoped the tropics would
free both Sandy and me. But it wasn't meant to be. No tension from Sandy's end: he
said the relationship could be whatever I wanted. Yet I felt myself back off in fear—
not quite Queen Cristina, since Sandy kept everything so unpressured and relaxed. I
also felt this hollow dread, that I'd finally meet the laughing man and let him slip
away because I didn't really believe I could bring it off. . . . But that week with Sandy
at Sea Island marked a profoundly important advance for me. It was the most I'd ever
shared with a man of my own kind. Our being gay was simply a given as Sandy and I
explored our hearts and writerly visions. Should we perfect the life or perfect the work,
and couldn't one have it both ways? It was the first time I'd ever considered that gay
might not just be about whom we slept with but a kind of sensibility, what survived
of feeling after all the fears and evasions of the closet. Sandy didn't quite buy that notion: he preferred to think of himself as a writer who happened to be gay rather than
a gay writer. But for me it was a watershed, to begin to think I could tap into that sensibility, however little I understood it yet. Certainly my writing would never be the
same, from this point on.

No tension from Sandy's end. How little he understood—which is as much as
to say how kind, how forgetful or forgiving, retrospection is. What Paul never
knew is that a few weeks after this trip, puzzled and frustrated, thinking now

of myself as undesirable and foolish, I read his journal and discovered the truth. I was visiting his Cambridge apartment, and when he went out to buy some wine for dinner, I stole into his bedroom, and madly thumbed through the diary I'd found under his balled socks in a bureau drawer. The most plausible entry said simply that there was no explanation for it but that I was just not his type. I closed the notebook, carefully put it back under the socks, returned to the living room, sat down with a novel and, like Patience on a monument, waited for Paul to return.

In any case, shortly after my discovery—which, after all, must only have told me what I'd long since guessed—Paul met Roger Horwitz at a friend's house and for the first time in his life fell in love. Though I never let on, I hated Roger for seducing Paul's heart away in an evening. I hated Paul for loving anyone but me—who had worked so hard, so "intelligently," to make it happen. It simply never occurred to me that Roger might be nicer, more sexy or supportive than I was. In time, it did. But in time, too, I had the sense to make a life of my own. Like Paul, I was tired of a half-hearted promiscuity, and decided to settle down. My way of doing that was walking into New Haven's one gay bar and deciding to strike it rich with the first person I could spot wearing a necktie—which I took to stand in for a whole set of convictions and repressions I'd find congenial. There was one over there, in a booth chatting with friends. I slid in and introduced myself. An hour later we were at my place, a month later we were a couple. And so began the slow waltz toward happiness, changing partners every dozen years, until the right one—at last!—came along.

In Roger, Paul had found *his* "right one." Roger changed his life gradually. And Roger's death changed it dramatically. In the years between these two events, other things changed as well—including our relationship. We were Best of Friends to the end, but the balance of emotion and interest shifted. Our friendship at the start was bound up with our shared desire to become Writers. Both of us were aquiver with literary pretensions and baffled resolves. Paul, of course, was the excitable one. He would send me a Xerox of the latest poem he was passionate about—by, say, Jean Garrigue—with a brisk note at the bottom: "I will *not* be your friend if you do not like this poem." His letters then were filled with the why-be-a-poet, how-be-anything-else blues. They were filled with accounts of his adventures with notebook and typewriter: the concentration, the frustration, the exaltation, and all of it garishly self-dramatizing. Here is a swatch from a 1973 letter to me, written from Milton Academy, where he was then forlornly teaching:

I have found a private place in the woods, only five minutes from my classroom, and I refuge there between classes, I wish so to avoid pontificating to the children. And I'm reading *Walden,* never have before (prompting my colleagues to shake their heads at me. Imagine, never having read Thoreau. I'll now admit that I've never read a Jane Austen novel either. Imagine.) I'm glad to have waited so long to decide, inevitably, that he is me.

The bravado of that—*he* is *me*—is characteristic, and at the time seemed only extravagant, even endearing.

One evening stands out in memory. At the invitation of my friend, the poet James Merrill, I brought Paul to dinner in Stonington, Connecticut, where Merrill had an apartment overlooking the harbor. Paul was eager to meet the famous poet. This would have been around 1974, Paul and I in our late twenties, Jimmy nearly fifty. It was just the three of us, for drinks and one of Jimmy's eccentric dinners: fish napped in blenderized leftovers, much vintage Puligny-Montrachet, and a sour cherry clafoutis with dollops of coffee yogurt that had gone off a week earlier. A dozen votive candles glistened in our wine and were doubled in the milk-glass tabletop under the ceiling's pressed-tin dome.

While they talked, I studied the pair. Most skittish young writers need mirrors in which to discover idealized—that is to say, false but useful—images of themselves. At least I did. In Paul, I saw a version of myself as I wanted to be, my brash and glamorous older twin. In Jimmy loomed what I wanted to be seen to have been, my much published, worldly wise uncle. My own moth-like uncertainties drew me to both men. Each filled in a piece of my puzzled sense of self.

The dinner lurched or glided along. Paul gushed, and at one point suggested we each read out our favorite poem. Did Jimmy wince? I could at least see in his eye a polite disdain for Paul's literary exuberance. And I could sense in Paul—who kept insisting—an impatience with Merrill's patrician reserve. Of course the host relented. So Paul read a tender monologue by Jarrell. I read something vatic by Yeats. Jimmy said he'd recite some Tennyson.

Paul and I sat up in our chairs. And from memory he recited a sonnet by Tennyson—but by Charles Tennyson, the laureate's nephew. It was "Letty's Globe," sentimental Victorian kitsch about a sleepy child's long golden hair falling across the Asia on her father's desktop globe. Merrill's reading was a splendid piece of leg-pulling—and a lesson too slowly taken to heart over the years. But then, as if to make amends, he extended the joke and suggested we all three take parts in a reading of Max Beerbohm's campy playlet "Savanarola Brown." Our timing was boozy, and the play's humor may have smelled of the sachet, but Paul and I—who'd never read it before—were convulsed. The evening was a success, at last, and at the door I should have known, as he smiled and waved, Jimmy had hours before decided it was not to be repeated. That my brother and uncle would never get along, while I could be the friend to each—this sort of family quarrel must have suited me at some level of mischief I confused with independence.

Then Paul moved to California. The visits continued back and forth. My fondness for Roger flourished. The letters and calls, though less frequent, were heartfelt and cheering. But within a few years, he abandoned poetry and took first to novels, then screenplays, then novelizations of films. The work grew charmlessly crass. Where before he longed to talk with me about Berryman or Lowell, now he bragged that he had lunched at a table near Barbra Streisand's or had bought the red convertible used by Richard Gere in *American Gigolo*. He boasted about an affair with a hustler. I instinctively—no, snobbishly—retreated.

Then AIDS hit. Roger died on October 22, 1986. Eight months later Paul had finished *Love Alone: Eighteen Elegies for Rog*, a sequence of poems that is a keening, a tumult of private and unrelenting force, and a moving historical document about the stricken soul. The preface to that book is his declaration of war. He first invokes the poet of the trenches, Wilfred Owen: "Above all I am not concerned with poetry. My subject is War, and the pity of War. The poetry is in the pity." Picking up Owen's negative urgency, Monette declares: "I would rather have this volume filed under AIDS than under Poetry, because if these words speak to anyone they are for those who are mad with loss, to let them know they are not alone." The poems spill their grief at the waste of love in long, thick columns of words, meant to invoke the inscriptions on a Greek stele. "I wanted a form," he wrote, continuing the military analogy with a terrorist twist, "that would move with breathless speed, so I could scream if I wanted and rattle on and empty my Uzi into the air." Finally, he offers his book to his fellow soldiers: "May it fuel the fire of those on the front lines who mean to prevail, and of their friends who stand in the fire with them."

It is heartbreaking to think of how many of those on the front lines in 1987 did prevail. And slowly I could see that Paul's definition of friends who stand in the fire was confined to the infected. I had by that time myself tested negative. That test result became a sort of translucent barrier between us. Paul let it be known that, from the Other Side, I could no longer understand him or the issues at stake. I daresay he was right, though I felt a tugging sadness at having been pushed to the perimeter of an inner circle I was once near the center of. This sense of a remove was only exaggerated later when, after Roger's death, Paul took new lovers—first Stephen Kolzak, a former television executive and AIDS activist who died in 1990 at age thirty-seven, and then young Winston Wilde who was with Paul devotedly at the end. Both men I found spiky and vulgar. (In the documentary, we're treated to Paul and Stevie's mincing video jokes about preferred sexual positions, and to Winston later remarking without a trace of irony, "That's when I realized. I told Paul we are a myth, we are enacting this great myth.") Yet, somehow, the friendship endured, though I had the sense then not of being with my friend but of watching him perform.

Some months after *Love Alone* was published, *Borrowed Time* appeared, with its classic opening sentence: "I don't know if I will live to finish this." It may be the best book he ever wrote; it is by far the most honest and harrowing. Its prequel, *Becoming a Man*, a memoir of his life until the day he met Roger, was published four years later in 1992 and given a National Book Award. It detailed all the losses that repression had occasioned, just as earlier he had dramatized the devastations of AIDS as the consequence of a political plot. Both books were his slave narratives, the account of his harsh masters, the closet and the government, and of his escape, his crossing over, into both openness and opposition. The danger lay in his becoming the cause's poster boy.

And that is precisely what happened. His bravery and dedication are undeniable. To some he gave hope, in others he stirred indignation. But when, playing the gadfly role, Paul took to the platform and preached to the converted, his targets were too bloated and easy: sissy Catholic cardinals and "wacko fundamentalists," Ronald Reagan and other "rat-brain politicians." His delivery was the televangelist's. His tone rarely modulated from *rage*. Rage is an emotion as calculated as any other, and particularly suited to drawing attention to one's self. His comparisons with the Holocaust only blurred rather than illuminated a dire public health crisis. But on he went, in his own eyes a guerrilla. His very last poems are saturated with bile. Everything is narrowed to one point. And on that point he spun like the star he had always longed to be. In ways that go beyond writing, of course, he had made his own condition into his text. He had traded ink for blood, images for sores, ideas for rage. He had achieved the celebrity he lived for by trading on his death.

Is rage righteousness? If this is what he had to do to stay alive as long as he could, who would gainsay it? Not I. Just as there is no blame to be attached to the course of a disease, so too should there be none directed at the means to combat that disease. And the standards for judging political rhetoric—the form Paul's rage assumed—are low. But if it is art one is after, if it is fiction or poetry one wants to use in the fight, then another set of standards is brought into play. Aristotle says somewhere that anger lives next door to the imagination. Certainly writers from Nietzsche to Celan, certainly poets from Ireland or Africa, say, have sharpened their pens on history's whetstone, though little of the literature of mere protest or resistance survives beyond the memory of whatever events occasioned it. A more private rage can result in more lasting work. Sylvia Plath is an example. In the swarming, suicidal hive of her bitterness she fashioned her own mythology of betrayal and isolation. The extremity of her circumstances and urges led not to a narrowing of poetic possibilities, but released an ironic lavishness of tone and metaphor. In the end, art wants clarity, subtlety, grace. This is not to say it need go gentle into the good night. Art wants fantasy and precision and force. It should mystify and scare. But finally, it wants moral weight and balance. To have made his death the meaning of his life and the sole subject of his writing left Paul without the means to achieve what he set out to do. His fear of death and hunger for life could only be channeled into fury at the lack of a cure. He couldn't make the time to catch at what was just out of reach. Art's afterlife eluded him.

Paul Monette died on February 10, 1995. Four days earlier, my friend James Merrill, one of this country's great poets, had died in Arizona. I had first met

James Merrill. Courtesy of J. D. McClatchy

him in 1973, at just about the same time I met Paul. And at the same time too, in the mid-eighties, both men were diagnosed with AIDS.

For years before he died, everyone knew that Paul was sick. It was his subject, his means to life. James Merrill had told no one—or no one but his lover, his longtime partner, and his lawyer, each sworn to secrecy. And until a slight physical erosion set in, years after his diagnosis, he kept the secret. In July of 1993, we traveled, together with my boyfriend of the time, to the Glimmerglass Opera Festival in Cooperstown. I remember sitting next to Jimmy the first night at a performance of *Così fan tutte* and out of the corner of my eye noticing in the light streaming from the stage how tired and wrinkled his face had become. The next afternoon, my friend and I went to a baseball game. When we returned to the hotel, Jimmy peeked from behind the window shade of his room, called to me in the parking lot, and asked if I'd stop by his room. He was sitting cross legged on his bed. I flopped in a chair in the corner. There was a bit of banter, then his face grew uncomfortably grim. "I want to lay something serious on you," he said. Again, I joked feebly, and said to go ahead. He paused a moment, then said flatly, "I've known for about seven years now that I have the virus."

Of course I didn't react. It was impossible to take in—*this* information from *this* man, my friend for twenty years, model and mentor, my ideal of integrity and order, discipline and artistry. So I numbly rambled on about doctors and medicines. He said he'd felt okay all along—until recently. The last blood test had told him his numbers were dropping fast. He had just begun, with reluctance, to take a course of AZT. Real weariness had set in. He said he'd decided to tell me because he wanted me to start covering for him, to give excuses to people, to mislead them in order to protect him. He was tired. And when I asked him if he wanted me to research new treatments, he said: "You know me. I'm one of those who just turn their faces to the wall when something like this happens."

A couple of years after his death, I read through Jimmy's journals, now housed in his archive at Washington University in St. Louis. One matter-of-fact entry notes that on April 1, 1986, at the Mayo Clinic, he was diagnosed with ARC. It is one of the few references to his disease he made in his journals, a series of notebooks kept over a lifetime and filled with intimate thoughts, astonishing dreams, and acid opinions, along with drafts of work-in-progress. Was he, in effect, keeping the secret even from himself? But what had struck me most forcibly that afternoon in Cooperstown was Jimmy's remarkable bravery: to have borne the news all those years by himself. A peculiarly iron will is required. In any case, having been entrusted with a dire secret, the first thing *I* did was tell someone else.

My own behavior having quickly grown erratic—alternately snappish and sullen—and for no apparent reason, there was a heightened tension at home. So I decided to tell my boyfriend. The bearer of A Secret, if he is to be of practical use, has himself to be secure, and I didn't want to live on intimate terms with someone and have a ghastly fact unspoken between us. That is one thing. But why, five years now after his death, tell the secret in public? Jimmy was by nature too polite ever to have extracted any sort of promise from me. But implicit in his revelation, his muffled *plea*, was my silence. While he was alive, I broke it two or three times as the situation deteriorated and I myself needed advice. But countless times I lied. I was untroubled by the deception, even in the presence of those who weren't taken in by it. After his death in 1995, I continued to lie—to old acquaintance, inquiring stranger, persistent reporter. I would be asked, "Did James Merrill die of AIDS?" And I would respond, "He died of a heart attack." Which was literally true—and I might then add off-handedly, "His father died of the same thing, and at the same age." Whether or not the questioner was convinced, for some reason he never then asked, "Well, did he *have* AIDS?" I kept thinking of my evasiveness as in service to what I had all along assumed Jimmy's own mixed motives to be: his mother, for instance, the embattled emotional center of his life, would have to be shielded, and by extension the rest of his family. His sense of decorum was inbred. Besides, he was part of a generation for whom dying is an embarrassment. I have a friend whose father, a man of Merrill's age, is dying of lung cancer and can't bring himself even to utter the C-word. And while cancer patients are thought of as the victims of implacable genetic forces, people with AIDS are often thought to have caused their own mortal situation. A death—at least this was true a decade ago—so stigmatized by the press and polite society, a disease so commingled in the common imagination with illicit sex . . . those of a certain temperament will reflexively shy from admitting or discussing it. As a man and also as a poet, his tone was that of high, serious comedy—the *dramma giocosa* of the Mozart operas, the dizzying paradox of the Wilde plays—and this is not a style that can readily deal with the AIDS epidemic or the earnest lugubriousness required of any "re-sponse" to it. After all, weren't Merrill's sessions at the Ouija board over the decades a kind of refusal to accept the gruesome circumstances and finality of death? Nothing is lost in translation to a conversation over lettered card-board and willowware cup.

I think he wanted as well to protect his lover from possible profes-sional handicaps (he was an actor) and from the certain opinions of his friends (with whom the young man was widely unpopular). But more than that, he wanted to protect himself, his time, his peace of mind. He didn't want to become a spokesman, a hero, a case study. He didn't want to run away with the AIDS circus, in the company of a menagerie of less than minor tal-ents hoisting a banner. He didn't want to have himself be the object of any-one's pity or praise because he was ill. Above all, he didn't want to be put on display, to be *shown* and thereby be made "monstrous." In our culture, with its appetite for intrusion and exposé, it may now be necessary to keep things secret merely in order to keep them private.

Or was it merely his "image" he wanted obscurely to protect, and is that why I continued to lie after his death? I think not. He knew what his renown rested on. I lied, first of all, because my friend, at a time of extreme distress, asked me to. My sense of moral responsibility has always radiated outward, from an inner circle of friends to more abstract spheres. Later I felt a continuing, though more tenuous, concern for his family. But after a few years, I began to wonder. For how long is such a promise made? How long must a secret be kept beyond the grave? Who exactly is being "protected," and from what—the truth? Shouldn't readers know the emotional circumstances in which his later poems were written? Wouldn't that knowledge affect, even enrich, their understanding of Merrill's work? In the end, I have come to feel an invisible hand nudging me forward to speak. I've come to think Jimmy would want the facts known. For once, he had had difficulty speaking about something; his lifelong frankness about his homosexuality never yielded to an ability to talk about the still more volatile subject of his AIDS. It was the only situation in which I'd ever found him literally speechless. Nor was it a matter we talked about between ourselves, behind closed doors. I've always felt that the initiative at such times, however indirect, lies with the dying. He spoke, with some bored reluctance, of medicines and regimes. I persisted with my research, and would report to him. There was a doctor in France . . .

I had a friend who was on such-and-such. . . . Merrill's interest always flagged, and the conversation was adroitly steered toward more companionable matters.

I remember, late in the game and for a clamorous reason, telling a close friend of his the news, and then telling Jimmy what I'd done and why. I waited for a scolding. But he only said how relieved he was, not so much that the friend now knew but that *he* didn't have to tell him.

In 1993 Merrill published his memoir, *A Different Person*, about a stay abroad in 1950. It's not a book "about" the events of that period, but about the effect of those events (and of his "difference") on a life that is slowly turned into art. His mother did not want him to publish the book. She'd had a cataract operation just in order to read the manuscript, found it too revealing, and begged him to suppress it. The poet's account of his own homosexuality, and of her hostility to his "tendencies," is frank and, in retrospect, slightly comical. Against his mother's wishes, Merrill decided to go ahead with it, and in March of 1993, he wrote her a letter to explain his decision. "Dearest Mama," it begins, "I would have liked to abide by your wishes, but the impulse—the *need*—to publish the memoir overcame my hesitation." The letter concludes this way:

You said the book made you see yourself as a bad mother. Don't believe it for a minute. I see my nature as my own—mine to discover, mine to express in what I've written and how I've lived; to be untrue to it would amount to suffocation. The longer I live, the more clearly secrecy strikes me as a great source of unhappiness. (I suppose I'm like Daddy in that.) Anyhow, the book begins with an unspecified estrangement between us, a mutual loss of trust. Bit by bit the story comes to light. Telling it in print may be the wrong thing to do; if it opens me to criticism, I'll just have to live with it. By the end of Chapter XIII—thanks in large part to its having been told—the story is laid to rest and our behavior (mine as well as yours) forgiven. You have prayed that our differences be resolved; I've written a book in that same hope. Between us we've done our best.

Of course the irony behind the eloquence here is that, while justifying his resolute honesty and declaring his abhorrence of secrecy, he is simultaneously keeping a fatal secret from her. But just beneath the letter's surface pounds an impulse he returned to again and again in his poetry: what he called "the unstiflement of the whole story." The broken home created by his parents' divorce, the carousel of erotic adventurism and domestic routine on which his life turned, the mess of self-illusion, the miracle of unconscious forces—all of these motifs his poems stitched and unstitched on the fire screen he placed between himself and the world. Early on, his poems indulged in an obscurity he presumed his ideal readers would penetrate. Later, a sometimes startling openness prevailed.

At one point in the memoir, he has an imaginary conversation with his mother, who admonishes him: "Why, why does all this have to be spelled out? . . . Don't imagine, son, that these are things people need to know." "But," he replies, "they are things I need to tell." It is no wonder, he goes on, that over the years the forbidden fruit of self-disclosure grew ever more tempting.

The spirit of the times ripened it like a kind of sunlight. The very language was changing. An article saying that I "lived with my lover in Athens" sickened you—what would the world think?—until I was able to point out that by 1970 "lover" denoted, as it hadn't in your girlhood, either a man or a woman. . . . Came the day when even the behavior you find so shocking, which by then lay decently buried in my past, or in my poems, was clear to anyone who still cared. As in the classic account of Sarah Bernhardt descending a spiral staircase—she stood still and *it* revolved about her— my good fortune was to stay in one place while the closet simply disintegrated.

Or all but. There was one shock he still withheld. If he couldn't bring himself quite yet to reveal it then, I can no longer think—given the pattern of his art, and the uses to which he put his experience—he would want it stifled now.

Two days after he told me the news, I started keeping a diary. If Jimmy now feared that time was turning against him, and because I needed some way to order my feelings, a record of things might be useful, I thought. Now that I glance over its pages, are they themselves a sort of documentary film? Here are some black-and-white excerpts:

3.viii.93 Stonington
Last Thursday, having returned from Chattanooga, I saw JM on the street and asked him to dinner that night. After the meal, he went by himself into my darkened living room (I stayed with DJ in the dining room) and listened to Mozart's four-hand

sonata, the one he and DK used to play. Two days later, he asked me over for dinner and told me he'd "turned a huge corner" while listening to the Mozart. For the longest time, he said, he hadn't been able to listen to music at all, or write—anything. Suddenly the pills kicked in. He's on Zoloft, a Prozac-like mood stabilizer. That night he seemed nearly manic, but it's a lot better than the deep, deep depression he's been in.

15.ix.93 Stonington

J saw a new doctor in Norwich yesterday. The point was to have a local doctor to hand, in case. He knew who J is, and was flattered by the visit. Given the records he'd read, he'd expected to see someone in worse shape. He "approved" of the medicine J is taking (limited AZT, and a drug to replace the Bactrim which made him turn red), and told him to return in six months. J had seen Dr. Montana in NYC the week before. His T-cell count is unchanged, but his "proportions" (?) are lower: 0.9. Not great, but stable . . . is the sense I have from his tone.

Tony Parigory has died in Athens. JM has watched his two closest friends—Tony and DK—die of the same disease: both of them unsparing mirrors for JM to stare into.

4.x.93 Stonington

JM has named me, he says, his Health Care Partner, which I guess is the term for the person who has final responsibility for medical decisions if he's incapacitated. Ray has been named the back-up.

Last week, Jimmy gave a reading at Yale, and we spoke together beforehand in my office. He's been saying how tired he is nowadays. He's OK in the morning, but the least strain exhausts him—a block-long walk, say. He wonders if the medicine may be the cause. He's on something called Darzone (?), a replacement for the Bactrim. He's going today to ask the NYC doctor about buying one of those machines that treat the lungs. This has the advantage of the medicine not going into the system; but the medicine also protects against intestinal trouble and dementia. He mentioned that at his last routine visit his T-cell count was the same (he didn't tell me the numbers) but that his platelets had fallen from 200,000 to 100,000 in three months. When it comes to hospitals he said he'd take himself off to the one in Pittsburgh. He has a doctor there. And he distrusts NYC hospitals. Another reason, he said, is that his old psychiatrist Tom Detre told him that "Katherine and I will see you through." He wonders if—and hopes?—this means Detre would give him pills to end it if the situation deteriorates badly.

JM has—or seems to have—only a moderate will to fight. One heard—or I heard—that same melancholy undercurrent in his reading that night. "Prose of Departure," of course, with its line "Nobody has to live, dear boy." JM's face looked tired.

He napped when he arrived at my office in the afternoon; didn't meet with students; went to bed as soon as he returned to Woodbridge with John and Natalie.

21.xi.93 Stonington

When I returned here yesterday, there was a message from J on the answering machine. His voice sounded stricken. I telephoned him in NYC at once, and he sounded—a day later—much better. He said the doctor (I presume on the basis of results from last week's blood work) had ordered an immediate series of tests. Spinal tap, CAT scan, etc. I'd guess they're looking for brain trouble, associated with the trouble he has with his balance. He was to go to Cabrini Hospital, but Tom Detre has persuaded him to fly to Pittsburgh.

This is the first outward sign of trouble, and the cover-up gets slightly more awkward.

18.xii.93 Stonington

J (in NYC) went today to have his blood oxygenated, something his nutritionist (to whom he regularly sends hair samples for analysis) recommended. He told me yesterday his T-cell count had dropped from 100 to 70, and the white count along with it.

He is perceptibly weaker. On Monday night (the 13th), he gave a reading at the 92nd Street Y. He had a cold and a sore throat. Even so, it was a dramatic sight— and I wondered if it was his last Y reading, nearly fifty years after his first. He stumbled a little as he walked; had forgotten to bring a copy of one poem he'd meant to read; looked thoroughly weary. PH, in a high hysteria he mistakes for helpfulness, canceled the party (given by someone else) planned for afterwards. The next night I substituted for J at an Academy event, just reading the introduction he'd written for Rick Kenney and Trude Schnackenberg. At the 72nd Street apartment that afternoon (to pick up the speech), he and P were arguing over the need for help. I don't see that J needs to be made a patient before his time. The point is to keep things normal, without exhausting him. But in fact, he's tired all the time now: two or three naps a day, etc. Perhaps Key West will help. Eleanor's told me a couple of times: I hope there's nothing really wrong with him that he's not telling us.

4.i.94 Key West

JM, DJ, and Barbara Hersey were here for dinner last night. ("Here" is 1424 Washington Street, my rental for the next month.) J looked terrible: haggard and listless. From the kitchen I overheard him—again—fail to come up with a word. He doesn't seem frustrated at such a moment, just utterly blank. He spends most of his days now in bed. He is most himself on the telephone, and social occasions rouse his old self—or a slower version of it. I've been trying to stay close without hovering. I've taken him shopping—and watched him unable to come up with the term "chicken broth." I've made phone calls for him, and helped him sort through the accumulated mail. He just manages. He complains of being cold. I went with him yesterday to the drugstore to buy a heating pad (also pills made of a marijuana derivative, meant to prompt his appetite: he says he has none, that food tastes bad). In temperate weather he's wearing silk long underwear and sweaters.

8.i.94

Two days ago, I felt under siege with the problems of others—Jimmy, arrangements for DJ, my mother's tears in Sea Island, S's wife begging for help, etc. Besides, I feel isolated and lonely in this empty house. I called Mawrdew for advice about S and ended up telling him about J. His advice is always sensible. He in turn urged me to tell Eleanor. I'll have to live with her long after the fact; it's not fair; she's my friend; etc. So I called. A long difficult conversation—listening to someone else's shock. At once she was convinced that [X] gave it to J. I keep repeating to her that it doesn't matter; that only J and the future matter. I pledged her to silence; she said she'd be guided by me. (I must say, J's own stories about how he was infected seem far-fetched. But it's in the nature of this disease that the accounts of its onset are shrouded in repression, lies, half-truths, forgotten circumstances, etc.)

17.i.94 Key West

As part of the Key West Literary Seminar, J gave a reading from the memoir two days ago to a packed house. He looked thin, and his voice is weaker, higher in pitch. He brought it off well—though immediately afterwards Charlee Wilbur drew me aside to say how worried everyone is about him, his looks. Ed White, who had dinner here with J the next night, called me up later to say the same thing: JM's decline is startling.

I'm taking him to the gym three times a week, and want to get him out in the sun to improve his color. His hair seems to be thinning, and the white scalp adds to the overall pallor.

He seems, though, a little better than when he arrived. He went yesterday to the local doctor for a Pentamadine treatment.

23.i.94 Key West

Though he looked bright at a dinner party last night given by Barbara Hersey, J reports himself continually exhausted. Ray told me on the phone this morning that he plans to tell his mother in Palm Beach in February that he has leukemia. Nearly everyone now—after they call J—telephones me, to ask what's wrong. The slurred speech, the vacant pauses, etc. I retail the familiar line. Still, there are calls that stop one. Charlee Wilbur the other day: "Dick and I have figured out, without anybody saying anything to us, that Jimmy is very sick. You seem to be in charge. Is there anything we could do?" I notice at cocktail parties with Ed White and Hubert how much and how bluntly Ed talks about AIDS. J is silent as he does so.

I made the mistake of asking J if he wanted to go see the movie Shadowlands. "Not a film for me now." I could have slit my own throat. He's giving a little dinner party tonight—Dorothea Tanning and friend, Marie-Claire Blais, the Weeks's. I've bought all the dinner for him, and will help him "do" the evening. It's good to keep up—for his sake—a semblance of the old routines, though he takes little interest in them, and is done in by them.

15.ii.94 Stonington
J is back in Pittsburgh. . . . When I asked him what the P'burgh report on his blood work had been, he shrugged. He didn't know. "If it had been good, I suppose they would have said so." He seems very weak and absent. Resigned, passive even. There's every reason to believe the AZT will provide some respite. But for how long?

20.ii.94 Stonington
J is back from P'burgh. And says he feels good, though the fatigue remains. The doctors say he is anemic—and AZT may exacerbate that. So he has shots of Epigen, to counteract that tendency. He'll now go to P'burgh once a month, for examination, Pentamadine, etc., doing everything at once.

17.iii.94 Stonington
JM much improved since starting AZT again. Still looks frail, but is steadier on his feet and mentally much clearer. The fact that he feels better, in turn, raises his spirits. March 3rd was his 68th birthday. PH gave a party for ten. A very jolly occasion, and topped off with a cake decorated with a laurel crown. P very solicitous—and one has to give him all credit.

But underneath, and as I knew, all is not well, and it exploded on Sunday night the 13th. I was in NYC, asleep, and had a call from Ray in S'ton, saying that P had called, out of his mind, but that J had gotten on the phone to say everything was under control. Ray was worried. So I called—heard the same thing, and told J I'd be up in a taxi. When I arrived, near midnight, the apartment was a ruin. Furniture upended, pictures thrown from the wall, J's bedroom door smashed in, glass and broken lamps all over the place. P was red in the face, frothing at the mouth, ranting about how ungrateful and slave-masterish J is, how he'll commit suicide, etc. My first impulse was to get J out of harm's way. The sight of him obviously infuriated P, and I only provided a new audience for his scene-making. I took JM back with me to 16th Street, put him to bed, pulled out the sofabed for myself and tried to sleep—though P called three times during what was left of the night, raving. JM was scheduled to fly the next day to P'burgh. I persuaded him instead to return with me to S'ton. I think he was glad for the peace, though he was (at the time) eerily exhilarated by the melodrama. EP may be right to think that a fight, a scene, is urgent with life—and so, unconsciously, desired, even provoked. Certainly J's "co-dependency" will get them back together again, in ways the average observer would think intolerable.

Hubert Sorin—Ed White's dear lover—died yesterday in Marrakesh.

8.iv.94 Stonington

JM had an attack of pancreatitis a couple of weeks ago. The doctor thought it a result of AZT toxicity. This must have been a psychological blow to JM—the medicine itself (which had given him such a boost) seeming now to turn against him. His pancreas count was very high: 1400.

31.v.94 Stonington

JM has looked well these last weeks. His numbers, though, don't look as good. His platelets have dropped; so too his hemoglobin count. Dr. Montana has told him to stop the AZT—which J did last week (to his great relief). He'll see the doctors in P'burgh on the 6th, but right now thinks that, because of his greater practical experience, Montana's caution is better than P'burgh's advocacy of AZT. Besides, Montana thinks there is something else to be tried—D14 or some such name. The statistics are, I think, about so: hemoglobin, below 10; T4's in the high 60s; T8's in the 70–80 range.

23.xi.94 Stonington

I haven't made an entry here for a long time because JM has been well. Today, though, on the phone from NYC (and just back from a trip to Chicago, St. Louis, Ohio, and P'burgh) he said that he thought he'd turned a corner in the disease—headed in the wrong direction. For the most part he's normal, though he tires easily. On some days he looks better than on others. As usual, those who haven't seen him for a while are struck by his "fragility." But most of the time he passes quite handily. A couple of weeks ago, though, there was an episode that bothered him. He found himself suddenly in a muddle: disorientation, not making sense of his calendar, etc. He knew something was up, and Montana suggested that at such times he resume the AZT. (He's been taking a substitute that begins with Z.) Dr. Hunt has now said that if these episodes recur, he's to go back on AZT "for the rest of his days." She's also putting him on a pill to prevent or forestall the onset of—is it MIA? A brain disorder that clouds the minds of, say, 20% of AIDS patients. I'd guess this is JM's fear, though he also realizes it's a benign fate from one point of view. His numbers, I gather, have drifted a bit lower, but the doctors are content.

He's ever more dependent on PH and on their relationship, on P's "caring" for him. P has moved to Hadlyme; Cosmo the dog very much completes the family. That JM feels part of a "family" seems tonic in itself.

There are no more entries because he seemed happily to improve, or at least to have stabilized, which is why his death a couple of months later came as a shock. He and his lover had rented a house in Tucson for January and February—a move that made an odd kind of sense when one realizes that, as a child with a vaguely asthmatic condition, Jimmy had been sent to live in Tucson one winter. A new book was scheduled for publication in March. He was writing new poems. His voice and prose were both strong. His calendar for later that spring was already filling up—he was even planning to take a new young friend to his first opera at the Met in April. A few days before his death, he was writing long, witty letters. Then, a sudden attack of pancreatitis. He's admitted to the hospital. The bother is, it means a long-planned cataract operation will have to be postponed, though no one expects this to be a hospital stay of more than a week. On February 4, we speak by telephone of this and that. But his breathing seems labored. And early in the morning of February 6, 1995, while he is sitting in a chair in his room, perhaps aware that if it was not soon it would be now, his heart just stops.

"Freedom to be oneself," he once wrote, "is all very well; the greater freedom is not to be oneself."

There are those, flushed with the fashionable jargon, who would claim that James Merrill lived in a state of denial. (Myself, I'm in favor of a good deal of denial.) But he was acutely aware of his disease, of its course and its consequences. After that last diary entry, I remember going with him to purchase a plot in the Stonington graveyard. I know that many of the bequests he had made in his will—these rare Japanese prints to one friend, that painting or statue, Fabergé letter opener or bronze Buddha hand for another—he began giving away to their intended recipients while he could see the delighted smiles on their faces. All the arrangements for his papers and literary executors were updated. Then he went on living.

In the decade between his diagnosis and his death, he published two new collections of poems, *The Inner Room* in 1988 and *A Scattering of Salts* in

1995, plus a new *Selected Poems* in 1992, his memoir, *A Different Person*, in 1993, and an abundance of incidental prose. He was at his desk nearly every day; only travel or bouts of illness kept him from the routines he had established half a century earlier. Surprisingly, the disease rarely makes itself felt in his work. Or, as one villanelle opens:

> Upon reflection, as I dip my pen
> Tonight, forth ripple messages in code.
> In Now's black waters burn the stars of Then.

Most of the poems of his last years are flickering reflections on *Then*—his family, his crisscrossed love life, various states of grace occasioned by travel or domestic happenstance . . . a new dog or windbreaker, each made over into an emblem of the mysterious powers of life breeding beneath us, brooding over us. Memory is his muse. The work of memory is most grandly conspicuous in the book he jokingly called his *me*-moir. *A Different Person*, his most sustained self-examination, is an enchanting meditation of the growth of the poet's mind—or rather, his sensibility—that necessarily involves an account of his becoming a practicing homosexual. ("Practice makes perfect," he liked to say.) There is an openness here—wry but forthright, elegant but detailed—that is new, and startling to some more prudish readers. That the action of the book transpires at the very time—the fifties—he was writing his most bejewelled and opaque poetry suggests he wanted to turn the tapestry around, to show the scramble of threads, all knots and loose ends, out of which he wove the elaborated patterns that he hoped would implicate without revealing his secret life.

Something, as he says, collapsed. From the mid-1960s on, his poems are more candid. The dodge behind ambiguous pronouns or a scrim of lustrous adjectives disappears. The flush of erotic passion, the maneuvers of romance, the cold wisdom of heartache—these are the pulse of his poetry. And when, from the mid-1980s on, Merrill wrote about AIDS, he did so in a way few of its victims ever have. There is no rage, no sentimentality, no up-close-and-personal. He writes about how he and his friends took their leave of life. He writes an apologetics of aftermath. He is the supreme elegist of AIDS.

His first such poems—and they are placed last in *The Inner Room*—are a pair of elegies in sapphics for his friend David Kalstone. They are poems that have attracted composers to set, critics to analyze. One is a dream, the other a metaphor in which art "cures affliction," the dead friend's ashes scattered onto the Sound, the box held underwater by the poet to free all it contained: "that gruel of selfhood / taking manlike shape for one last jeté on / ghostly—wait, ah!—point into darkness vanished." In that same collection is a more extended elegy for Kalstone called "Prose of Departure," a Basho-like travel journal about a trip to Japan undertaken while his friend was dying back home in New York. (At the time, I was darkly puzzled why he would undertake such a trip despite Kalstone's imminent death. Now I can understand Merrill's reluctance to face what awaited both men.) It is filled with petals and cemeteries, and ends with a fabulous kimono, "dark, dark purple traversed by a winding, starry path," the bolt of death flung outward from the vats of night and wound loosely around the body. But my favorite little allegory about death in "Prose of Departure" is one Merrill pretends that Kalstone once told him. I prefer to think of it as the way one friend departed from the other:

The Emperor's boyhood friend was convicted of treason and sentenced to death by decapitation. In honor of their former intimacy, the Emperor ordered the execution before dawn, after a banquet for his friend at which the Court dancers would appear. That legendary troupe could perform anything: the Spider Web, A Storm at Sea, the Nuptials of the Phoenix. On this occasion they outdid themselves. Yet well before the stars had set, the doomed man turned to his host: "The Son of Heaven has shown unmerited consideration, but really, can't we call it a night and conclude our business without further ado?" The Emperor raised his eyebrows: "My poor friend," he smiled, "haven't you understood? Your head was cut off an hour ago."

The poems he wrote in his last months (in his journal, one can see he was working on a new poem just the day before he died) there are a few sidelong glances at his condition, but it's as if he had better things to write up. One poem, "Days of 1994," seems sweetly valedictory. Another, "Christmas Tree," is a tiny parable in which he imagines himself as the holiday centerpiece, the cord for his electric lights "a primitive IV / To keep the whole show going."

> Yes, yes, what lay ahead
> Was clear: the stripping, the cold street, my chemicals

Plowed back into the Earth for lives to come—
No doubt a blessing, a harvest, but one that doesn't bear,
Now or ever, dwelling upon. To have grown so thin.
Needles and bone.

But looking out, he sees an image of himself as a child, the little boy whose mother thinks *Holding up wonderfully!* "No dread. No bitterness. The end beginning. . . . Still to be so poised, so / Receptive. Still to recall, to praise." It's not that the resignation in these lines is blind, but that it has turned to look backwards: necessity swaddled in nostalgia. In much the same way, it's not that Merrill was keeping something a secret for the decade after his diagnosis, but that he was keeping something private. His health was crucial to his life but not to the art that continually transformed that life into literature.

It may be that his strongest words on the matter are in poems from *A Scattering of Salts*. The strength is, first of all, a kind of rawness. "Tony: Ending the Life" remembers his old Alexandria-born friend from Athens, Tony Parigory. Their louche times together, cruising the bars in Athens, are one memory, along with a beard Merrill sported at the time: "over throat and lips had spread a doormat / On which to wipe the filth brought in from the street."

"Just see," the mirror breathed, "see who's alive,
Who hasn't forfeited the common touch,

The longing to lead everybody's life"
—Lifelong daydream of precisely those
Whom privilege or talent set apart:
How to atone for the achieved uniqueness?
By dying everybody's death, dear heart . . . .

In Tony's case, it was first a botched suicide attempt:

Blood-red ribbon where you'd struck your face.
Pills washed down with ouzo hadn't worked.
Now while the whole street buzzed and lurked
The paramedics left you there,
Returning costumed for a walk in Space.

The nurse thrust forms at you to sign,
Then flung away her tainted pen.

At last, the peaceful end, in a dull delirium of memories. Merrill's fantasy of an afterlife—its props familiar enough from his Ouija board writings, though with all their color drained away—is another version of the purple kimono with its wash of stars:

The sea is dark here at day's end
And the moon gaunt, half-dead
Like an old woman—like Madame Curie
Above her vats of pitchblende
Stirred dawn to dusk religiously
Out in the freezing garden shed.

It is a boot camp large and stark
To which you will be going.
Wave upon wave of you. The halls are crowded,
Unlit, the ceiling fixtures shrouded.
Advancing through the crush, the matriarch
Holds something up, mysteriously glowing.

Fruit of her dream and labor, see, it's here
(See too how scarred her fingertips):
The elemental silver
Of matter heading for its own eclipse
And ours—this "lumière de l'avenir"
Passed hand to hand with a faint shiver:

Light that confutes the noonday blaze.
A cool uncanny blue streams from her vial,
Bathing the disappearers
Who asked no better than to gaze and gaze . . .
Too soon your own turn came. Denial
No longer fogged the mirrors.

You stumbled forth into the glare— . . . .

But the book also includes a poem in quite another key. "Vol. XLIV, No. 3" is an earlier version of the diseased self as decorated Christmas tree. It's an eerie trope: the symbol of the redemptive Nativity used to embody one's mortality. This sonnet—the form of many of Merrill's greatest poetic triumphs—is not unlike so many of his poems that open with him gazing into a mirror, a mirror that is itself sometimes described as an open grave. Here the mirror is a slide under a microscope. In a poem that deals in microcosmics, the infinitesimal is described galactically.

> Room set at infrared,
> Mind at ultraviolet,
> Organisms even stranger,
> Hallucinated on the slide, fluoresce:
>
> Chains of gold tinsel, baubles of green fire
> For the arterial branches—
> Here at *Microcosmics Illustrated*, why,
> Christmas goes on all year!

He is looking at the enemy, his murderer, and his first impulse is to duck behind a metaphor. By the end of the poem that metaphor will yield to myth. But first, in the next stanza, he seems to let down his guard, and mix his metaphor—except when the reader remembers one version of history: that Christianity brought about the fall of Rome.

> Defenseless, the patrician cells await
> Invasion by barbaric viruses,
> Another sack of Rome.
> A new age. Everything we dread.

The poem's clinching couplet, with a gesture and diction that are positively Yeatsian, takes the Christian myth—that in the end is our beginning—and makes a defiant affirmation, at once fierce, numinous, and consoling:

> Dread? It crows for joy in the manger.
> Joy? The tree sparkles on which it will die.

For both James Merrill and Paul Monette, death—or rather their slow dy-ings—distilled their lives, wrung out an essence. Paul's activism, even his ex-tremism, was a part of the extravagance that had marked his style as a writer and as a friend. His outsize gestures pushed his death away by forcing others to confront it. Would it be fair then to characterize Jimmy's behavior as "paci-fist"? I think not. His fatalism was as much an attitude, a protective col-oration, as Paul's defiance. To the end, he wanted to view his condition as just another (albeit mortal) stage on which life acted out its terms. He treated his disease as he treated every other occurence: as a phenomenon to be ob-served, absorbed, pondered, transformed. AIDS was not the end of life. Though he died on the verge of pharmacological advances that have since prolonged the lives of patients, he lived as they do, with a wary confidence and due resignation, and the determination to work as if there were no to-morrow, to return to us by way of his art all that life had given him.

Scott Burton

Robert Rosenblum

Scott Burton streaked through our lives like a comet, a human phenomenon of such blazing intelligence and energy that, when he left a room, everything seemed to get dim as we returned to dull, familiar earth. Even if he hadn't given the art world a legacy of masterful, three-dimensional public and private works that, against all odds, fused sculpture and furniture in what he referred to as "pragmatic sculptures," he would have left an unforgettable dent in the memory of everyone who knew him.

He himself was small, neat, and wiry, perhaps the most compressed nugget of energy I ever knew; and, like his own lapidary art, he had an unyielding presence. Extremely well educated in all the humanities, with a B.A. in English from Columbia University (1962) and an M.A. from New York University (1963), he never stopped reading, looking, and learning with the zeal of a new graduate student. From this, he acquired plenty of ammunition for the frequent announcements of his latest enthusiasms and hates, which usually went against the grain of all shared beliefs. In the 1970s, for instance, he would claim that his friend Philip Pearlstein's neorealist canvases of nude models, objectively recorded with scrupulous detail, were far more avant-garde than any of the minimal art (including his own) we were cheering. He could surprise you, too, by asserting that such almost forgotten American painters as Guy Pène du Bois or Kenneth Hayes Miller were major artists; or, contrariwise, he could make you wonder whether you and everybody else hadn't been overestimating Matisse and Picasso, who were ripe for a reality check. His seemingly perverse opinions were not pronounced for the sake of camp, but because Scott had genuinely been smitten by new enthusiasms and new challenges to inherited prejudices. To know him was to be constantly disarmed by his fierce passions and loathings, which could quickly move from the realm of art to the realm of people. For Scott, there were no shades of gray.

His range of experience and knowledge was vast. I remember, for ex-

Scott Burton, from the Equitable Center project. Courtesy Max Protech Gallery, New York.

ample, our taking him to visit Gilbert & George's astonishing neo-Victorian home in East London, a domestic shrine crammed with what most would consider brutally ugly furniture and liturgical objects, from candlestick holders and chalices to coatracks and iron garden benches. Scott was already familiar with it all, amazing us and his hosts with a specialist's knowledge of the history of Victorian design. And reaching in different directions, I remember, too, his wild excitement about new television shows such as *Pee Wee's Playhouse*, which for him opened up a delirious world of furniture and decoration.

Of the many unforgettable things about Scott was his almost insane mix of old-fashioned propriety and new-fashioned sexual liberation. For us northerners, the fact that he came from Alabama seemed to account not only for his slightly southern accent but for a politeness and measured grace that in New York seemed to be an endangered species of behavior with antebellum roots. But the reverse side of this coin was his wild streak of 1960s-style rebellion. Back in the early 1970s, for example, when Scott and I were on the same ocean crossing, his public displays of same-sex kissing and fondling dropped the jaws of many passengers and crew on the SS *France*. Looking like a right-wing preppy in his conservative and expensive clothing, Scott, as the saying goes, could make a truck driver blush.

His seesawing balance between outrageous behavior and the most aristocratic good manners was very much part of Scott's particular role in the world of our family. Throughout the 1980s, he was an essential part of our domestic life—virtually a godfather to our two children and a frequent dinner guest. As for the children, his supply of affection and generosity was endless. He would shop for hours to find the perfect policeman's uniform or cowboy belt for Theo; and when Sophie was all of eight or nine years old, he would arrange Saturday afternoon tête-à-tête dates of old-fashioned ritual—first, lunch in some ladies' restaurant, the kind that served popovers; and then, a matinee which might introduce her to the Broadway musicals he cherished and knew by heart. Such gentility, I recall, even extended to the lemonade he once offered when we visited him and his boyfriend, Jon Erlitz, at their summer rental in Greenport, Long Island. Instead of buying his lemonade in a carton or a bottle, as the rest of us might have done, Scott had meticulously followed a recipe for the homemade variety that he had looked up in an ancient cookbook. For a moment, we seemed to be back in his birthplace, Greensboro, Alabama.

As for his boyfriend, Jon seemed to provide the id to Scott's superego. Greasy, bearded, leather-jacketed, booted, and tattooed, he was first sighted by Scott on one of the West Village piers, and when they finally connected, it was a marriage made in heaven or, for many of their hosts, in hell. Scott's impeccable manners (when he wanted them to be so) were instantly and grossly contradicted by Jon's appearance and demeanor, which might have passed muster in a lowdown leather bar, but which barely reached the level expected of housebroken guests. They would always arrive as a clinging pair, but while Scott would scintillate with ferociously and brilliantly delivered opinions, Jon would come and go from the table in yawning boredom, usually taking a handful of magazines to read in the nearest toilet, a habit which Scott indulgently overlooked or perhaps even admired. As amateur shrinks, we decided that Scott liked to impose his beloved Jon on higher society in a slightly sadistic way, in order to make us all squirm while he smiled proudly at Jon's antisocial antics. He took Jon everywhere, which included a memorable weekend at our own summer rental on Shelter Island, where we were members of a small and stuffy beach club conveniently located down the road. When we arrived there with Scott and Jon in tow, many eyebrows were raised. But the focus was even sharper when they stripped to their bathing suits, an event that made even us sit up and take notice and that we guessed must have been traumatic for the other club members. Suddenly, in this time capsule of American beachside exclusivity and decorum, there appeared an S/M fantasy of nipple rings and tattoos, of which the most startling were the blue spiderwebs in the shaved skin of both of Scott's armpits, now fully exposed to the sun and to everybody else. It was hard to reconcile this with the Scott who, in London, insisted on staying at the most stuffy, old-fashioned hotels, such as the Cadogan (where Oscar Wilde, in fact, was arrested), and who haunted Savile Row, where he would order, say, six pairs of specially tailored corduroy trousers. And then, giving America equal time, he would order, on trips west of the Mississippi, the most extravagant pairs of fitted cowboy boots.

Scott and Jon together always ended up being something of a circus, and the minute they left, you knew you had accumulated enough riotous stories for a morning of phone calls. But throughout the eighties, the shadow of AIDS kept darkening over Scott, perhaps accounting in some part for the last-ditch extremities of his behavior. His condition worsened, and in the summer of 1989, while he was having a major retrospective in Stuttgart, he suddenly fell so ill that he had to be hospitalized there. Our whole family was in Europe at the time and, not being able to leave the children alone, first Jane and then I paid Scott a visit. The German doctors and nurses seemed to be fascinated by him, not only because of their eagerness to learn more about AIDS patients, but simply because he was a mesmerizing person. When I nervously approached his hospital bed for our first conversation, which I feared would be awkward and maybe tearful, he immediately picked up the ball and started running, giving a loud discourse on what he most objected to in James Stirling's new and highly praised art museum in Stuttgart. He presented his critique like a lawyer for the prosecution, in lucid, informed sequence. I think he wanted to show me right off that his mind, if not his body, was still functioning perfectly, and it was.

Thereafter, his body weakened rapidly. He knew he would die soon, and he gave himself a heartbreakingly elegant adieu. On December 18, 1989, in his huge and stylish loft on West 36th Street, he pulled together a small but lavish party for a handful of friends. The event was appropriate, of course, to the holiday season, but also to the clock he must have felt ticking inside him. Surrounded by the fancy caterers he had hired for this poignant occasion, he held court like an aging southern gentleman. Too weak to stand, he summoned us up one at a time for what we all knew might be a final conversation. Eleven days later, on December 29, he died, fifty years old. His obituary appeared in the *New York Times* on January 1, 1990, sadly marking the beginning of our first decade without Scott.

Robert Farber

Patrick Moore

As I write this, I am flying to Europe to negotiate with local authorities for an exhibition of my friend Robert Farber's paintings in a historic building in a city that received pilgrims during the time of plague. I will discuss his work with people who never knew him, who will not understand why he was important to me. Robert would have been astonished to think of his paintings moving around the world, carefully held in crates, the subject of innumerable shipping documents and insurance policies. The happiness this would have brought him is the happiness that I feel in helping to make sure that his work is remembered. The story of my life over the past ten years weaves in and out of Robert's story as we moved to different cities, seeking different things; he running out of time and me unaccountably being given some more.

My only real chance at remembering Robert here is that every person whom I've loved is embedded in me forever, with all their glory and their faults, so in telling my story perhaps there will be glimpses of his.

The generation that survived the plague could not believe but did not dare deny. It groped myopically towards the future, with one nervous eye always peering over its shoulder towards the past. Medieval man during the Black Death had seemed as if silhouetted against a background of Wagnerian tempest. All around him loomed inchoate shapes redolent with menace. Thunder crashed, lightning blazed, hail cascaded; evil forces were at work, bent on his destruction. He was no Siegfried, no Brunnehilde heroically defying the elements. Rather, it was as if he had wandered in from another play: an Edgar crying plaintively, "Poor Tom's a-cold; poor Tom's a-cold," and seeking what shelter he could against the elements. Poor Tom survived, but he was never to be quite the same again. (Research notes from Robert Farber's journal, 1991)

On the cusp of a new millennium, I live the life of a medieval man. I talk with spirits at night when the cold darkness of desert air surrounds me in Los Angeles. I look for signs in the playlists of Southern California radio stations. I visit a woman on La Cienega to buy candles in honor of obscure saints or with pictures of Shiva on them. I leave food for the dead on full moons. I sit with my brothers and sisters in moaning, soaring sweat lodges praying for healing, praying for others, praying for myself, praying in gratitude. All this from a hardened New Yorker, bitter and cynical, who used to march the streets in rage. Los Angeles is a wondrous and ridiculous place, much misunderstood by New Yorkers until they flee here, burned-out. When I came to Los Angeles, I was running from many deaths, including that of an unlikely friend named Robert Farber. In a way, I was also fleeing a kind of hardened quality in my soul that seemed much like death in its finality and resignation. I had come to a shallow place looking for deep answers.

In the end, I think I care more about artists than I do about art. The passing fashions of greatness seem always to be wrong but I can say, without doubt, that artists and, in particular, visual artists, have always affected me as people. I cherish their willfulness, the inherent lack of definition in what they do with their lives, and wish that I could be less rational, less coherent myself. Robert found his way to the art world late in his life after having pursued a career in the theater for ten years. I too started out in the theater but found it a little too collegiate and friendly and quickly found myself attracted to the cold, mysterious ways of the art world. I love that the art world is about money, and I've always been fascinated by the "house of cards" aspect of selling objects of intangible value. I was once sitting at dinner with two friends who are considered important in the museum community and asked them what it felt like to really be at the white hot center of the art world. One of them said, "You are at the center. You're soaking in it." It's like going to Disneyland, slipping through an employee door, and seeing Snow White sitting there having a cigarette and Mickey washing out the sweat stains in his costume. Perhaps that is why I value the person more than the work with most artists; I can see in myself how my view of objects changes from year to year and, in the end, I trust my aesthetic judgment less than my feelings for a person.

Convergent forces in Robert's life led him to a burst of creativity that belied the distractions that surrounded him. I think it is a terrible thing to have to make a statement while the pressure of death builds behind you. Robert made his statement with one group of works, the Western Blot series, but I have a feeling his heart was more in the last few abstracted pictures done just before his death. These pictures picked up again his love of abstraction and physical beauty but with a power and emotional maturity lacking in his early work. The polemics and thought that he poured into the Western Blot pictures were very much of a moment, and they are his lasting contribution. They are his legacy because he did not have time to make a more complex one. I knew, however, during the last few times that I visited his studio, that his oeuvre could have been even greater since he had begun to find his voice and his eye and his hand just as he was forced to abandon his work.

Both Robert and I had lives that were alternately serious and superficial, and I find that I have let many things into my life that I would have thought myself too refined for several years ago. (Although the theater remains in exile for the moment.) The fact is that neither Robert nor I really fit into that terribly cool New York art world that we both aspired to and lived on the fringes of. If there is one thing that I know without a doubt that Robert and I shared, it is a deep yearning to belong. I am struck by passages from Robert's journals that could have been my own in describing a childhood spent trying to contain his homosexuality, trying to keep a lid on the effeminacy that inevitably seeped out, revealing him despite his efforts to hide. The fag beaten in high school, the adolescent resenting his father—these roles are hardly unique, but what surprises me is how they persist into adulthood. Robert and I both resented the hell out of the beautiful, butch boys in ACT UP and the effete, successful art dealers who had no time for us. Always being on the outside becomes very tiresome after a while and, eventually, I chose to be on the inside of a new life in Los Angeles. Robert and I spoke by phone after I left New York, but I regret that I was never able to share with him many of my experiences in L.A.

Robert and I were both addicts of the cocaine variety and our addictions were marked by lofts and vacations and jobs and cars and souls so spiritually wounded that we filled them with the pleasures of the material world. We required these pleasures as a poultice for our wounds in a world that often seems unaccountably empty in its splendor. Robert recovered from his addiction many years before I did but I understand, reading his journals, that he continued to reach out his arms to other comforts. His fears and needs were increased by his awareness of his HIV status.

Monday 1/27/92
Round Hill, Montego Bay
Away from New York, away from my studio, my routine, I see it's with me every
minute. Even as I sit under a huge rubber tree on the beach with the turquoise blue
sea and distant mountains, I feel it more than ever, that there's no help, that I'm in a
field of danger that separates me from others, that gives my life, no matter where I go,
an air of desperation and fear. No matter how beautiful and peaceful the setting, I sit
up straight, super aware, waiting in the dark for a glimmer of hope, knowing it's a matter of time. (From Robert Farber's journal, 1992)

Robert's few surviving journals are extraordinary in their mix of historical research, drug trial summaries, ACT UP meeting notes, investment reports, rent
calculations, travel magazine clippings, and ruminations from Fire Island
and other luxe settings. Reading the descriptions of Tuscany, Venice, Paris,
and the Pines, I realize that I resent Robert's wealth even as it benefits me. (I
am the director of the Estate Project for Artists with AIDS, and Robert's foundation has been extremely generous to our work.) I also recognize in retrospect how similar our wounds were and that our responses to the world were
differentiated mostly by the disparity in our bank accounts rather than our
spiritual inclinations. I wonder, if he had survived, what he would have made
of the new me. He most likely would have joined me in the cabala classes and
I would have happily accepted his invitations for weekends in a grand house
on Fire Island. Robert was reading about Schopenhauer in 1991 and, in his
journal, he copied a paragraph from Roger Kimball's essay "The Legacy of
Nietzsche," in the *New Criterion:*

Since willing springs from a lack, from deficiency, from suffering, he (Schopenhauer)
had a pessimistic view—all satisfaction is a prelude to fresh desire. Willing and its a
priori sense of lack is the condition of man.

In other words, nothing from the outside can fix it. It is clear to me that
Robert understood, quite aside from his medical condition, that the houses
and trips and purchases could not save him from the lonely emptiness that
was at his center. In depicting his family, particularly his father, in his paintings, Robert consistently portrayed a sense of isolation. Robert never really
belonged to anything, but it seems to me that, in a terrible way, Robert be-

longed to AIDS. It was his defining moment, and the drama of the time pushed away many of the barriers that stood consistently between him and the rest of the world. Looking at his work, speaking with his family and friends, I have to say that Robert's illness provided him with direction for the first time in his life. That direction was to have a terrible and tragic finality, but I think that it also revealed him at his best and kindest.

I should write of Robert's work because it always irritated him that I seemed more interested in him than in his art. Robert was not a frivolous person and his work was terribly important to him. I must keep in mind another thing that Robert wrote in his journal as he watched the perfect waves from his beach house: "The only thing I can hope to achieve is to leave a record that says I am here. I was here."

In my opinion, one of Robert's best works was a video installation entitled *Sorry for the Interruption* that depicts an idealized beach scene in an unspecified location that could be Fire Island, Provincetown, South Beach, Laguna, or any other hyper-beautiful beach resort where gay men flock in the summer. The sand is the color of a sexy tan, a beach chair arches out in architectural perfection, and an umbrella has been planted at a jaunty angle. The sky and sea are that tone of blue that is limitless, promising that this beauty is eternal. As the theme song for *A Summer Place* plays and the oversaturated colors sparkle, a shrill siren builds and a small circle of black appears on the horizon. The black circle grows, not unlike a lesion, and the sky slowly reverses out to a nightmarish and toxic landscape. As the screen goes blank, text appears—"Please Stand By"—and the loop begins again. Over and over, year after year, we gay men have returned to these beautiful settings that are beset by almost unbelievable loss; we are desperate to attain the sense of casual abandon that existed years before. I think of how it must have been for Robert in that beach house, incapable in all of its art-directed splendor of chasing away the ever present dread.

Another word about *Sorry for the Interruption* . . . it is extremely irritating. Imagine that music and siren over and over and over again. Robert seemed to revel in his ability to grate on people's nerves; he was a natural member of ACT UP. When Paula Cooper installed the piece in her Wooster Street window for Day Without Art in 1994, the audience in SoHo found the piece a bit too effective. An artist named Renee, whose particular contribution to art history has been endlessly to spray paint "I Am The Best Artist" all over SoHo, immediately complained. Apparently being the best artist took a great deal of concentration in his studio. Robert took as much joy in annoying Renee as in having his work displayed in one of the most respected galleries in New York.

Robert was fascinated by the power of sound; three years before the stridency of *Sorry for the Interruption,* he had created a sound installation titled *Every Ten Minutes* that was shown in museums and galleries around the world for the 1991 Day Without Art. *Every Ten Minutes* consists of a recording of a bell ringing at an interval that, at the time, indicated the frequency of AIDS deaths in America. The idea was so simple and so powerful, the rich tone of the bell drawing in listeners before reminding them of the horror it represented. It marked a time before Robert's anger took over and, although mournful, was not without hope. The bell had something of a medieval tone that would occur later in visual form in his Western Blot series.

Robert's research notes indicate that it was the view of historians that the mood of a plague period is best reflected in the art produced immediately after the plague. I disagree. The immediacy of the experience reflected in Robert's pictures speaks to me, pulls me back into tumbling emotions that I yearn to discard. Robert's pictures could be more accurately described as composites, floating grids of images, voices, and architecture that span centuries of fear. There is little redemption in these pictures, almost no hope. From his most significant body of work—the Western Blots with their cold modern medical references tearing into ornate medieval architectural elements—to the final paintings in a resolved dead blue, red or, most sadly, concrete, this is work about resignation. The flood of voices in these paintings sometimes terrifies me when I think about Robert, makes me believe that, for him, there was no rest in his resignation. Although the text in these pictures is quite affecting, it is when Robert revealed his hand as a painter that I am most moved. For example, in *Western Blot #11,* there is a sad, sleepy eye that watches over a white-on-white panel filled with little cross-hatchings, lines to count the dead. Then there are strange departures from the tomblike style of the other Western Blots. In #15, one half of the painting contains a roughly life-sized portrait of Robert on a wood panel but the other half is made on reflective Mylar, forcing the viewer to stand in the picture while reading the following text:

To look at me, you'd never know that I was HIV+. I mean I look okay. You'd never know that I have lost 400 T-cells since last summer. I mean I could be standing here beside you right now, reading this like any other person who happened to walk into the gallery and you'd never know the chaos and menace I carry within me 24 hours a day. You'd never know that I must take Bactrim, AZT and ddI and many different vitamins throughout the day just to keep my head above water. For now I'm managing to stay afloat. But I'm treading water every minute of the day hoping that I do not tire before a life-boat comes to bring me back to dry land. What a joy it would be to feel my feet planted on the sureness of firm ground where expectation and anticipation didn't always include a core of darkness and fear.

Robert's body of work concluded with a series of abstracted works such as *Narrow Escape* or *Concrete Painting* or *Solitude* or *Fly Away*, and these pieces articulate his experience in an even more profound way than his textual paintings. In *Narrow Escape*, a canvas is painted in concrete with the exception of a thin strip where a photograph of fluffy white clouds against a blue sky shows through. These were the clouds that Robert watched on Fire Island while feeling the concrete heaviness of his situation pressing down. I take comfort in the simple but incredibly rich blue field that is *Fly Away*. (I don't know if Robert had seen Derek Jarman's extraordinary last film, *Blue*, in which the filmmaker simply projected a screen of flickering blue while talking and talking and making his peace.) But between the abstraction and the words and the images, I think Robert left us with an indelible memory of New York in the late eighties and early nineties as it was being ripped to shreds by AIDS.

Three images of Robert haunt me—one from before his death and two more, either imagined or real, from beyond. I feel the necessity to describe the first although it causes me pain to remember it and it would have caused him pain to think of it in print. By describing it I hope somehow to drain the power from it and exorcise it from the reality of how he died, so in conflict with how he lived. Robert was one of the first artists who seized upon the Estate Project's work. He was as voracious about the estate planning information my colleague Randy Bourscheidt and I were developing as he was about data from drug trials. Long before we published our report and guide to estate planning, Robert was asking me for rough drafts to show to his lawyer. I can see the information scattered through his journals, influencing his plans as he faced death. He was so resolute, so driven. I remember the sharp slope of his nose, the intensity of his eyes, and the cut of his voice when the world did not suit him. He faced death with such fearlessness that it turned death into something different—a project, I guess. In my own pain, I never once considered that he was terrified. This was partly because Dino, my lover who died about two years before Robert, had reacted so differently to death. The loss of Dino, the one man whom I loved who returned my love unconditionally, scarred me in ways that are only now revealing themselves, and the sorrow of his loss became, for many years, my persona, the thing that I had to hang on to because it defined me. If I let go, I thought, what would be left of me? But Dino's death did not prepare me for Robert's because Dino was not afraid. Gentle, kind soul that he was, Dino reached up to death and let it take him. Not Robert. That same resolute quality that served him so well for much of his life turned on him as he died because he felt, perhaps even more than in his surrender to addiction, that he had lost.

The experience that I hate remembering was his last stay in the hospital. I was, by that time, living in Los Angeles, and I went to New York, not ready to venture back into a hospital. I must confess that, after Dino died, one of my greatest reliefs was no longer having to go to hospitals—and yet I found Robert imprisoned in one. There is so little humanity in the cold blue walls of hospital corridors, littered with random equipment resting after invading countless bodies. The pieces of equipment always remind me of abandoned cars, evidence of terrible accidents. I stood that day outside his private room at NYU Medical Center, dreading going in. When I did, I was confronted with what remained of my friend, surrounded by his family and those to whom he had entrusted his work and his money. I will never forget the terror in that man's eyes. The flesh was mostly gone from his face and all I could see were his huge, dark eyes darting back and forth, searching for something to hold on to. I wonder what he was seeing at that moment. Surely he did not see some shining beacon welcoming him to the next world, because he was clawing so desperately, trying to stay in this one. His strength was gone except for one last remarkable act. There were certain decisions that still needed to be made and, aside from legal necessity, all of us wanted them to be his decisions after he had spent so much time setting up the framework to carry them out. When I asked my friend those last questions, I saw him summon up something from deep inside and his eyes became sharp. In those few moments, I saw him one last time, he saw me one last time, and the plans were completed so that he could finally let go. Later, sitting in the lobby of NYU Medical Center, where I had sat so many times before, I put on my newly acquired L.A. sunglasses and rocked back and forth, crying. There was no fixing this.

Robert came twice to me after his death. Once in his New York loft, I felt that I was losing my mind when a photograph of him began to look a little too three-dimensional and I found myself sobbing uncontrollably. A more powerful event, though, occurred one night when I was deep asleep and saw a door in my dream. As the door opened and Robert stepped through, it was as if I were driving a convertible on a road by the ocean and accidentally hit the button to retract the roof. Air rushed past me like warm water, enveloping me, as I sat up in bed, wide-awake and crying. Robert would have said that I'd inhaled too much incense at yoga, but I know that these things are real . . . for me. And, if they're not real, I don't really care in the end because they have changed me somehow into a person with hope again.

I met Robert in 1989 when I was working for the wild and wonderful Anne Livet in New York. Her firm, Livet Reichard, had created Art Against AIDS as a fundraising vehicle for the American Foundation for AIDS Research (AmFAR), and I was hired as the Project Manager. I immediately hated the job, primarily because the abhorrent politics of AmFAR clashed so resoundingly with the ACT UP platform that I had endorsed. Robert called up and offered to volunteer for the project. From his first appearance I was leery of him because it was clear that Ms. Farber was not going to be stuffing envelopes. He was dispatched instead to try to find donations of salable art. What Robert brought back was a quite beautiful abstract painting of his own that he donated to our Washington, D.C., sale. I don't think Robert had sold many pieces and, when I sold his painting to a nice couple from Virginia for a sizable amount, I won his heart. We continued to work together later on the second ACT UP Auction for Action where he managed to piss off a number of important people in the art world by demanding that his painting be hung in a better position. Robert also bought several pieces from that auction including work from Nan Goldin, Jean-Michel Basquiat, and Kevin Larmon (not a bad investment in retrospect, as there were no reserves at the auction).

I was enamored of anything cold, conceptual, and expensive in New

Robert Farber, Western Blot #19. *Courtesy of Patrick Moore and the estate of Robert D. Farber.*

York. Consequently, I was deeply ambivalent about Robert's work. He asked me to write an essay for the catalog for his solo exhibition at Artists Space in 1992. After reading it, he said, "It's not clear whether or not you actually like my work." Today, though, I have no difficulty in saying that this is work worthy of attention. Perhaps time is giving it the distance it needs to be bearable. In the same way that movies about the Holocaust sometimes make me shut down because the horror of it is almost too great to grasp, I am sometimes overwhelmed by these paintings. Robert left me a painting, *Western Blot #19,* and it is an extraordinary work, filled with significance and meaning. The two main elements of the painting are texts. The first text reads:

I, as among the dead, waiting till death do come, have put into writing truthfully what I have heard and verified. And that the writing not perish with the scribe, I add parch-

ment to continue it, if by chance anyone be left in the future, and any child of Adam may escape this pestilence and continue the work thus commenced.
John Clyn of Kilkenny, Ireland, 1349 A.D.

Written in another hand, the chronicle continued, "Here it seems the author died."

Below this text, Robert included another field of words reading:

Someday the AIDS crisis will be over, and when that day has come and gone, there will be people alive on this earth who will hear that once there was a terrible disease and that a brave group of people stood up and fought, and in some cases died so that others might live.
Vito Russo, New York City, d. November 1990 A.D., 44 years old

Here, it seems to me, is the essence of being an artist, and the true intention of Robert's work. His stated wish was to have it known that he was here, but the real legacy is that he continues that discussion begun in 1349 by John Clyn. These paintings are a repository for history and, if on first viewing, they seem too much or too obvious, they are also incredibly brave. One day I will donate Robert's painting to a museum and, hundreds of years from now, someone else will feel a pain that seems unbearable. That person will believe his or her suffering is so great that no one else could ever have felt something similar. Perhaps that person will look at Robert's words and John Clyn's words and my words here and take some comfort in knowing that everything that happens has happened before. What a comfort to know that we are not unique, not even in our suffering.

Homage to Joe
Keith McDermott

In a photograph taken in 1980, Joe wears his shirt—as always—unbuttoned to expose a moderately hairy chest and a very flat stomach. His lips are parted in a sexy dumb way, but dark-framed glasses slightly nurdify the whole open-shirted, open-mouthed look. Next to him—upside down—is another figure, identifiable only as a pair of high-top sneakers, blue jeans and T-shirted torso cropped at the nipple line. With one arm around the airborne legs of the figure, Joe looks like he's posing with a prize catch.

I was that catch, standing on my hands for this portrait, taken during our first year as boyfriends. Showing off. Or perhaps, knowing Joe's pervasive shyness, I had dived out of frame to give him focus.

I still do. "Joe Brainard was an artist," I explain to people who have never heard of him, "The Tibor de Nagy Gallery mounted a retrospective of his work two years ago: paintings, drawings, and incredible collages—once, he had a show with 1,500 collages!" Since the number sounds implausible even to me, I may add that Joe, like many of his contemporaries, did speed. "He was also a writer," I add, "best known for a book called *I Remember*, a memoir, full of short personal reminiscences, all beginning with the words 'I remember.'" I may even move to bottom-of-the-barrel bragging which feels very un-Joe. "*People* magazine once did a story on him as a sort of nutty New York artist sitting in a loft full of paper bits obsessively making collages."

I rarely mention he was my lover.

The truth is that even during our years together, Joe had someone else in his life, which is a lot like saying he had another life. Every year from May through September he lived in Calais, Vermont, with his friend of some twenty years, Kenward Elmslie. During our months apart Joe and I wrote letters.

I accepted the arrangement. As an actor, my life—even where I lived—often changed from job to job. A marriage, especially to someone older, someone who had already made a reputation and had more money, threat-

Christopher Cox, untitled photograph of Joe Brainard. Courtesy of Nancy Cox.

ened to swallow my fragile sense of independence. The summer separations
came as a welcome respite. But by July my letters to Joe ached with the anger
and hurt of missing him. Late in August, the second summer after we met, a
journal entry written from the tarred roof of an East Village rooming house,
reminds me of my feelings: *Tonight Joe and Kenward gaze into the very same
evening sky, I am jealous of the moon.*

     I remember a feeling, the spring evening I met Joe in 1979, of floating
on other people's plans. After two years in Los Angeles, I had just returned to
New York to rehearse for "Meeting by the River, " a play written by Christopher Isherwood and his lover, the painter, Don Bachardy, which had an
eye-blink run on Broadway. The friend I was staying with had organized a
welcome home event, supposedly on my behalf, but the guests were all
friends of his who barely knew me. I was relieved when my ex-roommate, Edmund White, stopped by on his way to another party and in the hushed tones
he reserves for literary praise or gossip, told me, "Joe Brainard is giving this
fiftieth birthday poetry gala for his friend, Kenward. You remember Joe—the
collagist? Shy and has a stutter? And they'll be lots of cute poets and painters."
Without hesitation, I followed him down to the street and into a cab.

At one end of the crowded loft where the party was in progress, a small stage had been built. Occasionally someone went up, rang a little bell to get the crowd's attention, and offered a tribute or poem to the guest of honor. I met Kenward, a pleasant, heavyset man with thick glasses and congratulated him. And I met Joe.

Joe was tall, lean, and elegantly dressed in a sports coat and a silk shirt unbuttoned to the waist. He was friends with Isherwood and Bachardy: he had seen the play and told me I was good. He spoke so softly I had to turn my ear closer to hear him, close enough to catch his smell of Oil of Olay and tobacco.

An Andy Warhol superstar, looking oddly dowdy out of drag, lurched onto the platform to deliver a long, barely intelligible tribute to Kenward, before being encouraged back into the party.

"He gets a little drunk," Joe explained, unnecessarily, "but he means well." A renegade consonant—the "b" in "but"—stuck in a short volley of stutter as Joe's lips froze in the trumpet shape of the sound, his hazel eyes fluttering wildly, as if to blink out the word.

Joe offered me a cigarette, shaking one from his pack, and lightly touched my hand as he lit it. We both took guilty puffs and twisted our heads to the side to blow out the smoke. I glanced at his open shirt, wondering about this touch of flamboyance in a man so shy—or nervous. (Later, he told me that he'd worn it unbuttoned ever since a friend had complimented his stomach.) Looking up, I caught him staring. He said my eyes matched my blue shirt—a silly compliment to cover an undercurrent of attraction: the unmistakable vibration reminding us, even in polite circumstances, that we are animals.

We chatted. Joe was going to Vermont in two days. I wished him a good summer, thanked him for the party and said goodbye.

"Hello Edmund? Sorry I didn't say goodbye last night. No, I didn't stay long, I had to get back to my own party. . . . by the way, I liked your friend, Joe."

The message, as intended, reached Joe before he left the city. Ten days later, I received a letter written in clear grammar-school caps generously spaced across lined paper and peppered with underlinings, exclamation marks, *SIGHS!s,* and *GULP!s.* In this first letter, as in all his later letters, Joe misspelled words, drew hearts or rays around the word *you* and shaky letters to indicate turning into jelly.

My address, which Edmund had given him, "has been burning a hole in my pants, or . . . er . . . pocket." Seeing me in the play and later at the party ". . . flipped me out so much I can't even recall the experience." Then he went on to describe our brief meeting in some detail. He claimed he'd had a thing for me even before he'd seen me, but didn't explain how or why. He also told me he was "a ripe 37 (tho not all that ripe)," that he had been persuaded by his friend, the poet Ann Waldman, to quit using sugar and coffee, which had made him "ga-ga," and that was why he hadn't replied immediately. He also wrote proudly of gaining five pounds and asked me if I wanted a "pen pal."

I wrote back, telling him, as he'd asked me to, a little about my life at the time: how I'd just moved back to the city from L.A., how I was staying with a friend but searching for my own apartment, about the Robert Wilson play in which I'd just been cast. I imagine I saw-and-raised his innuendo about the hole in his pants "er . . . pocket." And then I didn't hear from him. I sent a postcard asking, "Where are you." The reply in his next letter, "right here," and the rather flat description of his activities made me feel I'd somehow scared him off with neediness. A few days later I received a thick letter containing his *actual* second letter, which had been returned to him, along with a note explaining the drama of crossed letters and cursing himself for mis-printing my address. This tiny misunderstanding and its resolution began the meltdown of our emotional reserve. "Lots of Love" became "Love" which became—if not "I love you"—an open acknowledgment that our letter-writing romance had become the dearest part that summer for both of us.

For me, this epistolary relationship was as exciting and as fraught with self-doubt as any face-to-face love affair I had ever had. A letter to Joe might be composed and carried with me during the course of several days. There was the thrill/anxiety as it fell from my hand into the postbox. Then came the anticipation of receiving a reply, cursing the casual tardiness of the mail carrier, or imagining, during a busy day away from home, a thick envelope addressed in Joe's familiar script consecrating the mailbox.

Joe often placed himself at the start of a letter on the lawn, in a chaise, near the lake or house and told me what he was wearing. I selected certain images, to picture him as I read: Joe, tanned, in a black nylon bathing suit against a Vermont lawn of violent green; or by the lake, dressed in khakis and a crisp white shirt (unbuttoned, of course), the last sharp light of a setting sun caught within his glass of Campari and soda. Later, photographs and paintings by Joe substantiated my idea of his summer retreat, but the house and grounds, given his friend's wealth, were more modest than I had imagined.

My favorite part of a Joe Brainard letter, often its climax, was some perfectly observed happening in the course of his nothing-much-going-on summer day in Vermont. And he wasn't unaware of his effect. The following passage from a letter written to me later appeared in a book of collected writings, aptly titled, *Nothing To Write Home About:*

A thrilling and tragic thing happened this morning on the front porch, where some sparrows built a nest under the eave, to lay their eggs in, which hatched into babies, that kept getting bigger and bigger, until finally this morning, right in front of my very eyes, they just got up and flew the coop! As though there was nothing to it. (Or as though they'd been sneaking out at night, secretly rehearsing behind our human backs.) And so as though by some pre-arranged signal—like "One, two, three, go!"— they got up and went. Fanning themselves out, each into a different direction, each into a life of its own. All except for one, that is, who flew right into the side of the house with a tiny "thud" and—alas—is of this particular world no more.

During the summer, Joe asked me to send a photo, "Tho *please* not a flattering one (a guy can take only so much you know) and I kid you only half." Actors have hundreds of glossy photos, but I chose a few "civilian" snapshots to send, none of them unflattering. In return, I received a small envelope marked "*YESTERYEAR,* A PHOTO-PUZZLE FOR KEITH WITH *LOVE,* JOE." Inside was a photograph of Joe, taken, judging by the tie-dyed T-shirt (his single article of clothing) and the hair (lots), in the sixties, and cut into heart-shaped jigsaw pieces.

We both added enclosures to our letters. He sent me Vermont leaves, drawings, rare postcards in glassine envelopes, old deeds, foreign currency and bits of interesting papers, tiny collages, Speedo bathing suits, and money. I was slightly shocked, when I went through the letters, to find how often Joe sent me cash: new hundred dollar bills or checks. Not long ago I discovered a two-hundred-dollar check still tucked into a poetry brochure and an uncashed thirty-dollar check so he could "be the first to buy flowers" for my latest sublet. Rereading the letters, I now see that Joe anticipated my embarrassment by including a postscript detailing his pleasure in giving me money, how he had "too much" and besides "I'm older than you" (though he was only seven years my senior). At some point, he told me frankly, he'd been given stocks or bonds, enough to live off the interest—I kept my understanding of this arrangement vague.

I nearly always cashed Joe's checks. Initially, I suggested the money was a loan. Even now I'd like to qualify, to describe my actor's life back then—but having said that much is probably saying enough. Joe wrote back explaining he never made "loans." He felt they were unhealthy between friends, so only gave "with no strings attached!"

Twice that summer, Joe sent letters to friends we both knew, requesting an "invisible date." The enclosed cash, he explained, was to pay for a dinner for three, including himself in absentia. Afterwards, the friend was to write back, describing the evening—and me. "I got a letter this morning from Jonathan, telling me all about our date—(even what you wore: down to the red tie)—and I never dreamed I could not go on a date and enjoy it so much: *so much!*"

Our letters grew more romantic and more spiced with sex. Joe cast himself in the role of "raunchy" older brother, and we both felt free to include pages of pornography. In the foreword to a book of Joe's drawings, the poet and art critic John Ashbery might also have been describing Joe's writing when he said Joe's porn studies show "how a 'hot' subject would appear to a mind uncluttered by notions of it (pornography)."

Recounting a "wet dream," Joe wrote, "I took you back to my modern white home—(very Frank Lloyd Wright)—with a shower as large as a big room . . . but before we took a shower, you said you wanted a breath mint, and so from a conveniently located box of sugared violet flowers, I began literally pouring them in your mouth and down your throat. Moments later, in the shower, during one (our first!) long kiss, I started (couldn't hold back) coming all over you."

By August, our letters were full of references to that "first!" kiss, but the anticipation was not always comforting. Joe worried a September meeting could never live up to the heights reached in our epistolary courtship. He was no bargain, he hinted: skinny, stuttered, smoked too much. At the same time he never doubted my allure and continued to praise my good looks and desirability.

It was very flattering, but I was also full of insecurities—and the air is thin in Paradise. I did, however, possess an actor's professional distance regarding my looks and a physical confidence that made *sex* seem as uncomplicated as rain. My letters to Joe grew *more* romantic, suggestive, and relaxed. "Look," I was saying, "let's not slow down—this is too much fun."

Then I got a job that took me out of town until November.

While I was away, we continued to exchange letters. Joe mailed "care packages" to my hotel filled with books, pictures, and odd postcards. Finally, on a clear fall day in November, six months after Joe and I met, I returned to the city—and our first date.

Joe came downstairs to let me in the street door, I gave him flowers, and when we briefly kissed, I recognized the smell of recently gargled Scope mouthwash. His Greene Street loft was divided into two big rooms. He led me quickly through an unlit back area, used for storage, muttering something about the mess, into a large, sparely furnished living area with big windows facing the street. This room included a small open kitchen and a bathroom behind double stained-glass doors installed by the previous tenant. There was no showing around to be done; the desk, couch, and floor-level mattress were visible from any point. Joe poured us wine, and we stood in the kitchen alcove to avoid the last harsh rays of a sun setting beyond Canal Street. The loft was dark when we broke from our first real kiss. On the way to dinner, I felt exhilarated and silly, with the odd sensation of having *flown* with time.

On our first restaurant date and on many after, Joe brought along little homemade books. In lieu of talk, we wrote back and forth like Beethoven and his nephew or documented meals with tiny drawings of the food: an oyster on the half shell, inky lines of wine cascading from a bottle, tiny french fries and a miniature steak.

"We had a great time," a friend once told me after a dinner date with Joe, "but I felt like such a chatterbox because he never said a word."

Joe's silences were not bred from overfamiliarity—a dead space between people who have nothing much left to say—but were full of nervous mannerisms: lip-popping, nodding slightly to a silent tune, a stuttering of eyelids when he saw me watching; often, he appeared *about* to speak. When he did, his mouth would hold the form of the first word for several seconds before he made a sound.

He always aped my order, swearing, "that's *just* what I was thinking of!" If I pushed him to choose an entrée first, he'd change his mind after hearing my selection and, in a barely audible voice, whisper to the waiter, "I'll have that, too."

We began to see each other every night: made love, slept, ate big breakfasts—enormous for such skinny guys—then parted to go about our days, until, dressed and shaved, we'd meet again for an evening date. Our restaurant routine varied with an occasional movie, a documentary if possible; we both found the vulnerability of real people more rewarding than a plot. Once, passing a group of the over-dressed tourists who had just begun to invade SoHo, I asked Joe, "*What* do you make of *them?*"

"Touching," he said, "that they try so hard."

In December, I began rehearsals to play Harold in a Broadway adaptation of *Harold and Maude* which left me very little time to see Joe. By previews, I sensed the production was doomed. After the opening night show, Joe joined five of my friends and me for dinner at the Russian Tea Room. Unknotted by Negronis (a lethal, ruby-colored cocktail), I recounted rehearsal horrors. My friends, all fellow actors, added hilarious, unkind reenactments of worst moments in the play. They felt an extra degree of performance energy in front of my new boyfriend, the sweet but nervous artist, who barely said a word. Yet during the course of the evening, Joe found opportunities for one-on-one exchanges with every person at the table.

Since Joe refused help to pay the enormous bill, we christened ourselves the "Negroni Diners Club," and each member pledged to arrange and pay for a future dinner out. None of us had as much money as Joe, but we made good on our promises and picked interesting dives we could afford (one memorable evening included Quaaludes and a tap lesson).

When my show closed two weeks after the opening, I found a tiny envelope in my dressing room. Inside was a chunk of gold and a note from Joe: "If closing night is too sad, might a little gold nugget and *lots of love* help?"

Joe's generosity became legendary among my friends. Andrea (our tap teacher) told me she'd run into Joe carrying a huge bunch of flowers. "Oh! These are for you," he'd said and handed them to her. He sent an antique tiara made of tiny seed pearls after another friend's heirloom jewelry had been stolen in a break-in. When Joe learned a performer friend of mine was checking coats at a Village bar, he stopped by to have a drink and leave a fifty-dollar tip. And when our favorite waiter, ill from AIDS, was forced to leave his job, Joe sent generous checks.

I met Joe's friends in more formal circumstances: at art openings or readings.

"They're a perfect couple," a friend of Joe's gossiped to a friend of mine, "Joe's a dreamer and Keith's a dream."

Our honeymoon period was not always dreamy. Both of us had too much time, and Joe was trying to break through a long unproductive spell. Though he seemed busy enough to me—designing covers for a friend's book, drawing or writing pieces for small press publications—he hadn't had a solo show in New York since 1976 and was anxious to enter his next big phase of making art. Unemployed again, I spent my time hounding agents, going on auditions, and looking for a permanent place to live. I seemed to move weekly, and not long after my show closed, I was once again between sublets. Joe suggested a temporary move into his loft.

Since half my unemployed days were spent riding a bicycle around Manhattan, suddenly living with someone made the errands around which I loosely structured my travels seem bogus excuses for escape. Joe, during his workday, could spend literally hours pacing around his loft. In my presence, the habit made him self-conscious and distracted me from projects I'd invented to keep me indoors. Neither of us complained about the quirkiness of the other, but we both felt on trial. To make matters worse, we picked that period to give up smoking.

Our domestic experiment ended when Joe paused during his routine loft-pacing to smash the heel of his boot through a record playing Patsy Cline's "Crazy." He immediately apologized for his uncharacteristic act, but I was relieved, soon after, to accept a three-week "dog-sit." I later referred to the "crazy" episode as "the time you turned the record player off with your foot."

Living apart we resumed our romantic dinner-to-breakfast dates. And that spring, for the first time in over ten years, Joe declined his standing invitation to Vermont. I worried he'd regret the choice and begin to resent me. Joe swore his decision was based on career frustration and a mid-life call for change, not on "us." But work frustration and a lingering guilt continued to plague him in the summer-empty city.

We began to find our evening dinner dates dispiriting. I resented the amount of money spent in restaurants even though *I* wasn't spending it, I and grew intolerant of our daily drinking. Let's eat at home, I pleaded, stocking Joe's pitiful kitchen with basic cooking supplies. While I made a meal, Joe, who'd spent all day at home working on collages he wouldn't show me, paced the loft like a high-strung pet. If Joe spent the night at my most recent sublet, unable to sleep, he'd tiptoe out at four in the morning. When I stayed at his loft, I found excuses to run off before the big ritual breakfast, which we both had loved. We began to make excuses for nights off. Joe needed to "get his head together," I needed to study for an audition.

In mid-July, Joe wrote to Kenward asking ("begging," he later admitted) to join him in Vermont for the remainder of the summer. We both felt a sad relief.

Our last evening was a bittersweet but celebratory night of good food, wine, and love-making. Joe gave me the "Homage to Keith" collages about which he had been so secretive. Among these obsessively beautiful images of Joe's affection were a bed embossed with roses and two pillows labeled "you" and "me"; photo-realistic drawings of two Vermont–New York envelopes, addressed in our respective hands and carried by gulls across an ocean horizon; a "portrait," in which my torso was a big heart studded with pink roses and two pink nipples, floating above a Rorschach splash of come and a pair of jeans unbuttoned at the top.

I had Joe's keys and promised to forward his mail. I spent hours alone in his loft, remembered none of our discomfort, and ached to have him back. I began projects: fixing a dripping faucet, repairing the bathroom tiles, cleaning the refrigerator. I moved on to organize the back room, first dragging everything out into the front, then sanding and polyurethaning the floor, and building yards of floor-to-ceiling metal shelving.

The neighbors complained about the noise at night, so in the evenings I stopped my work to root through the boxes and trunks now stacked in the living area of the loft. I discovered copies of Joe's writing, the original *I Remember, New Work, Selected Writings, The Friendly Way, Some Drawings of Some Notes to Myself,* and *The Vermont Notebook,* which he wrote with John Ashbery. I read literary magazines containing his interviews, drawings, and writings: *Little Caesar, Unmuzzled Ox, Z,* and the *Paris Review,* articles in art magazines, reviews of Joe's shows with pictures of his early "altarpieces" assembled from religious paraphernalia he'd found in his neighborhood on the Lower East Side. I found mimeographed issues of Ted Berrigan's *C* magazine, with covers by Joe and its adjunct *C* comics, where the balloons over Joe's cartoon sketches were supplied with text by writers like Frank O'Hara, Ashbery, Bill Berkson, Barbara Guest, Kenneth Koch, Peter Schjeldahl, Ron Padgett, and James Schuyler. (I had met some of the collaborators: James Schuyler; Kenward, of course; Ron Padgett and his wife Pat. Joe once took me to a party hosted by Ted Berrigan, a large man with a beard and very few teeth. He was warm and almost embarrassingly interested in whatever I had to say. Allen Ginsberg was there too, and a young man nobody mentioned was passed out on the floor, which made the evening seem very beatnik to me.)

The backroom stock included paintings by Fairfield Porter, Jane Freilicher, a tattoo artist named "Art," Larry Rivers, John Button, and Jim Dine. Also Joe's own paintings: scenes from his Vermont summers, "garden" paintings, grass cutouts, a collaborative painting with Jasper Johns. I found crates of small collages and trunks of paper bits from all over the world or picked off Manhattan streets, all painstakingly organized by color. And jewel cases and boxes of small treasures—a belt strung with solid gold coins (Gypsy gold), a stack of jokers culled from antique decks, ancient rings of soft gold, cigarette cases, a tiny head carved from a nut, "hobo" art made from matches, miniature dolls, furniture, china, pairs of dice—all collected with Joe's amazing eye.

When I was at Catholic school, I'd been fascinated by the reliquary of saints: fragments of skin, bone or hair, or an item touched or worn by the holy man or woman. Though I shaped a clearer image of Joe through these backroom artifacts, the relic which brought him close was not a painting or a book, but an unwashed shirt I pulled from his laundry bag in a dark walk-in closet, which still held the musty smell of perspiration in its cloth.

During the fifteen years I knew him, Joe got rid of everything. Most things he gave away—to me, to friends, to a man who sold things on the street—until, near the end of his life, his nearly empty loft looked as if it were inhabited by a Zen squatter. The gifts to me, things almost too beautiful to own, were haunted by his non-attachment; I gave them all away except for the collages and other pieces that I sold in an eternal struggle to pay my rent.

My relics now are letters. Joe's to me. A hundred and thirty-two over the nine years we were lovers, most written during the nine summers we spent apart. I don't have my replies. After Joe died, I thought of asking for them, but I was afraid they'd been destroyed or, less tolerable, that Joe, in his mania to divest himself of things, had thrown them out.

The letters I have from Joe are love letters, even the replies sadly accepting my annual decisions to break up during the frustrating abandoned summers. Finally, in the summer of 1989—our ninth season apart—I met a young Israeli painter who wasn't much interested in moving aside for a part-time boyfriend's return in the fall. I sent a real "Dear Joe" letter to Vermont. Neither of us was surprised or, I think, loved each other less, but for the first time in nine years, we didn't make our ritual first date upon Joe's return to the city. We still met for dinner often, enjoying each other's company, but we were careful when we kissed at the beginning or end of an evening, not wanting to spark the familiar electricity that might ignite painful emotions. We continued to write for the next five summers, but less frequently. Joe still recounted dreams of me. He always sent his love to Eric and often included money for a dinner out.

As early as 1982 Joe had written asking about my health. I'd had a strange summer flu accompanied by an awful sore throat. That year, shortly before GRID (Gay-Related Immune Deficiency) was renamed AIDS, I entered a clinical trial studying a connection between this "new" disease and people—mainly gay men—whose lymph glands remained mysteriously swollen. The swelling eventually subsided and I remained asymptomatic, but by 1984 our letters were full of news about hospitalized friends and sad reports of their agonizing deaths. A hysterical press, when it reported the epidemic at all, published editorials from people like William Buckley, who suggested "tattooing" the infected, or placing them in internment camps. I refused to get tested until 1989 or 1990 and only then because my blood work indicated a T-cell level far above what any doctor expected from a person exposed to the virus. The high count turned out to be a false reading, and I tested positive to the HIV virus.

I have two telling letters from the nineties; in one, Joe mentions losing five pounds from a severe sore throat; in the other, after offering condolences for the deaths of four of my closest friends, he writes of his own continued bad health and a change his protocol to include AZT.

Joe was in New York when he first told me he had AIDS. I don't think he'd told anyone else yet, except perhaps his friends Ron and Pat Padgett. I remember he was worried about the effect of the news on Kenward, but not much worried for himself. "I've had a great life," he told me, "no regrets." Convinced my own continued health was due to an army of alternative medicines—Chinese herbs, acupuncture, vitamins, yoga—I encouraged him to include some of them along with the Western medicines. "I think for now I'll just do what the doctor orders," he offered apologetically. When I began to cry, he held me. "Do you think you got it from me, Joe?" I asked. "Oh, probably," he said, "But you don't think I care about *that*, do you?"

His last letter to me, sent at the end of September in 1993, was brief: "Dear Keith, *Happy Birthday!* & LOTS OF LOVE, Joe. P.S. Having a horrible summer! Will tell you all about it in mid-October. Love to Eric!"

The stomach problems Joe had written about were due to CMV, a virulent opportunistic virus. He spent much of the winter in the hospital. For a while he was in a "care partner" facility at New York University Hospital, where still ambulatory patients have private rooms and must be partnered by a friend or mate.

When Joe left the facility, he could no longer climb the long flights of stairs to his loft and needed constant care. He moved into the apartment of his younger brother John. I visited him there several times. Joe was in constant pain and spent most of his time in a fitful sleep. On my last visit he hobbled in from his bed to lie down on the living room couch. I sat awkwardly in one armchair, John sat in another. Joe had written a check, which he was giving to me now, he explained, because he was worried nothing would go to me after his death. I felt full of opposition: to the check, to the presence of his brother, of whom I am fond, and most of all to a feeling that this conversation was our last. But I knew he was too sick to suffer my objects; I kissed him and said good-bye.

When Joe returned to the hospital, this time to a private room, I rode over each day and sat outside on my bike, counting up to the floor where I knew Joe lay in a room, dying. The day before he died I went inside. Ron, Pat, and John were there. They left the room to give me time alone with Joe. He was in a coma, struggling for breath beneath an oxygen mask. Over the past ten years I'd seen so many friends assume that gaunt, bearded look. And I'd watched mothers calmly stroke a sunken cheek and maintain a bedside manner well beyond the hope of a son's convalescence. Perhaps that was why with my head close to his, I could tell Joe how much I loved him—and not break down until I left the room.

Ron Padgett notified me of the memorial service for Joe held in November 1994, six months after Joe's death. I called our friends—Joe's and mine—and we sat together at the back of St. Mark's Church listening to a list of speakers read poems and eulogies. The alienation I felt during the ceremony was broken afterwards by a man I didn't know—though he looked strangely familiar. He introduced himself as Jim, Joe's older brother, who lived in St. Louis. He said Joe had spoken of our relationship and told him how much I meant to him.

The Poetry Project dedicated the next issue of their newsletter to Joe, with more remembrances, many of them from the speakers at his memorial. The following year Penguin reissued the complete *I Remember*. When Joe's retrospective was mounted in 1997, art critics and poets wrote in reverent terms about the timeless modesty of his work. Edmund White titled his piece in *Art in America* "Saint Joe."

In a 1977 interview, given at the beginning of what many posthumous reviews of his work referred to as the period he "quit making art," Joe said, "I don't believe in things I want, like being famous and making money. All that stuff is—I'd like to do it, but I don't believe in it as much as I used to. . . . I think what I'd love to do is fall madly in love with someone. I still think it might happen. . . . But I don't know if it's realistic or not. . . . I mean, I'd have to go really bananas. And I think the chances of meeting someone that you go bananas over like that are slim. So the odds are against you, though I'm sure it's possible."

When we first met in 1979, no one had heard of AIDS. Even if we had known about the disease, known that one or both of us were brimming with the virus, we'd have still fallen in love, still clung to each other for as long as our passion held. Our romance began in ardent letters, but really bloomed with a first kiss.

And if I collage that kiss with sensations from the next eight autumn evenings, following every summer apart, I do so because each reunion kiss left us dazed, laughing, reaching for a cigarette to re-ground us in the world or making love on the spot, several spots—sometimes we didn't get beyond the storage room. I loved him, and against all odds, he went bananas over me.

The Art of Losing
Andrew Solomon

There is always the Mozart story out there: someone died young with a whole lifetime already achieved. Then there are the rest: those who slowly, over perhaps three score years and ten, built up bodies of work informed by experience. Beethoven? If he'd died in his thirties, there would for all intents and purposes be no Beethoven. Verdi? My father used to shake his head with wonder when he told me how Verdi had composed *Falstaff* at the age of eighty. I loved the story of Verdi, because it seemed to me that the only way one could tolerate time was to believe that life was getting steadily better, to imagine growing rich in the mind even as the body went creaky. There are elements of youth that are hard for any of us to let go, but a true artist, I thought, achieved not only the immortality of his work, but also the persistent burgeoning of his genius. When I decided to be a writer, it was my idea to arrive at fulfillment simply by continuing myself indefinitely. I was a kid, and patient. There were so many days left.I was shocked when it turned out that there weren't necessarily so many days, that there might in fact be almost no time at all. All around me, artists whose enterprise required thousands of hours started dropping a hundred hours in. If you weren't Mozart, you had no chance; there would never be a *Falstaff* again. The brilliance of maturity was a thing of the past. I watched artists struggling to pack into their dense work not only the experience they had had but also the experiences they had once expected to have, and now wouldn't: people dying in the throes of their own potential. Nipped in the bud, many of these young sick people were bereft of voices before they knew what their voices were. It is all very well to mourn the distinguished men whose genius had manifested itself early, the ones interrupted halfway through; but I weep at the tomb of the unknown soldiers, the ones whose work, hardly begun, would with just a decade or two more have become something that we cannot imagine well enough to miss. We mourn the dinosaurs who perished in a sudden ice age, but our dead young artists are not pterodactyls; they are dragons whose would-be accomplishments never passed beyond the barrier of myth. We do not have enough information to begin to catalog the losses imposed on us. Writing panegyrics for individual artists whose names we know, we forget how much actually went with the acquired immuno-deficiency syndrome. Here is the tragedy: we have no idea what passed. We are never told what might have been.

The crisis consumed us. We got used to living with fear, and its chill effect changed everything for us: how we lived, what we made, and, of course, how we loved. Though some remarkable art was inspired by the intensity of ever-present accumulating deaths, we mostly lost in the battle against fear. Terror freezes creativity, and none of us had the purchase on gladness that should be the essence of young work. Coming of age in AIDS's cold climate, I lived with a perpetual residual neuropathy, a compromised mind. There are so many people who would have been my friends if they had not died before I had a chance to meet them, much less love them. There are so many who would have inspired me in my own work and thoughts. There are so many who would have changed the world. Who can forgive these losses? How is it that they failed to break the heart of God, when they broke the hearts even of those among us who were spared the plague?

I first heard of AIDS (GRID at the time) in the office of my ophthalmologist, Dr. Maurice G. Poster, at 71 Park Avenue South on a Wednesday afternoon in 1981 at about 4:45. I was in eleventh grade, and had just decided to wear contact lenses instead of glasses, so it was before I cut my hair shorter and after I got my Frye boots. It was then I'd resolved that I wanted to be attractive, and it was indeed that quest for attractiveness (a quest whose object I had not yet defined to myself) that had led me to the waiting room of Dr. Poster, who specialized in soft contact lenses for people with sensitive eyes. I do not have a good visual memory, but I can recall in living sepia that waiting room, the other myopic people reading copies of *National Geographic*, the nurses coming out from time to time to escort someone with dilated pupils to the doctor's room. I remember the brownish sofas and the yellowed lampshades and the hush that obtains in waiting rooms even when the patients are not particularly ill. I had leafed through several magazines and had haphazardly picked up a copy of *Time*. There, I happened on a brief description of a mysterious illness that killed Haitians and homosexuals.

The gay part didn't entirely surprise me. There were already so many bad things about being gay that the additional information that some people were dying from it seemed almost logical to me. On the other hand, I found the mortality of the Haitians somewhat bewildering. I couldn't think of any Haitians I knew; I'd had a protected liberal New York childhood and though I had black friends, they were all American blacks with approximately middle-class lives. My mother said, when I asked her later that day, that there were lots of Haitians in New York. She mentioned Mr. Leon (as we called him), who worked in the garage and drove a big Cadillac with a license plate that said MRLEON. I wondered whether Leon was going to disappear any time soon. Leon was in general grumpy and a little scary and I had always suspected that he did cultish voodoo with strangled chickens in some hidden part of the Bronx, but on good days he had a huge gold-toothed smile, and though he made me nervous, he was also the first person who ever called me Mr. Solomon (perhaps just because he'd forgotten my name, but when I was seven it made me feel wildly important). I had known him for a long time and I was sorry to think of him going. I was sorrier still about the gays of my life: my art history teacher and a pair of old family friends whom I thought of as surrogate uncles. Why would any illness be threatening Leon, Mr. Yates, and Willie and Elmer? The logic of it kept me up night after night, ruminating.

I remember wondering what I was going to do. I was not ready at the time to opt out of safe virginity. Still, it was a considerable disappointment that I would never be able to have sex with a man, though I had already sort of decided that I would never have sex with a man anyway, since gay men were social outcasts, sad figures, lonely, prone to undignified aging, childless, and null. I had, a few months earlier, been approached by a man (he told me his name was Dwayne, and showed me his credit card to prove it) while I was walking the family dog, and he had been unusually aggressive, taking my hand and putting it in his trousers. Dwayne lived in the big new building that had gone up on the corner of 72nd and Third. I had acutely wanted, for a few seconds at least, to go home with him, but I couldn't bear the fact that we might have to walk past the building where I lived and the doormen who knew me; and I knew that it would be complicated for the dog, who didn't really like new places, and that my parents would wonder what had happened to me, and that Dwayne might be a crazed ax-murderer. I left Dwayne and his pederastic ambitions on the corner. I hoped at that time that with practice and a little coaching, I would learn how to have sex with women, and I thought that *not* having sex with men was a good opening measure. I knew that women's sexuality scared me; I hoped that that would pass, as my childhood fear of the color orange had passed. I knew that I found men attractive, but I didn't find homosexuality itself attractive. Well, it was a puzzle. I'd perhaps never have sex at all; I had a spinster great aunt who had lived a good life in the world, and it seemed to me that one could do worse than she had done. This illness described in the pages of *Time* seemed to me relatively insignificant in this grand scheme of things, though I felt awfully sad for Leon and Mr. Yates and Willie and Elmer.

In the months that followed, I scanned newspapers for mentions of this illness. It fascinated me and scared me, and it also seemed to add to the alluring madness and evil and sensuality and pleasure of men loving men. I thought about the people who had done forbidden things and were now paying the price, and the images were curiously erotic. Everything was even more forbidden, even more dangerous, even more fascinating than I had dared to suppose. I didn't know much about sexually transmitted diseases (then called venereal diseases), and the question of what bodily fluids mixed with what other bodily fluids under what circumstances was one that no one in the press had yet thought to ask. What I understood was simply the fatal consequence of difference, and I wondered what other illness might strike some other world within my world. The groups it affected might be as haphazard as the legionnaires who had suffered Legionnaire's Disease. I concentrated on fear of the erratic to distract myself from terror of the erotic.

The first time I had sex was later that year, in the Metropolitan Museum of Art, where I was a summer intern. By that time, I knew a lot more about venereal diseases, though much of it was vague and some of it was wrong. I had sex with one of the museum guards, in the medieval sculpture court, after the museum was closed. I wanted him to do the things he wanted to do to me, but I did not allow it. Instead of violating the limitations imposed by the possibility of disease, I violated the security regulations of the Metropolitan Museum of Art and maintained some bodily integrity. As I reached that eternally memorable, never-equaled release, I saw saints and angels gazing down on me with expressions of pure benevolence. I was suddenly terrified by this sculpture that had witnessed my giving way to temptation (Christ on his Cross, in the far corner of the room, had resisted temptation—and was much admired for it, I knew). I pulled up my khakis and I ran from that place as though there were eight winds at my back.

During my undergraduate years, I prayed a lot. It was kind of an abstract notion for me, since I didn't really believe in God and hadn't grown up with anything much like faith. I prayed to my own future, that it not allow me to turn into one of those people who wore tight jeans and smoked cigarettes and were snidely girlish and died. I had a series of girlfriends with whom I didn't really have sex, though with one I felt excitement and with another I felt an adoration never equaled since. I had lots of gay friends, and I envied them their public freedom and wildness, though I never wanted to participate in it. My friendships were emotional, intellectual, monumental, physical in the embrace—but not sexual. I was safe against my will, so I was promiscuous in keeping with my yearning. Was promiscuity itself not a violation of the code of restraint and ethics to which AIDS made us subject? I often met men, really often, maybe six times a day, and had some kind of contact with them. I would let them suck me or feel me. Under duress, I would touch them. No fucking ever. I sucked once or twice but was too upset afterward. It was not about love or even about desire; the guys were often old or ugly or both. I expected that I would die from it, but I couldn't manage to believe that enough to change what I did.

I wondered what it would be like to be Brett, a year ahead of me in college, gay as Christmas, friends with James or Max (who were not really out of the closet but who were a lot closer to out than I was). Brett's mother was gay too, and they both had that strange and kind of ugly red hair. Brett was off having sex with everyone and taking drugs and talking about it. I found him vulgar and alarming and fascinating. He was a good singer and really cynical and came from Texas, and he had a garish limp-wristedness that didn't seem to bother him much. He tried to cheer on everyone whom he thought might be gay; he was a kind of mascot for gayness. I also wondered about what it would be like to be Hugh, haughty and imperious and beautiful, who was gay as though it were a birthright, who was so bitter, and so nasty, and who regarded the rest of us struggling with our identities as ludicrous and faintly embarrassing—if he regarded us at all. It was a time of wondering. I wondered, also, who would die. I retained with some pride an unconvincing facade of relatively unscathed asexuality.

Senior year, I went to see a sexual surrogate from the back page ads of

New York magazine because I wanted to practice having sex with girls and felt I should get the basics down before trying the experiment at home. That went better than I'd anticipated, and I kind of liked my surrogate, a blond southern woman who eventually told me that she'd been a prostitute for a while but that her real thing was necrophilia. She told me I was pretty good and alive and reminded her of whoring days, but that a lot of the guys she met were "kind of like dead people but so *sweaty.* And a lot of them are gays who are just *not* going to manage to put it in me, no matter how much they want that." We talked about whether she was afraid of AIDS, and she said she assumed she'd been exposed and if she was gonna go she was just gonna go. We used condoms together, though who was being protected from what was never really clear. I was glad for what I'd learned with her, but I couldn't yet translate it into a convincing passion.

Shortly after the end of college, I told a good friend all about my sexual history and she had said, "Listen, it doesn't matter that much whether it's girls or boys. It *really* matters whether it's inside or outside, and whether it's with people you know or with total strangers. And it *really* matters whether it's *totally* safe." By the time I was in graduate school, there were tests for HIV; and you had to be crazy to take risks. My mother spoke only occasionally about grandchildren, about having a family, about all the ways she would have liked my sexuality to fall in line with hers. She spoke to me instead about how scary it was to be gay—scary now not only because one would grow old alone and unloved, but also because one would not grow old at all. I went to get a test and I expected bad news and I thought that I might deal with it by killing myself. When I heard I was negative, I thought they must have made a mistake; I'd been careful, but I'd been careful with two thousand people, and I couldn't see how that was careful. I went to a party in New York at around that time and met a friend of a friend, a cheery fellow, Nick, who was cute as a button. "I just thought you should know," another friend whispered, watching us flirt, "that he's positive." I was shocked—this guy was about twenty, and well educated, and if I had known enough so soon, hadn't he known enough too? A little later I heard that Brett had AIDS. I hadn't seen him in years, but I thanked whatever God I had once beseeched for freedom that I had been too repressed to do damage to myself when I had wanted so badly to do all the dangerous things. Time passed.

I was not in a gay world when I started living with Michael, my first serious boyfriend, a year later. I was not infected. He and I knew about the epidemic mostly from the press, since we had no ill friends. Nonetheless, AIDS was one of the dominant realities of our life. I took the test again and again to make sure about the results, and I waited for the bomb to go off. Friends of mine had joined ACT UP. I was living in England then; I never went to ACT UP events, but I watched the protests happen.

I never once had sex with anyone the way I wanted. I never once did everything I wanted when and as I wanted. I was unacquainted with that reckless abandon that sounded like it had been so much fun a generation earlier. All the struggle to be frank and open about sexuality—and for what?

When Michael and I broke up, I was released back into peril. I remet a friend from grad school, Mark, some eight months later, the week my mother died. He was someone I'd almost slept with when I was in grad school, but at that time he'd been sharing an apartment with the guy with whom I was in love, and in my doe-eyed grad school way, I had chosen to pine after the roommate instead of seizing the moment with Mark. I'd afterward regretted the lost opportunity, since the roommate was repressed as all England, and Mark was hotly available. When I met Mark again, when my mother was newly dead and I wanted to die myself, I was exhilarated by his sexual energy. He lived on all the edges. He'd grown up in South Africa and was now attracted exclusively to inner-city black men, whom he picked up at night in neighborhoods where I was afraid to drive by day. He let them do anything to him. He was bruised with that, and he was also HIV-positive. I kind of wanted to be him.

I fell in love with a friend of his (I liked his friends), and we all went away for a weekend in Montauk. We were all the same out there until I dropped a glass in the bottom of our rowboat and Mark stepped on it. Blood came out of his foot and began to pool on the bottom of the boat. "Jump," he said to us. "Jump!" he said again, and I realized that there was broken glass all over the bottom of the boat, that I could have cut my foot too, that our bloods could have mixed. I jumped. So did the other guy. We swam as if there were piranhas in Long Island Sound. From the shore, we watched Mark picking up the pieces of broken glass and dumping them over the side of the boat. On the safe soft sand, I felt a wave of nausea. I hadn't thought to jump myself. If Mark hadn't told me to jump, I could have died. You needed a life preserver *in* the boat, not out of it.

I went out, then, with Talcott, and after that with Carolina. I loved these women and I loved the escape from everything I disliked about being gay. I loved too how far we were outside the bleak world of AIDS. But I felt as though I had abandoned my comrades—as though this route I was taking had become, ironically, the easy way out.

Brett died. I'd never liked him much and had never much respected him, and though I bore him no malice, I felt sorry more for friends who had been fond of him than for him. At the time, I thought he was the first of a cascade of losses, and that made me very sad. I involved myself in the cause. I gave money to all the AIDS charities. I marched. I worried about my friends, and about people who weren't even friends. I mourned for the tens of thousands dead. I read about and wrote about the breakdown of the community. I made friends with people who were ill and waited to be called on, waited to stand by their deathbeds. I knew a thousand people who were positive. I said, dramatically, when one of them was difficult, "But he's dying," and I thought that was true. I went on like that for years. I heard that this person had converted, or that one, and I reached out to them and tried to give comfort. I hoped that if I learned how they lived, I'd be able to live when my turn came, and that if I helped them as they died, I'd be able to die when it was my day to go. I gave money to AmFar and GMHC as a talisman against my own demise.

I remet Hugh, the haughty guy from college, and he was now an *artist* and keen to be friends. That chill austerity of his was gone. Hugh Steers. He joked, "Well, maybe HIV has made me nicer"—as though he didn't remember that he had been absolutely and deliberately and grandly the least nice person in the world. I thought it was tragic. I don't think he was a great artist, but his art became all of what he had learned from being ill. That slight sadistic superiority remained, mediated now by a touching empathy. I was glad and sorry to see that art, and to know that it was about a process never fully realized, though what fascinated me in Hugh was still the horrible way he had been rather than the poignant way he was, the alive part of him and not the dying part.

I went through a depression and had unprotected sex a bunch of times during it. Even at the bottom of my emotional pit, I had to be the top if I was being unsafe because to be unprotected and the bottom seemed too much like suicide. All I wanted was to tempt fate, to give the gods a chance to knock me off if they'd really decided I wasn't worth it. I gave them ample opportunity and I thought, when the depression cleared, that I'd be dying soon. Then I tested negative again. The routine for the test, the forms to fill out, the vial with the purple top into which my blood spurted, the waiting, the phone calls, the paralytic fear between giving the blood and getting the result—it was a commonplace of my life. I took a test every year or so. I lived in terror of the tests even when I knew there was nothing to fear, because they were to my mind still tests of how angry fate was on a given day. I lived a life of tempered passions, mostly. When I got into a relationship I always went in for an extra test. Unfathomably, I was always fine.

I never bothered with safe sex in relationships; that much real intimacy I insisted on having. I was terrified that I was going to make girlfriends ill with the illness I didn't have, that doctors told me I didn't have, but—who could be so sure? I was terrified of my fluids. I worried less with boyfriends; our risk seemed mutual, part of a covenant that neither party should have entered. I met Søren and had a grand romance for two years, until I walked in on him as he was having unsafe sex with a stranger. I broke his nose and his jaw with my bare hands, and, feral with rage, bit a chunk of flesh out of his cheek. That was all about AIDS. I remember all that rage, all that blood, drenching his clothes and mine. Then I met brilliant, cherry-lipped, full-bosomed Julie, and fell really in love, and nearly married her. Shortly after that plan failed, I met Ernö. Eventually, we moved in together. Later, he rediscovered God and took up the cause of Christ, renouncing the body that had given us both so much pleasure.

The losses for which I prepared myself never happened. My friends were too young or too cautious or too lucky. The positive guy, Nick, Mr. Cute-as-a-Button, eventually got on protease inhibitors and he's still cute-as-a-button. Mark is doing fine. Mr. Yates is still teaching art history at my high school. Willie and Elmer eventually died in their eighties of old age. Leon is still working in my father's garage. The guys who were in on my house share one summer, my HIV-positive friends, are also on the meds of our time, and they look great. The rest of my crowd—well, they aren't even positive. If I hadn't been so cautious, so constantly restrained, would I have died? Would we all have died? Would it have been worth it, to forget ourselves entirely? In fantasy, it would have been worth it; in reality—who could even think it?

James Merrill

Allan Gurganus

James Merrill is widely considered the greatest poet of his generation. In work of wild imaginative force, employing an insouciant and unequaled technique, Merrill's voice continues to awe, charm, and instructively reverberate.

His poetry still contains the dewy force of a prodigy, alternating with the wisdom of some ancient courtier-sage. Merrill's first poems appeared while he was still an undergraduate at Amherst. His lifetime's work can now be seen as his age's most spiritually attuned, its most urbane and candidly human. James Merrill was always a public man fully at ease with his sexuality.

His father co-founded Merrill Lynch, the world's largest brokerage house. But born to wealth, James Merrill dedicated his life to work. He published more than fourteen books of poems. These won him two National Book Awards (for *Nights and Days* and *Mirabell*), the Bollingen Prize (for *Braving the Elements*), and the Pulitzer Prize (for *Divine Comedies*). *The Changing Light at Sandover* appeared in 1982. Composed of a cycle of books, the work in its entirety won the 1983 National Book Critics Circle Award. Merrill wrote two novels, *The (Diblos) Notebook* and *The Seraglio*. His other works include two plays, a book of essays, and the warmly received 1993 memoir, *A Different Person*.

Merrill set up the Ingram-Merrill Foundation, named in honor of his parents. Through it, he distributed grants to a generation of deserving younger artists. James Merrill lived in Stonington, Connecticut, in Key West, Florida, and in Manhattan. He and the novelist Allan Gurganus were friends for the last six years of Merrill's life. Gurganus visited the poet in New York and Connecticut; they often exchanged letters and work. Merrill dedicated his late poem "Rhapsody on Czech Themes" to Allan Gurganus. James Merrill died of AIDS-related complications in 1995.

Gurganus twice spoke publicly of Merrill. Once in 1993 when he introduced the poet reading his work at New York's 92nd Street YMHA. In 1995

Gurganus delivered a eulogy at Merrill's funeral in Stonington, Connecticut. Those two addresses chronicle fond stages of a friendship. They offer us a portrait-in-motion of the brilliant, sprightly, and richly missed James Merrill:

INTRODUCTION OF JAMES MERRILL, AT HIS READING: 92ND STREET YMHA, DECEMBER 13, 1993

A child sits drawing at a round table. Beside him, an older friend, sketching some subject. Say, an elephant. The child, tongue pressed between new teeth, renders a series of gray circles forming a sort of haystack. The friend's sketch depicts four baggy knees, a tail like a burned rope, the snout segmented as a caterpillar. When the child finally pulls this exquisite drawing across the table—a sketch surrendered with some seeming regret—he exclaims, "Boy, that's good." Celebrating anatomical accuracy and the wit to shape it, the child summons Virtue itself.

Maxim Gorky, in writing to his friend Anton Chekhov, states, "When I read your work, I feel I have been trying to write with a log."

As a linguistic draftsman, one whose line rivals those pencil portraits by Ingres, as someone whose Imagination constitutes a geographic Dante-esque principality, no poet today is so "good" as James Merrill. The discipline of his line balances and anticipates the acuity of his senses (five senses, then suddenly six, then oh around forty). "Good".

Merrill must feel like the novelist in Randall Jarrell's *Pictures From An Institution*: "She had been called brilliant so often that, five minutes after you called her that, she couldn't remember whether you had said that or remarked on yesterday's snow."

So, tonight, I seek to celebrate James Merrill's other form of "good"-ness—one perhaps even more original than his mind, than his art's mere artfulness. For years I was afraid of Merrill. He said kind things about my work. But I felt like some parochial tap-dance teacher meeting Fred Astaire. At first Merrill's respect felt like "noblesse oblige." It took me forever to test then trust such direct "goodness."

Behind Merrill's fourteen essential books of poems, his volume of essays, his two underappreciated works of fiction offering Jamesian pleasures (in both senses of that name), and certainly in his newly published memoir, a somewhat different person coalesces beneath the assumed persona. Its actual form only looks fragmented, as the image of a pencil sidesteps itself when resting in a clear water glass.

We all feel the genial, playful, schooled yet innocent host of *The Changing Light at Sandover*. Receiving the proffered voices of remaindered spirits—doing so with simple tact, Merrill later politely deigns to "versify" the ghostly visitors' messages. He does so with the good will most of us might exercise by washing our guests' dinner plates, or phoning next morning to say, "Are you missing a cashmere scarf, maroon?" A "good" host. Not just to his readers, not just to the restless souls who perceive him as their party-hive of choice. But Merrill seems a fine, quiet host to the noisy World itself.

Perhaps, like Gorky wielding his whittled log of a pencil, I am better qualified to speak of Merrill's prose than his poems. In his newest book, *A Different Person*, we find the older (if not old) Merrill introducing us to the very young Merrill who introduces us—Virgil, pretty, in the Old World with excellent letters of introduction—into the agony of first leave-taking, first love, the terror of learning that we all spend most time alone in rooms however crowded. The quiet subtext of *A Different Person* is, as the title suggests, the creation of a transforming moral entity—meaning here, an aesthetic one. We are present at the creation of a person with every excuse for indolence, snobbery, license, self-pity and disdain. And yet we encounter someone very young who founds and then embodies a man of such empathy and playfulness, such difficult scope and yet so easy an intimacy.

The memoir begins:

Meaning to stay as long as possible, I sailed for Europe. It was March 1950. New York and most of the people I knew had begun to close in. Or to put it differently, I felt that I alone in this or that circle of friends, could see no way into the next phase.

Hear how Merrill's tone confides without presumption? It admits without confessing. It intrigues without vamping. It assumes the reader's equality, and therefore concocts it. It lightly harkens to the title and theme in "Or to put it differently." It begins with an action, as writing teachers strictly instruct; *and* a date and place, as they advise. And yet the overwhelming sensation this launching paragraph conveys is our own fond friendly concern *for the speaker*: his dilemma and—crucially, mysteriously—a fascination for what must happen to him next. The prose functions with the word-weightedness of poetic decision-making, but without once revealing any of these hostly preparations.

If a poet could be compared to some single social event, Wallace Stevens's might be a disjunct fiduciary convention albeit held in Key West at riptide and full moon; if Whitman's is a bunting-draped Arbor Day platform dedicated to the topic of the Sovereigne Self as embodied coincidentally by Walter Whitman here himself, then James Merrill's governing social metier-metaphor—in verse and prose—could be a party, but, crucially, *a party for others*. It is his hostly—near deaconish—preparation in anticipating and predicting others' pleasure that, curiously, provides the very moral gravity that makes others' rejoicing possible then utterly necessary. His work frees us toward serious play in the world.

And so, Merrill's unparalleled technical gifts are but the visible trappings one sees on entering the great and always festive event. As an imaginer of gatherings in which the living and the dead regain each other, as a singer, as a creator of the indelible made out of the merely mortal, James Merrill's skills have all been recounted by my betters. What I, as his friend, wish to humbly add to the facets of a person who must be very bored with the diminishing, chilly term "gem-like"—is something simple, something simpler.

Something simple as a child's exclamation on looking at a friend's adjacent page, where some mutually agreed-upon subject, say, an elephant, has been created with the most effortful of effortlessness so as to seem almost god-given, not handmade. (Nothing is god-given in art, everything is handmade; and yet truest art makes the reverse seem true.) I know that the actual genius underwriting and inspiriting this, our "greatest" poet, is someone as simple and direct as his work is complex with its clear guesses and brocade layerings. For those of us who go on learning both from his beautiful work and from his changing light-filled company—the person himself outstrips in grace even his own most evolved description. His genius for friendship is, if possible, his single greatest genius. He has, almost secretly, created a foundation dedicated to encouraging gifted young painters and writers. The foundation makes raids of vigilante kindness. It has helped those young artists who are healthy and those who discover they are dying just as they've begun.

It might be imagined that a person so urbane, so in demand as James

Merrill, would delegate his friendships. Wrong. There is no secretary. The letters are hand addressed. When your heart is broken (as it is too often, right?) no one in your address book is readier to console you through the difficulties of one A.M. And no one is funnier when a joke can again begin to help you. Nobody in my acquaintance better qualifies for all exemptions you'd quite freely offer someone cloudy, mandarin, distant, rich, *and* a genius. And yet no soul is less likely to invoke (or accept) such privilege. Given the kimono collection, given the god-like talents, given the three home addresses, what I am about to say might seem unlikely, but it's true: of everyone I've ever met, James Merrill has achieved the most absolute and purified simplicity. Decency, accountability, utter heart. His work abounds with empathy for both the living and the dead. And oh he shows such joy and talent for that time called "Right This Second In This Room." I mean Fun. His achievements are not simply artistic; unless you expand that word to include Life lived with all art's care and meter and good sense, with art's quantum imaginative abandon.

"Artistic temperament," Sarah Bernhardt tells us, "is a disease that only afflicts amateurs."

Leave it then as a beginning: How a child, presented offhandedly with the dear, superior friend's drawing of, say, an elephant, how this child must exclaim, "Boy, but that's good. Boy, oh boy, how—just sitting here—can you know so much about how elephants look and just . . . *are*? Know what? I've got to say. You're real real *good.*"

Offering Art the ultimate compliment, the child compares it to our beauty most absolute: Ethical Human Behavior. Lines on a page become Virtue itself.

Please welcome, James Merrill . . .

EULOGY DELIVERED, CALVARY CHURCH, STONINGTON, CONNECTICUT,
FEBRUARY 13, 1995
JAMES MERRILL, 1926–1995

To call James Merrill "kind" is like calling James Merrill "verbal."

On the page and in the air, was any human ever better company? Ready as James was to laugh, *making* him laugh felt like the invention of happiness. There was no more pleasing review than "My mother adores your new joke. Is telling it to all her friends." Oh, to be thought talented or grace-ful or good by the one person alive most purely all those things!

Grace cannot be invited. It arrives, or no. Usually, no. Here, eternal, it abided, said, "Yes, yes, yes, *this* one."

Speaking at a beloved's funeral is rendered easier by knowing he is al-ready immortal; but not by much. In a last letter I received from Tucson, James remembered, "The old European scientist in 'Pictures from an Institu-tion,' saying: 'What I really want is for visitors from another planet to come and make me their pet.'"

They did. They have. But—we all know—James Merrill forever *was* that. People would say of him, in the slang, "Everybody adores Jimmy. Jimmy is absolutely divine."

He and David Jackson were the Ouija board's handpicked local repre-sentatives. And now perhaps he intervenes for and interprets us—we, jum-bled letters, scattered between the board's only sure mercies the word "Yes," the word "No."

There was, in James's work, a Dante-esque sense of parallel universe; there was a breeze always blowing through Jimmy from somewhere else, a force that felt immense, a finer cosmos that constituted, it seems to us now, more than one single human being's imagination.

His empathy contained us all. His dignity saved us ours. After my most recent disastrous love affair, James waited till he could finally say, "My dear, have you ever considered getting a *dog*?"

He possessed the authority of a great beauty who never quite believed he *was* one. No one born a genius, no one more famous and more modest, no one less likely to be bossy and didactic and therefore no one ever likelier to *teach* you, no one more brocaded with exquisite Proustian aftermaths, ever achieved such . . . simplicity.

The sweetness of this man! You all remember: There was a cresting sense of This Moment We Are In Together, this conspiracy of immediate pleasure, and how we both might decorate and inhabit it well, and now, the *next* moment ahead, with James, and rolling into it together shoulder-to-shoulder and you all laughing, giggling really.

With James, we each became the person he believed we might best and eventually become. Before him, I saw bores scintillate; I saw professional scintillators lulled into mere humanity, and discussing compost or back pain. I saw waiters become, by proximity, Nijinsky.

Some people contain their grace; James dispersed his. It was a molecular nimbus he lived within and he seemed, after nearly seven decades in there, largely unaware of its effervescent impact on the rest of us. But he was aware of everything. He is likely aware of this we are doing today. And if he's not, it's a damn shame. He would so enjoy being present, but he'd wisely abide *not* being. His whole work, we see now, was a preparation for this day. His letters of introduction to the World of the Shades, book length, preceded him. He has long been a favorite there, too.

A few years back, one spirit in his trilogy told James, "You're early."

What seemed odd—he, who had more reason to expect than anyone alive, forgave us. Forgave us everything.

Since you all loved him, you'll understand: If James had never written anything but exquisite thank-you notes, this church today would be just as crowded.

He had many names, all of them true, none of them complete. I mean, of course, "James." "Jamey." "James Merrill." "J. M." "Mr. Merrill." "Mr. James Merrill, the poet." And finally—so toylike an endearment for so radical and enormous a humanity—everybody's especial favorite, "Jimmy." The darling of our crew, the finest of us, our laureate and sage, our Virgil early, our light source . . . Jimmy.

How rare, when the **great** man is a **good** man.

Jimmy, we loved you so.

And yet, we have only just *begun* to love you.

The Estate Project for Artists with AIDS

Maya Angelou

There is a custom observed all over the South which is touching. When a hearse followed by a convoy of cars passes in the street, pedestrians stop. Men remove their hats and women hold themselves in silence until the cortege passes. Whites and Blacks equally observe this custom regardless of the race of the people who occupy the vehicles. I am reminded that there is a religious sect which believes that death levels all. There are no raised headstones in Moravian cemeteries since they believe that in death, the rich and poor are equal.

The artists, heartbreakingly numerous, who have died of AIDS have left us, the general community, bereaved and wanting. Grief-stricken at their absence and wanting to relive the time we had together, we wander, mull, and meditate over what we could have done to make their passing easier. Among my personal losses I must list my friend Samuel C. Floyd, for whom I wrote a poem:

AILEY, BALDWIN, FLOYD, KILLENS, AND MAYFIELD

> When great trees fall,
> rocks on distant hills shudder,
> lions hunker down
> in tall grasses,
> and even elephants
> lumber after safety.
> When great trees fall
> in forests,
> small things recoil into silence,
> their senses
> eroded beyond fear.

When great souls die,
the air around us becomes
light, rare, sterile.
We breathe, briefly.
Our eyes, briefly
see with
a hurtful clarity.
Our memory, suddenly sharpened,
examines,
gnaws on kind words
unsaid,
promised walks
never taken.

Great souls die and
our reality, bound to
them, takes leave on us.
Our souls,
dependent upon their
nurture,
now shrink, wizened.
Our minds, formed
and informed by their
radiance,
fall away.
We are not so much maddened
as reduced to the unutterable ignorance
of dark, cold
caves.

And when great souls die,
after a period peace blooms,
slowly and always
irregularly. Spaces fill
with a kind of

soothing electric vibration.
Our senses, restored, never
to be the same, whisper to us.
They existed. They existed.
We can be. Be and be
better. For they existed.

I credit Samuel Floyd for encouraging me to write *I Know Why the Caged Bird Sings*. He reminded me so much of my brother, Bailey Johnson, of whom I have said and believe, "My family came closest to making a genius when they made my brother and my brother had the kindness to tell me when I was nine years old, a voluntary mute and socially an outcast, a willing outcast, 'You are very smart—not as smart as I am naturally, but smarter than anybody else.'"

Sam Floyd told me I could write better than most people and he knew he was right because he read everything in English. As AIDS invaded his body and his life he became more serious about friendships, more attentive to birthdays, anniversaries, and celebratory dates of his friends. He sent cards and made phone calls to all of us. He, who had been a great cook, sent ideas for party menus. He, who had been an irresistible party dancer, became adamant about going to every dance concert that New York offered. The last year of Sam's life (before the dying weeks) were spent in reaching out to friends, reassuring them that he would love them forever.

Sam's absence introduces a large, lifeless gray area into my life. He was among the closest of my male friends. Certain events are almost impossible to live through because I don't have Sam's brilliant, succinct statements about the participants and about the occurrences.

Each time I hear of a friend, an acquaintance, or a stranger who has died from AIDS, I feel as if I am a pedestrian on the streets and a cortege is passing. I, out of love for my friend, am inspired by the loss that other families and friends are experiencing, stop dead still, put my hand on my heart as if watching a flag being raised, and I think of my friend. I experience the loss within a loss, within a loss and I know that my life will never be the same and the world will never right itself again.

Subject and
Contributor Biographies

Subject Biographies

ROBERT FRANK ANTON

Robert Frank Anton was born in 1949 in Fort Worth, Texas, and spent the first eighteen years of his life there. After studying theater arts for one year at Carnegie Mellon University, he made his way inevitably to New York City, where he worked as a scenic designer. By the mid-seventies, his early passion for puppetry had reasserted itself, and he began a now legendary series of performances in a walk-up apartment on West 70th Street. In the late seventies and early eighties he performed in France, Germany, and again in New York—this time in a loft on Spring Street—always to growing acclaim. Robert Anton died in Los Angeles in August of 1984.

JOE BRAINARD

Joe Brainard was born in Salem, Arkansas, in 1942. He was an artist, writer, set designer, and frequent collaborator with the New York School poets. As a writer he was best known for the memoir, *I Remember*. His paintings, collages, and assemblages are represented in the Museum of Modern Art and the Whitney Museum of American Art. He died in 1994.

HOWARD BROOKNER

Howard Brookner was a filmmaker whose first project, *Burroughs*, a documentary on the writer William Burroughs, debuted to much critical acclaim at the 1984 New York Film Festival and was shown at film festivals around the world. His next documentary, *Robert Wilson and the Civil Wars*, was shown on PBS in 1986. His first full-length feature film, *Bloodhounds of Broadway*, was released shortly after his death. Brookner died of AIDS in 1989 at the age of 34.

SCOTT BURTON

Scott Burton, born in 1939, was a fiercely intelligent and innovative artist who succeeded in completely fusing the separate domains of sculpture and furniture. Extremely knowledgeable about both historic and contemporary art (he also wrote highly original art criticism), he transformed traditions related to the design of chairs, benches, and tables into the parallel traditions of modern sculpture. The marriage produced works at once abstract and utilitarian, and often evoked unexpected psychological dimensions, with the positioning of his sculpture-furniture implying a scenario of human interactions. His work bridged many gulfs, including that between the ivory tower of abstract art and the need for public resting places, both indoors and outdoors. He died in 1989.

CHRIS DeBLASIO

Chris DeBlasio was born in Long Branch, New Jersey, in 1959. He almost immediately showed an aptitude for music and began composing at the age of six. He attended New York University and the Manhattan School of Music, where he studied composition with John Corigliano and Giampaolo Bracale. In his brief career as a freelance composer he wrote a wide variety of music, including church music, chamber music, and an operetta, *A Murder Is Foretold* with librettist Sharon Holland. Upon being diagnosed with HIV, he became intensely involved in AIDS activism and research. He died in July 1993. His music has since been performed throughout the United States and abroad and continues to reach new audiences with its eloquence and refined passion.

ROBERT FARBER

Robert Farber was a painter who lived in New York City and died in 1995 at the age of 47. By the time of his death he had completed numerous photographs, installations, and paintings, including a series relating the Black Death to AIDS—the *Western Blot* series. The most important exhibition during his lifetime, the *Western Blot* series was shown at Artists Space in New York City in 1992. Farber's sound installation, *Every Ten Minutes,* was created for A Day without Art in 1991 and shown in galleries and museums around the world. A posthumous retrospective of Farber's work has been seen in Boston, Los Angeles, and Portland, Maine. Garber was a valued advisor to the

Estate Project for Artists with AIDS and was heavily involved with ACT
UP New York.

ROBERT FERRO

Robert Ferro attended the University of Iowa Writers' Workshop, traveled much, lived in Italy periodically throughout his life, and in later
years taught writing at Adelphi University. In the late 1970s—along
with lifelong partner Michael Grumley, Andrew Holleran, Felice Picano,
George Whitmore, Edmund White, and Chris Cox—Ferro formed the
Violet Quill Club, credited for raising gay literature to national awareness. *Atlantis: Autobiography of a Search in 1971,* Ferro's first book, co-
written with Grumley, is based on their adventures and research. It
was followed by the novella, *The Others,* and his well-received, popular novels, *The Family of Max Desir, The Blue Star,* and *Second Son.* He
died of AIDS-related symptoms in 1988, surviving Grumley only
three months.

FRANK ISRAEL

Frank Israel is widely regarded as one of the most extravagantly gifted
architects of his generation, an architect whose designs for private
houses and offices for film production companies epitomized the creative ferment of contemporary Hollywood. Born in New York City in
1945, he moved to Los Angeles in 1979 to teach at the School of Architecture at UCLA. He is most widely celebrated for a series of private
houses that pushed the modern vernacular of Southern California architecture to a peak of innovation. Upon being diagnosed with AIDS,
he also took on the task of educating people about living with the disease. In magazine interviews, and in the catalogue for his show at the
Museum of Contemporary Art, he suggested that the illness had influenced his architecture by encouraging him to take greater risks. He
died of AIDS-related complications at the age of 50 in 1996.

DEREK JARMAN

Derek Jarman entered films in the early 1970s, designing sets for Ken
Russell's *The Devils* and *Savage Messiah.* After making numerous experimental shorts, mostly in Super-8, he began helming features in

1979 with *Sebastiane*. Over the next twenty years Jarman frequently interwove historical evocation and unexpected anachronisms, particularly in his biopics *Caravaggio* and *Wittgenstein*. Radical gay politics, a constant theme in his films, emerged most forcefully in the 1990s with *The Garden, Edward II,* and his last film, *Blue,* in which the sole visual element is an unchanging field of blue, while the soundtrack describes Jarman's thoughts and emotions in the face of his imminent death from AIDS.

PETER D. KELLORAN

Peter D. Kelloran, born on December 17, 1961, was a young visual artist and aspiring musician who was a part of the punk scene at the Firehouse in San Francisco. He made his living as a bartender at the Paradise Lounge. He was an AIDS activist during the birth of ACT UP and contributed visuals to campaigns waged against Jesse Helms, Marlboro Tobacco, and the Gulf War. He died on May 10, 1994, at the age of 32. At the time this was the median age of survival for PWA's. On the topic of this statistic, he often joked that Jesus died at the age of 33.

BRUCE KELLY

Bruce Kelly was born in Montgomery, Alabama, in 1948. He graduated from the University of Georgia with a degree in landscape architecture and earned a masters degree in historic preservation from Columbia University. In addition to his landscapes and his work as a Frederick Law Olmsted scholar, he served as president of the New York chapter of the American Society of Landscape Architects.

STAN LEVENTHAL

Stan Leventhal was born in Philadelphia in 1951 and raised in Queens and Roslyn, New York. After studying at Emerson College and Berklee College of Music, he moved to New York City and became a novelist and short fiction writer. He was the founding editor of Amethyst Books and edited *Torso* and *Honcho* magazines. He founded the Vito Russo/Pat Parker Memorial Library at the New York Lesbian and Gay Community Center as well as the Center's Literacy Project. He died of AIDS on January 15, 1995.

MARC LIDA

Marc Lida was born in 1957 and lived most of his life in New York City. He attended the State University of New York at Purchase and the Parsons School of Design. His illustrations were published in the *New York Times* and the *Village Voice,* but he was never able to support himself solely by selling his art. And so he became a social worker who worked with people with AIDS/HIV. His masterpiece, a suite of watercolors illustrating Marcel Proust's *Remembrance of Things Past,* was exhibited at the Yale University Art School Gallery in 1991. In the catalogue for the exhibition Maurice Sendak heralded Lida's "astonishing personal view that soars over and beyond the text."

JOAH LOWE

Joah Lowe was born August 1, 1953, and was raised in Henderson in provincial east Texas. He was a San Francisco choreographer and body worker who taught what he called "Lessons in the Art of Flying," based in part on his private therapeutic practice that combined elements of Aston-Patterning, Feldenkreis, and Laban techniques. After seeing performances by Alvin Ailey American Dance Theater at the University of Texas at Austin, he decided to become a dancer and sought training at the North Carolina School of the Arts. He received his B.A. in dance (with honors) from Connecticut College in 1976 as a protégé of Martha Myers and, that same year, danced with Pauline Koner Dance Consort in New York. Upon moving to the Bay Area in the late 1970s, he danced with Lucas Hoving and continued to create and perform in his own choreography, ranging from solos to large group works. He died of AIDS-related complications January 7, 1988, in a hospital in Longview, Texas, while visiting his family for the holidays.

JAMES MERRILL

James Merrill is widely considered the greatest poet of his generation. He published more than fourteen books of poems which won him two National Book Awards (*Nights and Days* and *Mirabell*), the Bollingen Prize in Poetry (*Braving the Elements*), and the Pulitzer Prize (*Divine Comedies*). Composed of a cycle of books, *The Changing Light at Sandover* won the 1983 National Book Critics Circle Award. Merrill wrote

two novels, *The (Diblos) Notebook* and *The Seraglio*. His other works include two plays, a book of essays, and the warmly received 1994 memoir, *A Different Person*. Merrill set up the Ingram-Merrill Foundation to
distribute grants to deserving younger artists. James Merrill lived in
Stonington, Connecticut, in Key West, Florida, and in Manhattan.
James Merrill died of AIDS-related complications in 1995.

PAUL MONETTE

Paul Monette is the author of four books of poetry and seven novels,
as well as several highly praised nonfiction works, including *Borrowed
Time* and the National Book Award winner *Becoming a Man*. He received, in addition to the National Book Award, the PEN Center West
Freedom to Write Award, three Lambda Literary Awards, numerous
civic awards for political activism in the fight against AIDS, as well as
honorary Doctor of Letters degrees from the State University of New
York at Oswego, Wesleyan University, and the City University of New
York. A leader in the battle against AIDS, he died of AIDS in 1995.

MARK MORRISROE

Mark Morrisroe was born in Massachusetts in 1959. In the late 1970s,
Morrisroe attended art school at the Museum of Fine Arts in Boston
where he experimented with performance, filmmaking, and photography. His style of documentary photography is now described as a
component of the famed Boston School that includes Morrisroe's
contemporaries Nan Goldin, Jack Pierson, Philip-Lorca DiCorcia,
David Armstrong, and Doug and Mike Starn. Mark Morrisroe died of
AIDS in July 1989. He was 30 years old.

JOHN C. RUSSELL

John C. Russell was born in 1963. A playwright whose works appeared in off-Broadway theaters in New York City, he was a member
of the New Dramatists and was the chairman of the Circle Repertory
Board. More than half a dozen of his plays were staged or read at numerous venues including BACA Downtown in Brooklyn, the Joseph
Papp Public Theater, and the Downtown Art Company in Greenwich

Village. His play, *Stupid Kids,* was performed at the WFA Theater in 1998. He died in 1994 from complications due to AIDS.

WARREN SONBERT

Warren Sonbert was one of the most prominent and gifted experimental filmmakers of the last thirty years. He began making films as a teenager, documenting the Downtown artist scene of the 1960s in lush, exhilarating sequences with dark ironies underneath, as indicated by his titles (*Where Did Our Love Go?, Hall of Mirrors, The Bad and The Beautiful,* and so on). A passionate opera buff, he wrote exuberantly and sometimes acidically about film and opera for various alternative newspapers. He relocated to San Francisco, where he took up residence in the Castro and participated in the gay renaissance there. His work was displayed in the New York Film Festival and in art film venues worldwide. Warren died at the age of forty-seven in 1995.

DAVID WOJNAROWICZ

David Wojnarowicz was born in 1955 in Red Bank, New Jersey, but was living in New York City by his early teens. Despite a rough existence that involved hustling and other kinds of street activities, he began keeping journals during his teenage years and taking photographs in his early twenties. Almost entirely self-trained, he became known in the East Village as an innovative and provocative artist in a variety of media including writing, photography, filmmaking, performance, and painting. He had his first solo exhibition in 1982. Two catalogues cover his work—*David Wojnarowicz: Tongues of Flame* (1990) and *Fever: The Art of David Wojnarowicz* (1999). He also published three books—*Close to the Knives, Memories that Smell Like Gasoline,* and *In the Shadow of the American Dream: The Waterfront Journals.* Discovering that he had HIV in 1987, much of his work thereafter addressed the experience of living with AIDS. Because of its transgressive imagery and brutal honesty, his work was the focus of many of the late 1980s battles between the political and religious right and the art world. He died in 1992.

Contributor Biographies

MAYA ANGELOU

Maya Angelou is the author of the bestselling *I Know Why the Caged Bird Sings, Gather Together in My Name,* and *The Heart of a Woman,* as well as five collections of poetry and the inaugural poem *On the Pulse of Morning.* In the sixties, at the request of Dr. Martin Luther King, Jr., she became the northern coordinator for the Southern Christian Leadership Conference, and in 1975 she received the *Ladies' Home Journal* Woman of the Year Award in communications. She is on the board of trustees of the American Film Institute and is also one of the few female members of the Directors Guild. She is currently Reynolds Professor at Wake Forest University, Winston-Salem, North Carolina.

JOHN BERENDT

John Berendt is the author of *Midnight in the Garden of Good and Evil.* Born in Syracuse, New York, he graduated from Harvard College in 1961 and since then has been an editor and columnist for *Esquire,* a television writer, and the editor of *New York Magazine.* He lives in New York.

WILLIAM BERGER

William Berger, a native of Los Angeles, studied Italian and Latin literature at University of California at Santa Cruz. A New Yorker since 1984, he is the author of *Wagner without Fear* and *Verdi with a Vengeance,* several contemporary hymn texts for both traditional and new settings, and the libretto for an opera, *The Wolf of Gubbio,* being set by composer Patrick Barnes. He lectures on music, opera, and architectural history, and is frequently heard on NPR's *Performance Today* and *At the Opera.*

ALEXANDER CHEE

Alexander Chee is a recipient of the 1999 Michener-Copernicus Society Fellowship for distinguished fiction. His poetry, short fiction, and memoirs have appeared in *Men on Men 2000, Boys Like Us, His 3, LIT,*

Interview, James White Review, Big, Barrow Street, and *Out.* He lives in Brooklyn and teaches for the New School University.

DAVID GERE

David Gere is co-editor of *Looking Out: Perspectives on Dance and Criticism in a Multicultural World,* has served as co-director of the Dance Critics Association from 1992 to 1995, and is currently writing a book on dance and corporeality in the AIDS era. He is an assistant professor in the Department of World Arts and Cultures at UCLA.

BRAD GOOCH

Brad Gooch is the author of *Finding the Boyfriend Within; City Poet: The Life and Times of Frank O'Hara; Jailbait and Other Stories;* a book of poems, *The Daily News;* and three novels, *Scary Kisses, The Golden Age of Promiscuity,* and most recently *Zombie00: A Fable.* His writing has appeared in the *Paris Review, Partisan Review, Bomb, New Republic, Harper's Bazzar, New Yorker, Vanity Fair, Out, New York, W, Travel and Leisure, Los Angeles Times Book Review, Nation,* and *American Poetry Review.* He is an associate professor of English at the William Paterson College of New Jersey and lives in New York City.

ALLAN GURGANUS

Allan Gurganus is the author of seven books, including *Oldest Living Confederate Widow Tells All* (winner of the Sue Kaufman Prize for Best First American Fiction from the American Academy of Arts and Letters), *White People* (Pen/Faulkner finalist and winner of the Los Angeles Times Book Prize), and *Plays Well with Others* (Lambda Literary Award finalist). *The Practical Heart,* a group of four novellas, is forthcoming. Living in his native North Carolina, he is co-founder of Writers Against Jesse Helms. Gurganus is represented in Patrick Merla's classic, *Boys Like Us.* Edmund White's *Faber Book of Gay Short Fiction* begins with Henry James and ends with Allan Gurganus. His fiction has been translated into twelve languages.

RANDALL KENAN

Randall Kenan is the author of a novel, *A Visitation of Spirits,* a collection of stories, *Let the Dead Bury Their Dead,* and a work of nonfiction,

Walking on Water: Black American Lives at the Turn of the Twenty-First Century.

PHILLIP LOPATE

Phillip Lopate is the author of several collections of personal essays, including *Bachelorhood, Against Joie de Vivre,* and *Portrait of My Body;* a novel, *The Rug Merchant;* and a book about his teaching experiences, *Being with Children.* He served on the New York Film Festival Committee, and his film criticism was recently published in the collection *Totally, Tenderly, Tragically: Essays and Criticism from a Lifelong Love Affair with the Movies.* He is a professor of English at Hofstra University, and lives in Brooklyn, New York, with his wife and daughter.

CRAIG LUCAS

Craig Lucas is the author of numerous plays, including *Prelude to a Kiss, Reckless, Blue Window,* and *Three Postcards* and is a contributing editor to *Bomb* magazine. He has been nominated for the Drama Desk three times, for a Tony once, has been a finalist for a Pulitzer, and received two Rockefeller Foundation grants as well as a Guggenheim fellowship and NEA/TCG fellowship. He is the recipient of the first George and Elisabeth Marton Award as well as the L.A. Drama Critics, Drama-Logue, Obie, Outer Critics' Circle, and the Burns Mantle Best Musical Awards. He lives in upstate New York and is partners with set designer John McDermott.

J. D. McCLATCHY

J. D. McClatchy is the author of four collections of poems and two collections of literary essays. He is also the editor of several other books, including *The Vintage Book of Contemporary World Poetry, The Vintage Book of Contemporary American Poetry,* and *Recitative: Prose by James Merrill.* Since 1991, he has served as editor of the *Yale Review.* In 1996 he was named a Chancellor of the Academy of American Poets, in 1998 was elected a Fellow of the American Academy of Arts and Sciences, and the following year was elected to membership in the American Academy of Arts and Letters. His work appears regularly in the *New Yorker, New York Times Book Review, Paris Review, New Republic,* and many other magazines.

KEITH McDERMOTT

Keith McDermott is an actor and writer living in New York. He has published stories in *Men On Men 7* and *Boys Like Us,* and is a contributor to the magazines *Nest, Out, Punch,* and the *James White Review.* In 1999 he won an award for fiction from the gay and lesbian group In Our Own Write. He is currently working on a novel and a book about acting with his longtime mentor, Michael Egan.

RAMSEY McPHILIPS

Ramsey McPhilips presently hosts a gardening television show called *Hugo! Gardener, The Television Hortivangilist.* When not living on his farm in Oregon, he travels about the world teaching the gospel of gardening to a variety of characters whom he occasionally renders in writing, photography, and film. Like the Greek goddess Persephone, he tends a garden to unveil, capitalize, and then cure the darker origins of the soul. Ramsey McPhilips was born on Halloween in 1957.

PATRICK MOORE

Patrick Moore is a cultural activist and writer with a specialization in digital imaging technology. After the publication of his acclaimed first novel, *This Every Night,* during a time when the impact of AIDS was being felt throughout the art world, the Alliance for the Arts asked Moore to research and write a study and legal guide on estate planning for artists. Following the success of *Future Safe: Estate Planning for Artists in a Time of AIDS* Moore stayed on as Director of the Estate Project and since 1992 has led the program from a small research effort to a national archival organization with an annual budget of more than $1,000,000. While directing the Estate Project Moore has continued his writing and, in 1996, published *Iowa,* his second novel. Moore currently divides his time between New York and Los Angeles.

HERBERT MUSCHAMP

Herbert Muschamp is the architecture critic of the New York Times and the author of *File Under Architecture* and *Man About Town: Frank Lloyd Wright in New York City.*

FELICE PICANO

Felice Picano is a much-translated, best-selling, prize-winning author of fiction, poetry, memoirs, and other nonfiction and is considered a founder of modern gay literature along with the six other members of the *Violet Quill Club*. His plays have been produced off-Broadway, around the United States, and abroad. Picano also began and operated the Seahorse Press and Gay Presses of New York for fifteen years. His highly praised novel, *The Book of Lies*, was published in 1999, and his earlier short fiction was collected and published in 2000 under the title *The New York Years*. He now lives in Los Angeles.

ROBERT ROSENBLUM

Robert Rosenblum has been a professor of fine arts at New York University since 1967, but has also taught in many other institutions, including the University of Michigan, Columbia University, Princeton, and Yale. Recently, he has also joined the curatorial staff at the Guggenheim Museum. Rosenblum is a prolific writer, with books, articles, and catalogue essays that cover a wide range of fields, from Neoclassic painting to art of the 1990s. Among his works are monographs on Ingres, Frank Stella, and Jeff Koons, as well as many specialized studies on Picasso. In 1999 he published *On Modern American Art*, an anthology of four decades of writing. It includes an essay on Scott Burton's *Last Tableau*.

SARAH SCHULMAN

Sarah Schulman is the author of eight novels, including *Shimmer, Rat Bohemia, Empathy,* and the forthcoming *The Child*, as well as two nonfiction books, *Stagestruck: Theater, AIDS, and the Marketing of Gay America* and *My American History: Lesbian and Gay Life during the Reagan/Bush Years*. She is the recipient of the American Library Association Gay/Lesbian Nonfiction Award (1998), the Ferro/Grumley Award for Lesbian Fiction (1995), the Gregory Kolovakos Memorial Prize for AIDS Fiction (1990), and the American Library Association Gay/Lesbian Fiction Award (1988). She is currently developing two plays and a musical based on her novel *Shimmer*.

ANDREW SOLOMON

Andrew Solomon was born in New York and studied at Yale University and then at Jesus College, Cambridge, in England. In 1988 he began his study of Russian artists, which culminated with the publication of *The Irony Tower: Soviet Artists in a Time of Glasnost.* He is a contributing writer for the *New York Times Magazine* and also writes regularly for the *New Yorker, Artforum,* and many other publications. He is now working on a book about depression, *The Noonday Demon,* to be published in the United States and the United Kingdom in 2001 as well as in France, Germany, Holland, Sweden, Italy, Brazil, Poland, and Portugal before the end of 2002. He now divides his time primarily between London and New York.

BENJAMIN TAYLOR

Benjamin Taylor has taught at Columbia University and Washington University in St. Louis, and is now on faculty at the Writing Program of the New School for Social Research. His essays and journalism have appeared in the *Los Angeles Times Book Review, Raritan, Threepenny Review, Salmagundi, Antaeus, Georgia Review, New England Review, Bomb, Bookforum,* and many other publications. He is the author of *Into the Open: Reflections on Genius and Modernity,* and a novel, *The Mercy Seat,* which received the 1996 Harold Ribalow Prize. His new novel, *Pax Americana,* is forthcoming.

JONATHAN WEINBERG

Jonathan Weinberg is a painter and associate professor in the History of Art Department of Yale University. He is the author of *Speaking for Vice: Homosexuality in the Art of Charles Demuth, Marsden Hartley and the First Avant-Garde.* His articles and reviews have appeared in *Arts, Art in America, Journal of Homosexuality, Yale Journal of Criticism,* and *Genders.* Weinberg's paintings are in several important collections including the Metropolitan Museum of Art and the Montclair Art Museum. His next book, *Famous Artists: Ambition and Love in Modern American Art* is forthcoming.

EDMUND WHITE

Edmund White has written a dozen books including most recently the novel, *The Married Man.* He is perhaps best known for his trilogy, *A Boy's Own Story, The Beautiful Room Is Empty,* and *The Farewell Symphony.* He teaches at Princeton.

PHILIP YENAWINE

Philip Yenawine has been engaged in museum education for thirty years, ten years of which were spent as director of education at the Museum of Modern Art, New York. He writes about art and is the author of several books that address issues germane to beginning viewers, including children. He has served on the boards of many contemporary arts organizations, including Visual AIDS and the foundation Art Matters. He is currently co-director (with cognitive psychologist Abigail Housen) of Visual Understanding in Education, a nonprofit organization that develops programs to instruct teachers how to use art to teach thinking.